Grant's Lieutenants

GRANT'S LIEUTENANTS

FROM CAIRO TO VICKSBURG

Edited by
Steven E. Woodworth

UNIVERSITY PRESS OF KANSAS

Published by the University Press of Kansas (Lawrence, Kansas 66045), which was
organized by the Kansas Board of Regents and is operated and funded by Emporia State
University, Fort Hays State University, Kansas State University, Pittsburg State University,
the University of Kansas, and Wichita State University

Library of Congress Cataloging-in-Publication Data
Grant's lieutenants / edited by Steven E. Woodworth.
     p.   cm. — (Modern war studies)
    Includes bibliographical references and index.
    Contents: From Cairo to Vicksburg
    ISBN 978-0-7006-1127-0 (cloth : alk. paper)
    ISBN 978-0-7006-3525-2 (pbk. : alk. paper)
    ISBN 978-0-7006-3526-9 (ebook)
    1. Grant, Ulysses S. (Ulysses Simpson), 1822–1885—Friends and associates.
2. Grant, Ulysses S. (Ulysses Simpson), 1822–1885.   3. United States.
Army—Biography.   4. United States. Navy—Biography.   5. Generals—United
States—Biography.   6. Admirals—United States—Biography.   7. United
States—History—Civil War, 1861–1865—Campaigns.   I. Woodworth, Steven E.
II. Series.
    E467 .G73   2001
    973.8′2′092—dc21   2001001685

British Library Cataloguing in Publication Data is available.

Contents

Introduction   1

"A Full Share of All the Credit"
Sherman and Grant to the Fall of Vicksburg   5
℮∽ *John F. Marszalek*

"Earned on the Field of Battle"
William H. L. Wallace   21
℮∽ *Steven E. Woodworth*

The Reliable First Team
Grant and Charles Ferguson Smith   43
℮∽ *Benjamin Franklin Cooling*

"If He Had Less Rank"
Lewis Wallace   63
℮∽ *Stacy D. Allen*

The Forging of Joint Army–Navy Operations
Andrew Hull Foote and Grant   91
℮∽ *Benjamin Franklin Cooling*

"I Could Not Make Him Do As I Wished"
The Failed Relationship of William S. Rosecrans and Grant   109
℮∽ *Lesley J. Gordon*

Fighting Politician
John A. McClernand   129
℮∽ *Terrence J. Winschel*

A Matter of Trust
Grant and James B. McPherson   151
℮ *Tamara A. Smith*

"We Had Lively Times up the Yazoo"
Admiral David Dixon Porter   169
℮ *R. Blake Dunnavent*

The War of Spies and Supplies
Grant and Grenville M. Dodge in the West, 1862–1864   183
℮ *William B. Feis*

Grant's Ethnic General
Peter J. Osterhaus   199
℮ *Earl J. Hess*

Notes   217

List of Contributors   251

Index   253

Introduction

Ulysses S. Grant did more than any other single Union general to secure the North's victory in the Civil War. Troops under his command
won one of the North's first truly significant victories at Forts Henry
and Donelson in February 1862, opening the way to almost all of the
subsequent Union successes west of the Appalachians. The greatest of
those successes were his as well. His army withstood the worst the rebels could do at Shiloh in April of that year and finally captured Vicksburg and its thirty thousand defenders in July 1863, breaking the back
of the western Confederacy and setting the scene for the great left-
wheel that would bring Union armies from the Mississippi to the Appalachians, to the Atlantic, and then northward into the very backyard of
Robert E. Lee's Virginia Confederates, locked in desperate struggle
with another of Grant's armies. When Lee finally surrendered at Appomattox, it was Grant who chivalrously declined to claim the vanquished
captain's sword. He could afford to be generous, for on that day the
common-looking sometime leather-goods clerk from Galena, Illinois,
bestrode the military world as the most successful general of the Western Hemisphere.

He certainly did not get there all by himself. Along the way he
had to find and learn to depend upon able subordinates. He had to learn
how to use these men and how to get rid of them if he found he could
not use them. At these tasks he proved extraordinarily successful, and
that success was no small part of the larger picture of Grant's victorious generalship. Clearly these men and their relationships with Grant
are worthwhile subjects for closely focused study, and that is what this
book sets out to do, with apologies to Douglas Southall Freeman,
whose earlier work, *Lee's Lieutenants,* was an obvious part of the inspiration for this one.[1]

This book differs from Freeman's in several ways, most apparently in that it is not a continuous narrative by a single author but a series of essays by several authors. Naturally, the different contributors have different styles of writing. Also, the chapters contain a certain unavoidable degree of redundancy. After all, a study of the relationship of Grant and Sherman must mention the battle of Shiloh, as must also, in their turns, the studies of Grant's relationships with Lew Wallace, William H. L. Wallace, John A. McClernand, or Charles F. Smith. The distinctive emphasis of each chapter is the relationship between Grant and the lieutenant in question. How did the lieutenant's service contribute to Grant's success and to his development as a general? Conversely, how did interaction with Grant affect the lieutenant's career? Finally, how did the relationship between them contribute to the course and outcome of the war? These are the questions we seek to address for each of the lieutenants in question. This volume focuses on the men who were Grant's lieutenants up to the fall of Vicksburg in July 1863; a second volume will address the men who served under him during the last two years of the war. In the case of generals who continued to interact with Grant during the second half of the war, another chapter in the second volume will cover their activities during that time. This volume, however, deals with the complete careers of those generals who did not have much direct contact with Grant after Vicksburg.

Naturally, it is not possible or desirable to include in a book such as this lengthy consideration of every single one of Grant's subordinate officers, even within the selected chronological period. The idea has been to include the most important as well as some who are representative of various types of officers and may therefore tell us something about how Grant dealt with those groups. Among those generals who were most important are three who by the time of the Vicksburg campaign commanded three of the Army of the Tennessee's four corps: William T. Sherman, John A. McClernand, and James B. McPherson. Of similar or even greater importance was the man who was almost a mentor to Grant during his early career, Charles F. Smith. A difficult subordinate whose career track crossed Grant's at a later crucial junction of the war was William S. Rosecrans.

Several other generals, though likewise important to Grant at various stages of his career, also show his interaction with specific types of officers. Citizen-soldiers in shoulder straps are represented by Lew Wallace, William H. L. Wallace, and Peter J. Osterhaus, as well as McClernand. Osterhaus is also unusual in that he was a foreign-born officer, lending a particular interest to our study of his dealings with Grant. Another special case is that of Grenville Dodge. Though only a division commander, Dodge played an important role in Grant's success by serving as the closest thing Grant had to a chief of intelligence. Two other unusual cases are those of men who were not, strictly speaking, Grant's lieutenants at all, or even officers of the U.S. Army. U.S. Navy Flag Officer Andrew H. Foote and Rear Adm. David Dixon Porter were nevertheless men whose relationships with Grant were vitally important, both to the latter's career and to the course of the war.

These were some of the men who were with Grant in his first two years of war. His ability to select them and to make use of their talents—and to avoid excessive damage from their faults—was as important to his rise to national fame as any other component of his success. The study of Grant and these men should reveal much about the nature of his road to victory from Cairo to Vicksburg.

"A Full Share of All the Credit"

Sherman and Grant to the Fall of Vicksburg

John F. Marszalek

The two men possessed completely different personalities. U. S. Grant was quiet and shy, able to write succinctly and clearly, but he was also an individual who found public speaking and most relationships with strangers painful. William T. Sherman, on the other hand, was exuberant and outgoing, his correspondence a string of excited run-on sentences, yet he was very much at home behind a podium, able to make friends easily, and pleased to carry on conversations with strangers. Even in appearance, they were different. Grant was stumpy; Sherman was tall and thin.[1]

Yet they had their similarities. Both men were born in Ohio, although Grant is more usually associated with Galena, Illinois. They both disliked their years at the U.S. Military Academy at West Point (though Sherman achieved much higher standing than Grant), and they both served in the pre–Civil War frontier army and found it boring. Each resigned his commission to go into business and suffered one failure after another. The coming of the Civil War gave each the opportunity to turn his life around and become successful. In truth, the two men, who hardly knew each other before the war, gained fame together, and each played an important role in the success of the other.

Grant was two years younger than Sherman, having been born in 1822, and he did not become a plebe at the U.S. Military Academy until Sherman was already in his final year. The two had virtually nothing to do with each other at West Point, although in that small late-1830s world on the Hudson River, they certainly had some contact. Grant was a careful observer of people, but others rarely recalled anything about him. Sherman made just such a point in a postwar speech. He said he

5

simply could not remember much about Grant from their West Point days together: "I hardly noticed him."[2]

After graduating in 1840, Sherman joined the Third Artillery Regiment in Florida, where he fought in the Second Seminole War. Later posted to garrisons in Alabama and South Carolina, he served in California during the Mexican War and the gold rush years, but he never saw any combat. When Grant gained his commission in 1843, he went into the infantry and served as a quartermaster during the Mexican War but also led a company in battle while serving under Zachary Taylor. In the early 1850s, Sherman held commissary posts in St. Louis and New Orleans and resigned his commission in 1854 to become a banker in California. After the Mexican War, Grant also served on the West Coast and similarly resigned his commission in 1854. He left the army under a cloud of rumors about excessive drinking, however, while Sherman resigned with a good reputation.

By 1854, then, Sherman and Grant had become civilians, and both proved unsuccessful in their economic endeavors. Sherman managed banks in California and in New York City, and they failed. He similarly found no success in Kansas real estate or law, and then, after declining to work in a family business, he found his footing as superintendent of the Louisiana Military Seminary. Unlike Sherman, Grant drew on his family connections for a livelihood. He unsuccessfully took up farming on the lands owned by his father-in-law, and after failing in a real estate business, he finally had to accept the humiliation of taking a clerkship in his family's leathergoods store in Galena.

Grant and Sherman bumped into each other on the streets of St. Louis during these lean years. In 1857 Sherman had just experienced his New York bank failure and had returned to St. Louis to see what to do next. One day, he ran into Grant, still reeling from his failure at farming. The two men spoke only briefly, both no doubt unhappy to meet a fellow West Pointer under such adverse conditions. In later years, Sherman said that all he remembered about that meeting was that, at the time, he "concluded that West Point and the regular army were not good schools for farmers [and] bankers." There is no record of Grant's response, but it must have been similar to Sherman's. They were failures and could see it in each other's faces.[3]

They both returned to the army to fight in the Civil War, but each did it in a different way. When secession came, Sherman left Louisiana and took a job as president of a St. Louis street railway company. His family pressured him to accept an army commission, but he was not convinced that the North was taking the Southern threat seriously enough for him to risk another failure. In mid-May 1861, however, no doubt owing to the influence of his foster father, the powerful Ohio politician Thomas Ewing, he was named colonel of the regular army's Thirteenth Infantry Regiment, refusing to serve with volunteers, whom he considered untrustworthy. Soon he was doing inspection work for U.S. Army commanding general Winfield Scott.

Sherman rose to brigade commander in the Union army before First Bull Run and distinguished himself by his exemplary conduct during and after the battle. He was named a brigadier general of volunteers. Worried that Bull Run proved just how chaotic the military situation around Washington really was, he contentedly left for Kentucky to become second-in-command to Gen. Robert B. Anderson, the hero of Fort Sumter and commanding general of the Cumberland region.

When the war began, Grant had only recently taken a clerkship in the family store in Galena and was at a low point in his life. He hoped the conflict would give him another chance to turn his fortunes around. When Fort Sumter fell, citizens of Galena held a meeting in support of the Union cause, and because Grant was the only West Pointer there (and the only person present with military experience), he was elected to serve as meeting chairman. He later recruited a company of volunteers in the community but refused to lead them into combat. As a West Point graduate, he thought it beneath him to serve under a civilian colonel. Besides, he believed, his previous army experience warranted his receiving a higher rank than captain. He was disappointed. It was only when Elihu Washburne, his district congressman, took him to see the Illinois governor that he received his colonelcy in the Twenty-first Illinois Regiment. He marched his unit to Missouri, where he soon was promoted to brigadier general in the volunteer forces, thanks again to Washburne's influence. He soon found himself commanding troops at Cairo, Illinois, where the Ohio and the Mississippi Rivers meet.

Both Grant and Sherman thus were firmly back in the army of the United States. Both performed well enough in their early days of service to gain the one star of brigadier general; the future looked promising. At this point, however, their careers diverged. Sherman almost lost his commission, but Grant began to gain national fame.

Although Sherman had done well at First Bull Run in late July 1861, the Union debacle there convinced him that he had indeed been correct in supposing that the government was not taking the crisis seriously enough. He accepted a post in Kentucky but only after insisting to Pres. Abraham Lincoln that no one ever ask him to assume full command of the department. Lincoln told him not to worry, but when Robert Anderson succumbed to physical and mental fatigue, Sherman was forced to the front. Under the pressure of increased responsibility and convinced that Northern newspaper reporters were providing the enemy with vital intelligence, he ordered all correspondents out of his military area. His usual perpetual motion also increased in intensity, and gossip swirled around the region that he was losing his mind, if he had not done so already.

When Secretary of War Simon Cameron paid a visit to Sherman's command, the worried general insisted that he would need two hundred thousand men if he were to have any success in Kentucky. He repeatedly wired George B. McClellan, Union army commanding general, warning of dangerous consequences for the Federals in the region. Louisville and even Cincinnati, he cautioned, were in danger. He demanded replacement, reminding his superiors that he had insisted on no command; yet here he was in just such a predicament.

Don Carlos Buell replaced Sherman in mid-November 1861, and the rattled brigadier joined Henry W. Halleck's command in Missouri. He then predicted dire consequences for Union arms there. He seemed on the verge of a breakdown, so his wife came to take him home for a rest. While recuperating in Lancaster, Ohio, he saw a *Cincinnati Commercial* headline: "General William T. Sherman Insane."[4] Other newspapers took up the chorus, and Sherman's reputation disintegrated. He returned to service in Missouri a broken man, fit only to train recruits at a camp outside St. Louis. Thoughts of suicide raced through his head, stayed only by concern for his family.

At the same time that Sherman's life seemed in disarray, Grant's military career improved—but only after a shaky interlude. With a sure, steady hand, in early September 1861, Grant took Paducah, Kentucky, at the confluence of the Ohio and the Tennessee Rivers, without having to fire a single shot. Then on November 7, he attacked Confederate general Gideon J. Pillow at Belmont, and although he was driven back, his confidence in his ability increased. When Henry W. Halleck became commander of the Army of the Missouri, Grant traveled to St. Louis in January 1862 to try to convince his new superior that instead of reorganizing his forces as Halleck was doing at the time, he should allow Grant to march on Fort Henry in Tennessee. Grant believed the capture of this military installation would serve as the opening blow in a campaign to control the Tennessee River. To his dismay, Halleck greeted Grant with "little cordiality" and "cut [me] short as if my plan was preposterous," Grant said. Halleck disdainfully determined to prepare his troops fully before committing them in battle, and perhaps he was also worried about trusting so many soldiers to a man whose reputation was still dominated by gossip of chronic drunkenness.[5]

Grant was crushed, but he did not give up. He and Navy Flag Officer Andrew H. Foote talked the matter over and were confident that a joint army–navy invasion could take Fort Henry. They sent separate telegrams to Halleck exuding confidence in their ability to take the fort, and this time Halleck agreed. Grant's fifteen-thousand-man force and Foote's seven river gunboats went into action, Foote's armada reaching the fort and capturing it on February 6, 1862, even before Grant's army could arrive. Wasting no time, Grant and Foote organized an attack on nearby Fort Donelson. Once again they were successful. Of even more significance, Fort Donelson resulted in Grant's becoming a national figure. When Confederate general Simon Buckner asked for a truce to discuss terms of capitulation, Grant responded that the only terms would be "unconditional and immediate surrender." He then became "Unconditional Surrender" Grant, a household name.[6]

Grant was a success while Sherman seemed to be continuing his prewar pattern of failure. When he returned to Missouri in late December 1861, Sherman knew the insanity charge was still reverberating around the nation. On December 23, Halleck placed him in command of recruit training at Benton Barracks, an assignment that provided him with little chance to do damage to the Union cause. He remained depressed, but slowly his work began to draw him out of his doldrums. Then, something significant happened. In mid-February 1862, when Halleck decided Sherman was ready for responsibility again, he sent him to Paducah as commander of the Department of Cairo. At the same time, he named Grant commander of the Department of West Tennessee.[7]

At the time, Halleck saw no special significance to this routine movement of officers, although he remained suspicious of Grant and worried about Sherman. In fact, Halleck had done something that would have a profound effect on the outcome of the war. He brought Grant and Sherman together militarily and thereby gave them a chance to forge a friendship that helped to determine how the war would ultimately be fought. And clearly he had no way of anticipating the consequences of his action.

Sherman, ordered from Paducah to the mouth of the Cumberland River, forwarded troops to Grant and watched with great appreciation as he used these soldiers to capture Fort Donelson; "a brilliant act . . . extraordinary and brilliant," Sherman marveled. He watched from a distance and liked what he saw. Here was a military man who confidently decided what had to be done and then just as confidently did it. For the first time in the war, Sherman saw a modicum of hope for the Union cause. He looked to Grant to provide the leadership he had always insisted the Federals exercise and that his own military career needed to be successful. At the same time, Grant appreciated Sherman, his senior, who waived rank to support him and always sent encouraging letters with any troops or supplies he pushed forward.[8]

Though Grant inspired Sherman, Henry W. Halleck was not similarly impressed. Old Brains was a stickler for detail and suspicious that his subordinate did not understand his precise role in the overall war effort. Halleck wanted to make sure that Grant made no move without his permission. The problem was that although Grant tried to stay in contact with Halleck, his messages were not reaching St. Louis. On March 3, 1861, an angry Halleck wrote Commanding General George B. McClellan in Washington that he had not heard from Grant in over a week. He accused Grant of resting on his laurels and allowing his men to become "demoralized." In a later letter, he accused him of drunkenness. "I am worn out and tired with the neglect and inefficiency," Halleck lamented, and McClellan was sympathetic in his response: "Do not hesitate to arrest him at once if the good of the service requires it." Halleck telegraphed Grant, ordering him to give his command to Maj. Gen. C. F. Smith. "Why do you not obey my orders to report strength and positions of your command?" Halleck demanded.[9]

Grant's earlier successes and his aggressiveness and determination to press forward had ironically earned him the animosity of his superior and the loss of his command. Fortunately, however, he had impressed Lincoln, who immediately told the secretary of war to demand of Halleck why he had shelved a successful general. Halleck, who was in a more confident mood because of his recent promotion to commanding general in the West, was not about to buck the president, so he reversed himself immediately. On March 13, after Grant had asked for leave so he could convince "those higher in authority" of his rectitude, Halleck wired back immediately that not only did he not want Grant to quit, but he also wanted him "to assume immediate command [of his force] & lead it on to new victories." Unconditional Surrender Grant had justified his name again, only this time it was because of the capitulation of his nit-picking and no doubt jealous superior.[10]

Sherman's military career also seemed to be progressing along a similarly promising path. He commanded a volunteer division, and when he reported to Gen. C. F. Smith at Fort Henry, Smith ordered him to destroy the railroad between Corinth and Iuka in Mississippi. Grant's capture of Forts Henry and Donelson had been instrumental in causing Confederate general Albert Sidney Johnston to abandon his long defense line from the Cumberland Gap in the East to New Madrid and Island No. 10 on the Mississippi River. Johnston fell back into Corinth, where the north-south Mobile and Ohio Railroad and the east-west Charleston and Memphis Railroad crossed. Sherman's job was to cut the east-west route in preparation for a Union attack on Corinth.[11]

During this so-called Yellow Creek expedition, the spring floods hampered Sherman, but he did notice a landing on the Tennessee River only twenty-two miles from Corinth. High ground loomed above it, thus making any campsites there immune to the flooding inundating other terrain below. Sherman recommended this spot to Smith as the bivouac area for Union troops preparing for the forthcoming attack on Corinth. When Grant took Smith's place, he agreed with Sherman's choice. Grant's army, including Sherman's and four other divisions, camped on the plateau between Pittsburg Landing and Shiloh Church, some three miles inland from the river. Another division camped at Crump's Landing, six miles away, and Grant had his headquarters at Savannah, Tennessee, nine miles distant.[12]

There was no sense of urgency in Grant's army at Pittsburg Landing. Halleck, in St. Louis, had ordered Grant to await the arrival of Don Carlos Buell's Army of the Ohio, and only then, when the two armies were massed and when Halleck had arrived to take command of the combined force, would the Union army march on Johnston's entrenched soldiers in Corinth. There was always the possibility that the Confederates might attack Grant before Buell arrived, but that seemed improbable. Why would Johnston leave his entrenchments and the railroads they defended to battle Union troops in the open field? Grant and the man he saw as his chief subordinate at Shiloh, William T. Sherman, could not conceive of a Confederate attack on the Union camps.[13]

Grant and Sherman thus reinforced each other's misconception. Sherman told his men not to worry about any Confederates attacking their camps and was pleased to read in an April 4 letter that Grant, his commander, "look[ed] for nothing of the kind," either. When, during that same period, Sherman's reconnaissance force ran into so many Confederates a few miles from Union camps that it had to be reinforced, the incident did not change his mind. "The enemy is saucy . . . [but] I do not apprehend anything like an attack on our position," he reported to his superior.[14] Grant was pleased to hear the news; after all, it buttressed his beliefs. Sherman was determined not to repeat the mistakes he had made in Kentucky and Missouri by insisting that there were Confederates everywhere preparing an assault. He could not bear being called insane again. As for Grant, his mind seemed focused only on getting his army ready to move forward when Buell and Halleck arrived. He did not consider the possibility that the enemy might beat him to the punch.

On April 6, 1862, both Grant and Sherman were proven wrong, almost disastrously so. Early that Sunday morning, Confederate soldiers came crashing through the woods, sending Sherman's division and those around him reeling back from Shiloh Church toward Pittsburg Landing and the Tennessee River. Grant, who had injured an ankle in a horse-riding accident on Friday, April 4, came hurrying from Savannah to the battlefield and hobbled all over it trying to stem the assault. Sherman did marvelous work rallying his troops while having three horses shot out from under him and minié balls tearing through his hat and a strap, the latter projectile causing a painful shoulder injury. Buckshot struck him in his right hand. As he traversed the battlefield in midmorning, Grant was impressed by Sherman's decisive actions. This man was providing effective battlefield leadership, and Grant never felt a need to give him any advice. He complimented Sherman on his good work and hurried away, recognizing that "his presence was more needed over at the left."[15] Sherman helped provide Grant with necessary time to establish a line to protect Pittsburg Landing. By the afternoon, because of Gen. Benjamin Prentiss's determined stand in the Sunken Road and the heroic work of Sherman, Grant had his defense line in place. Meanwhile the battlefield death of Confederate general Albert Sidney Johnston and the decision by his replacement,

P. G. T. Beauregard, not to continue the attack ended the fighting on that terrible first day.

A heavy rainstorm that night exacerbated the miserable sights and sounds of dead bodies and the moaning of wounded soldiers. The Confederates endured the shelling by Union gunboats from the Tennessee River all that long night, but many, at least, had shelter from the rain in Union tents they had captured. Union soldiers also suffered from the elements, but the arrival of Don Carlos Buell's Army of the Ohio lifted their spirits. They felt more secure about repelling the Confederate attack they knew had to be coming the next morning.

When Grant saw Sherman around 5:00 P.M. on that first day, however, he was not thinking of defense. He was planning to beat back the Confederates. He told Sherman about his success at Fort Donelson and predicted that an assault the next day would similarly defeat the Confederates here. Sherman thought he must have heard his friend wrong; was Grant really planning an offensive? When he saw Grant again at 11:00 P.M., he thought of asking him about retreat plans, but something told him not to broach that subject, even though the normally unimposing Grant looked even more unimpressive that night. He stood under a tree, holding a lantern, his clothes soaked and sticking to his skin. Yet something in his demeanor gave Sherman pause. "Well, Grant," he asked tentatively, "we've had the devil's own day, haven't we?" "Yes," Grant replied quietly but firmly, "lick 'em tomorrow, though." [16]

Grant proved himself to be a prophet. He threw his forces forward early Monday morning and drove the stubborn Confederates off the battlefield and all the way back to Corinth. Once again, his determination and aggressiveness turned the rebel tide. Once again, Sherman saw that this unimposing man was actually very impressive. Grant's leadership ability reinforced Sherman's emerging belief that the Union cause was not hopeless. For his part, Grant heaped profuse praise on Sherman after the battle, and even as an old man he believed that "Sherman was the hero of Shiloh." [17]

Grant and Sherman came away from Pittsburg Landing with their respect for each other tremendously enhanced. Grant had seen Sherman in action and saw that he could indeed rely on him. Sherman saw Grant turn the tide from disaster to success, and his belief in Union victory increased markedly. The two men liked what they saw in one another; an important bond was strengthened.

This bond was tested immediately. With the battle hardly over, Federal politicians and newspapermen launched a full-scale attack on the Union command. Grant received particular abuse for allowing his troops to be surprised at Shiloh. It was incompetence, the accusation insisted, made worse by another losing bout with the bottle. Conversely, Sherman received praise for his heroics. His hatred for the press and his respect for Grant, however, caused him to launch a counterattack against his journalistic enemies. His defense was so unyielding that reporters and politicians soon included him in their attack on the Union high command: both Grant and Sherman shared the public abuse.[18]

Henry W. Halleck also proved to be a problem. Immediately after Shiloh, he arrived to take command of the massed Union forces and lead them against the Confederates at Corinth. Halleck's troops consisted of Grant's Army of the Tennessee, Don Carlos Buell's Army of the Ohio, and John Pope's Army of the Mississippi. By the time Halleck finished reorganizing this force, however, George H. Thomas was in Grant's command slot, and Grant was Halleck's "second in command according to some French notion," Sherman noted, "with no clear, well-defined command or authority." Halleck disdained Grant almost completely. "I was ignored as much as if I had been at the most distant point of territory within my jurisdiction," he remembered. The controversial victor of Shiloh was clearly on a shelf. When Grant offered a suggestion for a tactical move, Halleck "silenced me so quickly that I felt that possibly I had suggested an unmilitary movement." Sherman and the other generals who had fought at Shiloh held command posts and played major roles in the campaign against and occupation of Corinth in late May 1862, but Halleck kept Grant completely out of the action.[19]

Halleck's treatment crushed the usually steadfast Grant. The only way out, he believed, was to resign his commission. Rumors to this effect spread throughout the army, and a worried Sherman decided to see for himself. He rode out to Grant's camp, and what he discovered was upsetting. Camp equipment was piled up, and in a tent he found Grant methodically tying correspondence into bundles for later transport. Was it true, he asked Grant, that he was planning to resign his post? "Yes," Grant replied. But why? Grant stammered in reply: "Sherman, you know. You know that I am in the way here. I have stood it as long as I can, and can endure it no longer." But where did he plan to go? "St. Louis," Grant replied. Did he have anything to do there? "Not a bit," Grant admitted.

Sherman would not accept Grant's pessimism. In his excitable manner, he told the normally subdued Grant that he would not hear of his leaving. Reporters had called Sherman crazy in Kentucky and Missouri, but Shiloh had restored his reputation, despite press attacks there. The same thing would happen to Grant; something would come along to restore him. Sherman insisted that his friend remain in the army and await a change of fortune.[20]

When Sherman finally left Grant to his thoughts, he did not believe he had convinced him to stay. In fact, he even asked higher authorities for Grant's escort company, once he resigned. Grant later recalled that Sherman "urged me so strongly not to think of going, that I concluded to remain." Now it was Sherman who was giving Grant confidence, and he "rejoice[d]" at Grant's decision to stay.[21] The two men once again reinforced one another, and their friendship further solidified and grew. From this point, their mutual affection and trust remained rock hard. Whatever problems might arise during the rest of the war, the two men confidently believed that they had each other's unwavering support. Considering how often Civil War generals on both sides mistrusted each other, the Grant-Sherman relationship allowed each man to act with the assurance that the other was completely trustworthy.

Problems remained, however. Halleck's capture of Corinth resulted in his being named commanding general of all Union armies. But before he left for Washington, he broke up his huge army and sent it, piecemeal, on a variety of housekeeping tasks. Grant became commander of the District of West Tennessee and later the Army of the Tennessee; Sherman became military governor of Memphis. Despite Sherman's pleasure in Grant's achievements, it is significant that he still considered Halleck to be a superior commander. He saw Grant as no "genius" but as an "honest truthful modest soldier." Halleck, however, was a man of significant military ability. With him gone, Sherman saw "no one here qualified to control large movements."[22] Whatever his misconception of Grant's intellectual ability, a common enemy in Union uniform refocused and reinforced his close ties to his unassuming friend.

On April 25, 1862, while Grant and Sherman had been moving with Halleck's army toward Corinth, Adm. David Farragut, with the aid of army units under Benjamin Butler, had captured New Orleans and pushed his way up the Mississippi River to Vicksburg. In late June, Farragut made it past Vicksburg's guns and linked up with the Union fleet above the city. Vicksburg remained in Confederate hands, however, and when the admiral withdrew south again, the Mississippi River between Vicksburg and Port Hudson in Louisiana returned to Confederate control.[23]

Following Farragut's failure, new plans for the capture of Vicksburg began in earnest when Grant and Sherman met in Columbus, Kentucky, on November 15.[24] John McClernand, a powerful southern Illinois congressman, had convinced Abraham Lincoln to give him command of a force he had recruited in the Midwest to try to capture Vicksburg. Grant and Sherman both knew McClernand well; he had commanded a division at Shiloh. They both found him offensive, largely because he was a politician-turned-general rather than a West Point graduate but also because he had a propensity for self-promotion.

The soldiers McClernand recruited in the Midwest arrived in Tennessee and Mississippi before he did. Grant knew he had to act quickly before McClernand came downriver with Lincoln's orders and took command of a Vicksburg expedition. Aided by a telegram from Halleck in Washington that allowed him to attack the enemy at his discretion, Grant moved immediately. He ordered Sherman in Memphis to lead a force down the Mississippi River against the Confederates who had dug in north of Vicksburg while he led a second prong from North Mississippi along the Mississippi Central Railroad to Jackson and then west toward Vicksburg. Grant also hoped that Nathaniel Banks in Louisiana would march north and attack the city from the south.[25]

Grant's subordinates were not happy with this arrangement. They wanted their commander to lead the main Vicksburg expedition because if it succeeded, Sherman would gain the credit, but if it failed, Grant would be held responsible. Besides, they were determined to gain martial glory for themselves. They appealed to Mrs. Grant, who was visiting her husband at the time. She immediately confronted him, but he only smiled at her concern. "We will hope that Sherman will be successful and, in that case, he will be entitled to the credit," he said. But what if he lost, Julia Dent Grant persisted. "Ah, we will not suppose that," he replied.[26]

Unfortunately, Banks never moved north, and Confederate cavalry raiders burned Grant's supply base at Holly Springs, thus preventing him from continuing south. Sherman attacked anyway, and his solo assault on Chickasaw Bayou in late December 1862 was a miserable failure. Vicksburg remained in Confederate hands. Even worse, from Sherman's viewpoint, McClernand arrived and took command of the expeditionary force. Grant did not reach the Vicksburg area until late January 1863, at which time he took over command of all the Union forces there. McClernand remained an irritant and a threat: he might gain higher command because of his ties to Abraham Lincoln.

Compounding the difficulties with McClernand's presence, Sherman became embroiled with a newsman, Thomas W. Knox of the *New York Herald*. He court-martialed Knox for accompanying the Vicksburg expedition against orders, citing the trial as a test case against all reporters, whom Sherman considered spies. Knox was sent out of the area but through Lincoln's intercession came back and asked Grant for permission to return to Sherman's army. Though Sherman's wife insisted Grant was secretly supporting Knox, Grant blasted the reporter for his journalistic attacks on Sherman and refused to allow him back into the area without Sherman's permission. Sherman told Knox, "Never," in the process lashing out at the press in general. He later thanked Grant "for the manner and substance of that response."[27] The two men thus remained close allies as they pondered what to do about Vicksburg.

It was an awful winter and spring, the wet weather adding to the misery Grant and Sherman felt over their failure to take the hill city. Grant implemented a variety of plans to capture the fortress. He had his soldiers continue an earlier attempt to dig a canal to divert the Mississippi River from its present channel, but the project was a miserable failure. Then he tried a variety of expeditions through the bayous and waterways, but these too came to naught. He had little real hope for any of these attempts, but he needed to keep his army busy and its morale up.

Sherman thought his friend was making a major mistake in this fruitless digging and trying to get ships and men through the swampy bayous and creeks. He worried that an increasingly impatient press would only step up its attacks, that Lincoln would grow tired of supporting Grant, and, chiefly, that McClernand would take his place. He also worried when Grant told him about his latest plan. He proposed running the fleet past Vicksburg's guns, marching his troops along the western side of the Mississippi River, ferrying his army to the eastern side below Vicksburg, and launching a campaign from there.

Sherman hurried to Grant's headquarters and asked to see the general alone. He told him he was worried about a possible disaster; Grant was placing his army in grave danger by implementing his risky plan. Sherman was convinced that the only logical thing to do was to take the troops back to Memphis and then repeat the failed attack plan, but this time to do it right.[28]

Grant understood that Sherman's advice made military sense, but he was sure that his friend was crucially wrong from a political point of view. The press, politicians, and the public in general would perceive any movement back to Memphis as a retreat, a failure. Unconvinced, Sherman sent Grant a letter repeating his suggestions. He read it and filed it in his pocket, secretly pleased, no doubt, that Sherman was concerned about him and so willing to do all he could, despite their disagreement over tactics.[29]

As part of his plan, Grant wanted Sherman to make a feint against Chickasaw Bayou to deceive the Confederates. Realizing that Sherman was still smarting from his repulse there in December, Grant displayed amazing sensitivity toward his friend. "I am loath to order it," he said, "because it would be so hard to make our own troops understand that only a demonstration was intended, and our people would characterize it as a repulse. I therefore leave it to you, whether to make such a demonstration." Sherman understood what Grant wanted, and he waved off his friend's concerns, although pleased with his kindness. He promised to do what Grant wanted because it had to be done. The two understood each other implicitly, and their trust and consideration for each other only intensified these good feelings and significantly worked to aid the Union cause. Even though Sherman did not agree with Grant's plan, calling it "one of the most hazardous & desperate enterprises that any army ever undertook," and even though he was concerned about having the public view him, once again, as a loser, he took on the assignment enthusiastically. He willingly risked more public censure—for Grant.[30]

Whether Sherman's feint to the north was instrumental in Grant's success below the city is debatable, but his willingness to do it with vigor was important. While Sherman feinted, Grant maneuvered magnificently to keep the Confederates off balance. Confederate cannon kept him from landing his troops at Grand Gulf; but undeterred, he confidently changed his plans. He crossed the river at Bruinsburg and placed his force between John Pemberton's army in Vicksburg and Joseph E. Johnston's troops in Jackson. Following victories at Port Gibson and Raymond, Grant drove Johnston out of Jackson and ordered Sherman, now on the scene, to destroy the city's warmaking capacity. He and Sherman personally visited a factory that continued to operate, despite the recent battle. They found the letters "CSA" on every bolt of tent cloth the factory produced. Grant immediately ordered the factory burned, and Sherman implemented the order.[31]

Then Grant turned west, won again at Champion Hill and Big Black River and captured Vicksburg and the army of John C. Pemberton on July 4, 1863, after a forty-seven-day siege. Sherman did everything Grant asked of him in the campaign: making the feint, racing back to rejoin the main force, damaging Jackson, participating in the May 22 attacks on the Vicksburg entrenchments, supporting the dismissal of John McClernand for violating orders, and establishing a defense line against Joseph E. Johnston along the Big Black River. Sherman did not share in the final capture of Vicksburg because he was on the Big Black ensuring that Confederate forces under Johnston did not try to relieve the siege from the east. He did it all gladly, giving Grant his total support. Grant welcomed this unselfish loyalty and felt strengthened.

Sherman was so elated about Vicksburg's capitulation and so proud of Grant that he excitedly told his friend, "I can hardly contain myself." A month before he had called Grant "deservedly a hero . . . [who was] entitled to all the credit of the movement which was risky and hazardous in the extreme and succeeded because of its hazard." To anyone who would listen, he explained how Grant had correctly read the situation while he himself had been wrong. He insisted to the Illinois governor and a delegation of state officials who visited the army that "Grant is entitled to every bit of the credit for the campaign; I opposed it. I wrote him a letter about it." Had Sherman not mentioned this letter, few would have known about it, because Grant had kept it confidential. Instead, Grant effusively praised Sherman at every opportunity. In his memoirs he wrote that Sherman's "untiring energy and great efficiency during the campaign entitle[d] him to a full share of all the credit due for its success. He could not have done more if the plan had been his own." The two men received promotion together, Grant to major general in the regular army, Sherman to brigadier.[32]

After Vicksburg, Grant traveled to New Orleans to confer with Gen. Nathaniel Banks, leaving Sherman in command of the troops in Mississippi. Sherman refused to take personal command, insisting that all orders go out under Grant's name. Once more, Grant could see that his absolute trust in Sherman was justified. He could depend on his friend Sherman as he moved to subdue the Confederacy.[33]

As for Sherman, he too benefited from his secure relationship with Grant. When the two stood on the Walnut Hills above Chickasaw Bayou, which Sherman had failed to capture in December 1862, he was overcome. He told Grant that "up to this minute, he had felt no positive assurance of success." Now he did, and clearly he realized that he owed it all to Grant.

Still, despite his solid admiration for Grant, Sherman did not consider his friend "a great man" or a "hero." He saw him as "a good, plain, sensible, kind-hearted fellow," those characteristics the essence of his strength.[34] Sherman never doubted that he was smarter than Grant, but he always deferred to him in military rank because he admired his no-nonsense military success. Grant was first, Sherman always believed, but he considered himself second.

The two men saw that in their friendship and their mutual trust they had created a successful military team. As they rose in rank and authority, this bond continued to influence Union success more and more. Ulysses S. Grant and William T. Sherman, two prewar failures, worked together to accomplish the success that had eluded them separately when they had not been friends. They brought out the best in each other, and they both understood this well. It was because of Sherman, Grant said, that "I have gained the little credit awarded me, and that our cause has triumphed to the extent it has."[35] He was right.

"Earned on the Field of Battle"

William H. L. Wallace

℮ Steven E. Woodworth

Ulysses S. Grant, still lame from an accident two days earlier, hobbled down the gangplank of the steamboat, mounted the horse an orderly held for him, and rode quickly up the road from Pittsburg Landing to the top of the bluffs. There, fifty feet or so above the surface of the Tennessee River, the roar of battle reached his ears in full fury. Several miles inland the scattered divisions of his army had sustained heavy attack that morning—Sunday, April 6, 1862—from the slightly larger Confederate army of Albert Sidney Johnston while Grant was at his headquarters in Savannah, Tennessee, several miles downstream. Hearing the distant firing but uncertain of its import, Grant had boarded a steamboat and set out for Pittsburg Landing. Passing the detached division of Maj. Gen. Lew Wallace at Crump's Landing on his way to the battlefield, Grant was still sufficiently uncertain of the situation to give no definite orders except that Wallace should have his division under arms and ready to march at a moment's notice.

The steamboat reached Pittsburg Landing at 8:00 A.M., and Grant rode inland from the landing, eager to learn the condition of his army. The roar of battle rose, closer and louder. One-half mile from the river, he met an officer whom he trusted to give him a solid and sensible account of the military situation. Brig. Gen. William H. L. Wallace had held that rank for just sixteen days, but Grant had confidence in him. After a brief conference with Wallace, Grant saw it all plainly. He had a major battle on his hands here at Pittsburg Landing, and he would try to arrange his army accordingly. Turning to a staff officer, he immediately sent word to Lew Wallace, down at Crump's Landing, to march his division to the battlefield at once.[1]

Perhaps the noise and smoke would have been enough to tell Grant all he needed to know, but his actions and statements over the previous several months had given evidence of a growing confidence in W. H. L. Wallace, a lawyer from Ottawa, Illinois, who was showing himself to have the makings of a first-rate officer. Their conference would probably have been enough to convince Grant to redeploy his forces even if the commanding general were still out of earshot of the battlefield. That was a circumstance worthy of note, for Grant, like all West Point–trained members of the Old Army's officer corps, had an in-bred suspicion of the eager novices and pompous politicians who provided much of the "leadership" for the nation's newly raised armies of volunteers. Somehow, W. H. L. Wallace had overcome at least a considerable degree of Grant's reservations and won for himself—and, by association, other volunteer officers—the respect of the businesslike, thoroughly professional general from Galena.

William Wallace was born in Urbana, Ohio, but moved to Illinois as a young child with his parents. The family settled in Mount Morris, where young Wallace attended the Rock River Seminary, a secondary school sponsored by the Methodist Church. From its stately building on a prominent swell of the prairie, a student could survey a long swath of the river valley, all the way to Rockford, twenty miles to the north. After graduating from the seminary and briefly teaching there, Wallace studied law and took up a practice in Ottawa, La Salle County, on the Illinois River between Springfield and Chicago, amid the waving prairies and rich farmlands of central Illinois.

When the Mexican War broke out, the twenty-five-year-old enlisted as a private in the La Salle County company of the First Illinois Regiment. He was soon promoted to lieutenant and the role of regimental adjutant, a position that kept him at regimental headquarters and allowed him to observe the actions of higher ranking officers in ways he could not have done as a line officer.

Sometimes dealing with the undisciplined volunteers could be difficult. While the regiment was still on its way to Mexico—indeed, on its way by steamboat down the Mississippi—some of the men got hold of a supply of Old Red Eye and got drunk. One of them, as Wallace recorded in his journal, "was particularly savage, and I was charged by Major Warren with the unpleasant duty of choking him into submission." Wallace got the job done, but no sooner had the drunk recovered from the rough treatment than he was raging and dangerous again. "Something must be done with the fellow," Wallace wrote. Something was. A few days later, the company's captain and Wallace's senior law partner, T. Lyle Dickey, had him drummed out of the army. "As he stepped on shore the band played the 'Rogues' March,' the other companies hissing and hooting him and hallooing to the people on shore 'not to stop that man but let him go, that he was drummed out,' etc., the sense of his disgrace seemed to force itself upon him, and he walked up the bank with tears in his eyes," Wallace recorded, adding, "The scene left an impression on the minds of all."[2]

Lieutenant Wallace was no romantic about war and its scenes. The regiment's journey to the seat of war took it past New Orleans, and they found themselves one night encamped on the field of Andrew Jackson's 1815 victory over the British, America's most celebrated battle to date. In his journal for July 25, 1846, Wallace wrote, "Slept upon the ground where Jackson achieved his glory . . . but felt none of Byron's enthusiasm upon the plains of Marathon, perhaps because I was very tired, probably because I am not Byron."[3]

Their journey took them onward by sea to the Texas coast, then inland to San Antonio, where they camped amid the ruins of the old Spanish Mission de Concepcion. From here they had only a small strip of Texas territory to traverse, and a mere twelve days' march brought them to the Rio Grande. Further marches took them deep into Mexico, where they joined the army of Gen. Zachary Taylor near Saltillo in the waning days of 1846. The main American effort had shifted to other theaters of the war by this time, and the Illinoisans feared they would see no fighting. On February 22, 1847, however, Mexican general Antonio Lopez de Santa Anna brought up a larger army to attack Taylor's outnumbered Americans.

"I've seen the elephant in every attitude, walking, running, at bay and fighting!" Wallace wrote to a friend back in Illinois a few days later. The First Illinois was in the thick of the battle. Early in the day it launched a successful bayonet charge, and Wallace noted of the enemy, "They could not stand the cold steel." Later the regiment found itself in a bad spot, with U.S. troops giving way on either side of it and the Mexicans turning both flanks and threatening to cut it off. At the last moment Col. John J. Hardin gave the order to fall back. Then U.S. artillery opened up to drive back a body of Mexican lancers who had nearly cut off the Illinoisans' retreat. "The first shell whistled close to me and burst within fifty yards of me," Wallace wrote, adding that it was the sweetest sound he ever heard.[4]

The lancers nevertheless succeeded in killing a number of the men, including Col. Hardin, and Wallace took the initiative in rallying the regiment and readying it to face the next Mexican advance. The day ended with the Americans still firmly in control of the battlefield, and that night Santa Anna's army slunk off to the south.[5]

Buena Vista was the First Illinois's great moment in the Mexican War, their one glimpse of "the elephant." Wallace was unimpressed with Taylor's generalship in the affair, believing that Santa Anna had the edge in skill—though not in courage—over "Old Rough and Ready"; "Nothing but the bull-dog courage and perseverance of the volunteers saved the day."[6]

When the war ended and the First Illinois went home, Wallace tried briefly to gain a commission in the regular army. Despite good recommendations from superiors who were impressed with his performance, the effort failed. So he went back to Ottawa and to his law practice with partner Lyle Dickey. It was not a bad life, and in 1851 he married Dickey's eighteen-year-old daughter Ann.[7]

By the time Southern secession plunged the nation into Civil War, Wallace was a mature man of nearly forty-one years, with a wife and family and an established law practice. Yet like tens of thousands of men across the North, he believed it was his duty to offer his services in the fight for the Union. In April 1861 he raised a company of volunteers in response to Pres. Abraham Lincoln's first call for seventy-five thousand militia—on ninety-day enlistments—to put down the rebellion. Along with companies from all over the central and southern portions of the state, Wallace and his La Salle County boys headed for Springfield, to be incorporated into regiments and dispatched to the seat of the war, wherever that might be. "Both justice & duty point the way," he explained in one of his first letters to his wife after leaving home, "and whatever may be the result to individuals . . . the right will prevail."[8]

Still, that did not mean Wallace was prepared to go to war in any capacity whatsoever. After all, he was no nineteen-year-old farm boy leaving home in hopes of "seeing the elephant" for the first time and content to shoulder a musket as a private soldier. On the contrary, as a man of some standing in the community as well as previous experience as an army officer, he was no more inclined to settle for his current rank of captain either. In an April 24 letter to his wife from Springfield, he explained that the companies present there were being organized into regiments; the members of each regiment would then elect their own colonel. Wallace believed he had a good chance to win that post within what would become his own regiment and added, "If I do not succeed I will return home immediately."[9] Serving the cause was all very well, but ambition must be served.

As it turned out, of course, he had no need to return home, easily winning election as colonel of his regiment. Nor was he the only man tempted to take counsel of his ambition that spring. Indeed, when one of the regiment's ten captains discovered that he had lost the race for lieutenant colonel, he pulled his company out of the regiment, necessitating a shake-up in organization of what became the Eleventh Illinois, delaying its formal mustering-in by several days. Lust for high rank and military glory was epidemic among both amateur and professional officers in those days. Wallace's case, though far from admirable, was actually one of the milder forms of the affliction.[10]

Wallace at once set to the task of training and disciplining his regiment. He found it no easy job, but he stuck to it with dogged persistence and, with the benefit of his experience in the Mexican War, gradually made progress. Within two weeks of the regiment's organization, another officer noticed a clear improvement in its performance on drill. Disciplining the rowdy farm boys—excited as they were at being embarked on the first great adventure of their lives—to behave themselves during their off-duty hours proved more difficult. The standard punishment for severe infractions in that stage of the war was being "drummed out of camp," a humiliating spectacle in which the offender was formally expelled from the army. One soldier noted in a letter home that he would rather be burned to death than drummed out of camp, but Wallace showed himself ready to use that penalty if pushed. A lieutenant in the Eleventh noted that two men suffered that fate on May 18.[11]

To keep his men in check, Wallace imposed a strict regime—roll call in each company at sunrise, Monday through Saturday, then squad drill, company drill, guard mount and inspection, a period of instruction for the officers while the noncommissioned officers gave the troops yet another dose of squad drill, and finally a couple of hours of battalion drill topped off by dress parade at 6:00 P.M. This schedule was relaxed on Sundays, with only the unavoidable morning and evening roll calls and the evening dress parade, but "the colonel earnestly recommend[ed] his command to attend divine service in camp on Sunday."[12] His willingness and capacity to impose thorough training and strict discipline were some of the most important qualities that marked him out for greater responsibilities.

The Eleventh's first movement as a regiment taught Wallace the difficulties of command but also showed him rising to the challenges with unusual diligence and ability. On May 4 the adjutant general of Illinois gave him orders to take his regiment to Villa Ridge, Illinois, near Cairo at the southern tip of the state. He carefully made preparations for the trip, receiving assurances from state military officials in Springfield that a ten-days' supply of food would accompany his regiment and giving orders to his commissary officer that the food be loaded onto the train. Before the regiment marched to the Springfield depot on the afternoon of May 5, Wallace checked with the commissary officer to make sure all the food was aboard. Assured that all was well, he boarded along with his men for the long ride south. It was crowded, and he was tired, and the men, of course, were excited and rowdy. With difficulty he got those in his section to pipe down as the train rattled on through the night and a pouring rain, across the sodden central Illinois prairies.

The next morning found them on the line of the Illinois Central, pulling into Carbondale, deep in the southern Illinois region known (for reasons now obscure) as Little Egypt. It was six o'clock, and the rain still fell, but the men took advantage of the stop to fan out from the depot and visit the shops of nearby Main Street. While his men were flocking into S. H. Freeland's grocery and other such establishments, Wallace made a disturbing discovery. Not ten-days' rations but only one had accompanied his regiment on the train, and despite all his orders and inquiries, no arrangements had been made for getting any more. Furthermore, he somehow learned that no provision had been made to house his troops at Villa Ridge, less than two hours away. Faced with the prospect of his men camping hungry and tentless in the dripping woods, Wallace took energetic action. He sent to the army commissary at Cairo, Illinois, for rations, and he began to inquire for all the local carpenters and any supplies of lumber that might be available. He repeated the process at every southern Illinois whistle-stop all the way to Villa Ridge, and by the time he got there he had some twenty carpenters aboard his train. He laid out the encampment, set the carpenters to building and his men to carrying lumber, and "before an hour the whole place was noisy with the sound of saws & hammers." Even these efforts were not sufficient, so Wallace commandeered several local buildings and ordered part of the railroad cars to be kept on a nearby siding until better shelter could be found. The officials of the Illinois Central were irate, and the state adjutant general's office was concerned about the effect this would have on the transportation of other troops within the state, but the men of the Eleventh appreciated it.

As for the state military bureaucracy, Wallace had a comment or two for them. He sent a strongly worded report about the difficulties he had encountered, and, still not satisfied, sent an even more strongly worded private letter to the adjutant general's first assistant, Maj. John B. Wyman. "There are some things I want to say stronger than official language will warrant," he explained to the hapless major. "By the eternal my men must be fed." How could he demand that his men show good discipline and refrain from pilfering food from civilians when they were going hungry? He also urged the speedy shipment of arms and accoutrements for his men, especially the new minié rifles.[13]

Of course, most of the regiments in the mushrooming army at that time were in want of such things, and minié rifles were at a premium from one end of the country to the other. It was also true that before the war was over—indeed, before it was a year older—Wallace and his men knew what it was to endure much greater portions of cold, hunger, and exposure to the elements without thinking their lot worse than that of all soldiers. Yet his efforts during the movement to southern Illinois showed, in early form, a number of the qualities that made him a successful officer during the first year of the war: energy, resourcefulness, attention to detail, and concern for the welfare of his troops.

That did not mean things were going to be easy for him. Shortly after arriving in Villa Ridge he received a letter from S. H. Freeland, a Carbondale merchant, complaining that goods had walked out of his store without payment the morning the Eleventh had passed through town—sixteen pieces of dried beef, sixteen and a half packs of patriotic Union envelopes, and a tin cup: total value, $5.75. Then there was the mayor of nearby Mound City, Illinois, who complained that some of the soldiers would come into the town frequently, "get drunk, insult ladies upon the street, and disturb the peace and quiet of our people generally." He sent three of the delinquents back to camp in care of the city marshal. There were also complaints that the men "have been engaged in lawlessly killing animals belonging to citizens living in the neighborhood of the camp." Again, Wallace reacted energetically, laying down stringent orders for the suppression of such activity and threatening the perpetrators with court-martial and drumming out, the punishment whose effectiveness he had seen demonstrated in the Mexican War. In short order he carried through on that threat in several cases.[14]

He also combated disorderliness through the positive means of keeping the men otherwise occupied. They "take great interest in drilling," he explained to his wife, "& I am giving them enough of it." To his delight, they began to take pride in themselves as soldiers and as members of the Eleventh Illinois. They were pleased when large crowds turned out to watch them drill. They were good, and they knew it. They knew their commander's worth as well. Drill was noticeably smarter when he directed it than when the lieutenant colonel commanded. One May evening a company of the Eleventh, the Rockford Zouaves, marched up to headquarters to give him "the Zouave Salute" and to sing patriotic songs.[15] Clearly the regiment was coming along well.

The summer passed without action for the Eleventh Illinois. Back east in Virginia, rival armies fought the battle of Bull Run that July, and the North suffered a humiliating defeat. The ninety-day enlistments expired, and Wallace persuaded his regiment to reenlist in a body, as several of Illinois's original ninety-day regiments did. Now they were in for three years.

Wallace also gained more authority and responsibility. Though still a colonel in rank, he came to command a brigade, including his own Eleventh Illinois, at the post of Bird's Point, Missouri, just across the Mississippi River from Cairo. In that capacity he negotiated an informal prisoner-of-war exchange with Confederate officers from down the river and otherwise performed with his usual quiet competence. His commanding officer was now the newly minted Brig. Gen. Ulysses S. Grant. Grant occasionally had Wallace lead forays into the interior of southeastern Missouri, reconnoitering rebel positions or vainly pursuing Confederate guerrilla leader M. Jeff Thompson. Nothing in this stage of their relationship denoted anything special. Wallace was just one more adequate nonprofessional subordinate for a West Point–trained general who had precious few professional officers to carry out his orders. Like fellow Illinois lawyers Richard Oglesby, Benjamin Prentiss, and John McClernand, Wallace did as he was told and committed no gaffes during this period. Grant was satisfied that the Ottawa lawyer was among his four or five best lieutenants at this point, for he made official Wallace's command of a brigade.[16]

Wallace's consistent efforts to maintain discipline began to pay off, though his efficiency in this area became visible generally through the contrasting lapses of other officers. When he took a brief leave in late October and Col. Richard J. Oglesby commanded the camp at Bird's Point, Wallace's crisp discipline was missed. The Eleventh's major, T. E. G. Ransom, wrote to Wallace from camp to inform him that Oglesby had unaccountably permitted a minstrel show to stage a series of performances in camp, something Ransom or Wallace could have predicted would get out of hand. The result of Oglesby's ineptitude was a disturbance in which some of the soldiers "got broken heads &c." As for the traveling exhibition, "This morning it is laid on the ground, a few broken benches alone indicating where once was a flourishing side show."[17]

Quiet competence and good discipline were qualities to impress U. S. Grant. When in early November 1861 he set in motion the series of movements that resulted in the battle of Belmont, Missouri, Wallace seems to have played an important part in Grant's thinking. He sent most of the Bird's Point garrison on another, and bigger, expedition into the interior of southeast Missouri, this one under the command of Colonel Oglesby and once again on the imagined trail of the elusive Jeff Thompson. Wallace's brother-in-law, Lt. Cyrus E. Dickey of the Eleventh, thought he had "good reason to believe that Gen. Grant intended to give [Wallace] the command of the expedition & waited for him to the last moment."[18] But Wallace was not yet due back from his leave, and Grant was eager to get on with the war.

Very eager. Grant apparently had in mind a plan to open the Mississippi deep into rebel-held territory. Besides Oglesby's force in southeast Missouri, he had several other detachments of his command in motion. Their apparent ultimate purpose was to take the river towns of Belmont and New Madrid, Missouri—the first opposite the Confederate stronghold at Columbus, Kentucky, and the second another thirty miles or so down the river. He may even have had designs on Columbus itself, if the operation should progress favorably. At the heart of this effort was a sizable expedition led by Grant himself, traveling down the Mississippi by steamboat transports from Cairo with the purpose of attacking and taking Belmont.[19]

When Wallace returned from his leave, Grant on November 6 sent him orders to take the five companies of the Eleventh that Oglesby had left behind at Bird's Point and march inland to join the colonel with specific orders from Grant. The new expedition, unavoidably commanded by Oglesby, who was several days Wallace's senior as a colonel, was to forget about Thompson—there had been precious little chance of catching him in the first place—and to turn its march southeastward toward New Madrid. Once Oglesby reached New Madrid, he was to "communicate with [Grant] at Belmont," which Grant obviously expected to seize from the rebels in the next day or two. Apparently the quiet general from Galena believed opportunity was beckoning him and was further developing his plan.[20]

Grant also had a useful notice from departmental headquarters in St. Louis to the effect that the Confederates might be crossing troops from Columbus over into southeastern Missouri. That was highly unlikely, but it gave Grant useful cover. If his grand plan miscarried, he could always claim that the dispatch of Oglesby and Wallace was simply an attempt to comply with headquarters' desire to stop such Confederate troop shifting.[21]

Wallace set out from Bird's Point as ordered on the evening of November 6, reached Charleston, Missouri, and encamped late that night. At this point a strange episode occurred in the Grant-Wallace relationship. As Grant later wrote in his report on the battle of Belmont, it was 2:00 A.M., November 7, when a steamboat came down the river bearing a messenger from Wallace. He had discovered from "a reliable Union man" in Charleston that the rebels were indeed transferring troops across the river from Columbus to Belmont, this time for the purpose of cutting off Oglesby. This, Grant explained in his report, seemed "more than probable" and made his demonstration down the Mississippi even more important. In fact, he concluded, "This information determined me to attack vigorously his forces at Belmont."[22]

Two o'clock in the morning would be about the right time for moonshine, and that is just what this story was. Grant had already given notice to Wallace and Oglesby that he would be in Belmont within the next day or two, a circumstance that would require him to "attack vigorously." Indeed, Belmont was the obvious first target of all Grant's early-November maneuvering. Furthermore, though it is true that Wallace was in Charleston and that there were a number of Union men there, he left no record of receiving any such report or of sending word of it to Grant. Even in his voluminous and detailed letters to Ann, he said nothing of the matter. Instead, he criticized Grant for what he saw as an ill-advised attack on Belmont and expressed doubts about the tall tale of needing to protect the Union forces in the interior of Missouri.[23] So Grant at least considered Wallace a credible source for a fictional story needed to make the Belmont operation look like something besides a grand plan that had ingloriously fizzled.

By November 8, however, that is clearly just what the Belmont operation was. Grant reached Belmont and attacked on the seventh, men fighting bravely and routing the Confederate defenders. Then, however, the green citizen-soldiers considered their task accomplished and began a highly disorganized celebration of the victory while the Confederates rallied and received major reinforcements from Columbus, just across the river. The rebel counterattack sent Grant's disorganized forces flying back to their transports with fairly heavy casualties. Numbers of Union troops, including Grant himself, narrowly avoided being nabbed by the rapidly advancing Confederates. For a sometime leathergoods store clerk turned Union general with plenty to prove, it was not a thing of beauty. If Wallace ever found out what Grant did to cover his flank back at departmental headquarters, he left no record of it. Since it is hard to imagine Wallace knowing about it and not confiding it in his letters to Ann, the odds are he went to his grave ignorant of the contents of Grant's report.

After the battle, back in the army's bases around Cairo, Grant confided to Wallace "that if he had had regular troops he would not have fought" the battle of Belmont once he landed and assessed the strength of the Confederate forces in the vicinity. He had believed, however, that if he had then left without fighting, "he never would have been able to convince his volunteer soldiers that he was not afraid to fight." To keep up the confidence and morale of his raw troops, Grant had led them into battle. Wallace was not impressed, but he expressed his skepticism in a letter to Ann rather than in conversation with Grant or, so far as any evidence reveals, with any other officers in the army. Grant "& his friends," Wallace told his wife (pointedly excluding himself from that group), "call it a victory," but the citizen-colonel from Ottawa thought "it cost too much."[24]

Yet along with Wallace's doubts about Grant's moral courage, another thing is evident in the aftermath of the battle of Belmont. Though Grant may have invented the story of Wallace's midnight messenger, he nevertheless showed respect for him in thus confiding his motivation for the action. He also showed that he considered Wallace as worth more than the rank amateurs he classed as volunteers. The latter might need an otherwise useless battle to keep their morale high, but Wallace could receive at least a part of the true explanation. In his memoirs, Grant described him as "a most estimable officer" and "a veteran too," basing that claim to veteran status in part on Wallace's Mexican War experience. It was, after all, more than many of Grant's colonels possessed.[25]

After Belmont, the forces around Cairo settled into winter quarters. With his accustomed concern for the health and comfort of his men, Wallace himself produced a design for a "very convenient & comfortable" style of log hut for his men to build and occupy. He encouraged diligent building and policing of the camps, sponsoring a contest in the Eleventh Illinois in which he offered an oyster supper to the company that had the neatest quarters. Company G took the prize. Wallace also took a direct interest in seeing that the brigade hospital was "overhauled & repaired to make it more comfortable" for the sick he expected that winter.[26]

Winter quarters did not mean complete inactivity, even as pertained to military operations. There were still rumors and reports of Jeff Thompson marauding in southeastern Missouri, and since Grant lacked adequate cavalry, the infantry—often as not Wallace's—drew the duty of chasing him. It would have been a questionable undertaking with mounted troops. For foot soldiers it was, in Wallace's words, a "wild goose chase" that served only to demonstrate "that we can move over any kind of roads & that we can stand any kind of weather." Through alternating rain, snow, mud, and intense cold, he and his troops made one foray after another into the wilds of Missouri. He had confidence neither in the success of his mission—"I have no idea we will catch him"—nor in his commander. "I am getting very tired of this," he confided in a letter to Ann, "& feel strongly the necessity of some head—some leading mind upon whom I can rely & feel that in so doing I am directed by a mind that conceives the crisis & comprehends the means of meeting it." The clear implication was that Grant's was not such a mind. "This feeling of doubt & distrust," Wallace concluded, "is terrible when there are such momentous issues at stake."

Still, Wallace performed as a faithful and reliable subordinate. He kept his doubts about Grant to himself and to Ann in his letters, and though he had no expectation of actually catching Thompson, he noted,

"I am ordered to try & of course will do my best." During these expeditions, too, his command showed good discipline, whereas other commands sometimes straggled and plundered. An officer who was loyal, did his best ("of course"), and kept his troops orderly and well in hand must have impressed Grant.[27]

On February 1 Wallace and his men received orders to prepare for another expedition, obviously much more significant than the others. In this case they were to board steamboats that would take them up the Ohio and Tennessee Rivers, through Kentucky, and to the borders of Tennessee, in which state, as Wallace proudly noted in his letter to Ann, "we will have the honor of being the first Federal troops." For him this was a new challenge of sorts. This time he would command a full brigade in the field, something his many small expeditions had not involved. He confided to Ann that he felt "a great deal of anxiety about details" but trusted that, with God's help, all would be well.[28]

Their objective was Fort Henry, a rebel stronghold on the Tennessee River, but they were not to meet the enemy in battle there after all. Landing several miles from the fort, Grant's troops began tramping overland to take up positions surrounding it on the landward side. The Tennessee roads were none too good to begin with, and recent heavy rains had not improved them. While the foot soldiers slogged through the mud, the accompanying naval flotilla attacked and subdued the poorly sited Confederate fort. Wallace's brigade had an especially hard time, since attached to it was Capt. Edward McAllister's battery D, First Illinois Artillery, consisting of four heavy siege guns. Wallace managed as best he could on what he called "the worst roads I ever saw." Under a new organization of Grant's forces, the brigade was now part of a division under the command of John A. McClernand, a political general from Illinois. McClernand was pleased with Wallace's performance, referring in his report to his "able and judicious" leadership in getting his brigade forward under trying conditions. Wallace and his men could hear the naval bombardment, lasting two hours with an impressive decibel level. His troops and the awkward heavy guns were still toiling through the mud three or four miles out when the firing stopped, marking the surrender of the fort. His men "didn't get under fire," he wrote, "but hope for better luck next time."[29] Wallace also noted in his letter to Ann, "Genl. Grant invited me to take a state room on his boat."[30] Grant apparently had a growing regard for the erstwhile lawyer from Ottawa.

As Wallace anticipated, the army's next move was to march east-ward toward Fort Donelson, the Confederate bastion guarding the Cumberland River. On February 11 orders came down from division headquarters to take up the march. Once again the prospect of battle loomed, and Wallace's frame of mind was again equal parts of devotion to duty and trust in God. To his wife he wrote that day, "I am de-termined to do my duty as I understand it & leave the event in His hands."[31]

They camped that night and marched on to Fort Donelson the next day, arriving before its frowning embankments shortly after noon. Along with the rest of McClernand's Division, Wallace's brigade took up a position on the Union right, helping to hem in the southern end of the Confederate position. On February 13 and 14 they sparred vigor-ously with the Confederates opposite them. Nights were misery as pickets kept up intermittent gunfire and a storm lashed the exposed troops with rain and snow.

Early on the morning of February 15 the rebels launched a furious assault in an attempt to break out of their enclave around the fort and withdraw to join other Confederate forces far to the south. The on-slaught struck the extreme right of the Union position, and as that end of the line began to give way, Wallace's brigade also came under at-tack, with the brigade-right taking the first and heaviest blow. Wallace maneuvered his troops skillfully to turn back several charges but found that the brigades to his right were giving way. The sounds of battle on that side were moving in an ominous direction. Worse, the brigade was beginning to receive fire from the right and rear. Wallace's orders were to hold the position "to the last extremity," and that point seemed to be approaching. When McClernand could find no reinforcements to bolster Wallace's line, he gave the brigade commander permission to retreat. Having held that ground as long as he could without being cut off, Wallace ordered his regiments to fall back.

The terrain was hilly and did not allow Wallace to see his entire brigade line at one time. In the confusion, the Eleventh Illinois, fighting on the brigade's hard-hit right flank, did not get the order to fall back, a circumstance that Wallace attributed to "the stupidity of an orderly." The regiment held its ground, fighting alongside the Thirty-first Illi-nois, the left-most and only remaining regiment of the neighboring bri-gade. Finally, the Thirty-first ran out of ammunition and withdrew, and the Eleventh fought on alone until, assailed in front and on both flanks, it barely managed to make its escape, having sustained the highest casualties in the brigade.[32]

The following morning the rebel force surrendered, and Wallace's troops marched forward and planted their colors on the now undefended breastworks, as other Federals were doing up and down the line. The battle of Fort Donelson was a major turning point of the war. It cost the Confederacy over thirteen thousand prisoners at a time when it could ill afford such a loss of manpower, and together with the victory at Fort Henry it opened up the major rivers of the Mississippi Valley to Union incursion. Half the state of Tennessee, including the cities of Nashville and shortly thereafter Memphis, fell to Union control as the result of these victories and the chain of events they set in motion.

With understandable exaggeration, Wallace called it "the greatest battle ever fought on this continent." Whether he knew it or not, his opinion coincided with that of Grant when he added, "I think it is the death blow of the rebellion if rapidly & judiciously followed up." Numerous Confederate strong points, including Columbus, would have to be abandoned as a result of the Union triumphs on the Tennessee and Cumberland Rivers. "Te Deum laudamus—Let the people praise Him," wrote Wallace. Yet the slaughter of the Eleventh Illinois disturbed him deeply. "When I look at my own regiment, whose long front I have so often looked upon with pride, now shortened of more than half its length," he wrote, he could not help thinking "that it is a dearly bought victory."[33]

Wallace's performance at Fort Donelson impressed Grant, and the latter's estimate of him continued to rise steadily. Later that month Wallace accompanied Grant, McClernand, and their staffs on steamboat excursions up the Cumberland River, first to Clarksville and then to Nashville. Wallace's presence on these jaunts may well indicate that Grant was including the Illinois colonel increasingly in his inner circle of what have been called "Grant men," though Wallace was not, in fact, a particular admirer of the general.[34]

In mid-March Grant recommended to the War Department four colonels in his command as highly deserving candidates for promotion to the rank of brigadier general. Two of these men were professionally trained soldiers. The other two were W. H. L. Wallace and Thirty-first Illinois commander John A. Logan. They were, as Grant admitted, "from civil pursuits," but he emphasized that he had "no hesitation in fully indorsing them as in every way qualified for the position of brigadier-general." Despite their lack of West Point educations, Grant explained, these two men had "fully earned the position on the field of battle."[35]

The army's next move took it back to Fort Henry, onto the steamboats, and up the Tennessee River until it was near the southern border of the state. Wallace's brigade halted for about a week near the river town of Savannah, then rode the steamboats farther upriver to Pittsburg Landing, on the west bank of the river just a few miles from the Mississippi and about thirty from the main Confederate base at Corinth, Mississippi.

"There will probably be some changes in our organization," he confided to Ann on March 22. "Genl Grant today intimated that he intended to put me in command of a division." Wallace was not sure whether such an event would actually take place or whether he really wanted it. True, "It would relieve me from my present division commander"—McClernand. Yet, on the other hand, it would take him away from his troops, especially the Eleventh Illinois, to whom he had a strong emotional attachment. He also felt his usual intense awareness of the responsibilities involved in higher commands. "In any event," he concluded, "I shall strive to do my duty relying on our Father for strength, courage, & wisdom to aid me."[36]

Grant was very much in earnest in what he told Wallace, though it is not clear which division command he had in mind on March 22. An additional division, composed primarily of new troops sent upriver, was soon put together in the camps around Pittsburg Landing, but its command went to another Illinois lawyer-soldier, Benjamin M. Prentiss of Quincy, who had been a brigadier general since the previous summer and thus much outranked Wallace, whose promotion to that rank dated only from March 21, 1862. Instead, Wallace succeeded to the command of another division.

Maj. Gen. Charles F. Smith had once been a West Point instructor to, among other cadets, Ulysses S. Grant. He was now Grant's subordinate, though much respected by his former student as well as by the rest of the Old Army's officer corps. Department commander Henry W. Halleck, eaten up with envy at Grant's success, had even tried to finagle Smith into Grant's job—good of the war effort be hanged—in order to sidetrack Grant's rising reputation. Thus Smith had briefly been the official commander of the expedition up the Tennessee River. All that changed when Smith fell seriously ill as a result of the infection from a minor injury sustained when he slipped while getting into a boat. On April 2, his condition had deteriorated to the point that he had to relinquish command, not only of the expedition but also of his own division, and take to his bed in Savannah. He did not live out the month. C. F. Smith was a promising officer who had helped Grant much and might have done much more for the Union had he lived, but he was no proper substitute for that general.

That same April 2, Grant, once again in command of the expedition, assigned Brig. Gen. W. H. L. Wallace to Smith's division, in theory to "be assigned to a brigade by Maj. Gen. C. F. Smith." In fact, since Smith was incapacitated, Wallace, who outranked the division's other officers, took command.[37]

On April 3 McClernand's division had a grand review. The weather was fine and balmy, the peach trees in nearby orchards in full bloom. Wallace commanded his brigade on review for the last time. The following day an officer of the Eleventh Illinois noted in his diary, "Gen. Wallace took leave of the . . . Brigade today to take charge of his new command."[38]

He was plunged immediately into responsibilities of the gravest character. The division whose command he had just taken over was the army's reserve, camped closest to the landing. It would be the first to respond to reinforce any portion of the army that might be attacked. This applied especially to one of the army's six divisions that was positioned at a distance of several miles from the other five. Maj. Gen. Lew Wallace's division was encamped near Crump's Landing, several miles north of Pittsburg Landing. Grant wished to hold Crump's Landing, but the garrison there would be an obvious target for Confederates hoping to isolate and destroy a portion of the Union army. It was therefore of the utmost importance that Lew Wallace be speedily reinforced if he should be attacked, and W. H. L. Wallace was the division commander who would have to do so. Grant lost no time in making this duty clear to Wallace but seemed comfortably confident in the latter's ability to carry out such a responsible task. On April 4, the same day Wallace assumed command of Smith's old division, Grant wrote to tell him, "It may be necessary to re-enforce General [Lew] Wallace to avoid his being attacked by a superior force. Should you find danger of this sort, re-enforce him at once with your entire division." Will Wallace immediately got in touch with the Indiana Wallace and the two exchanged dispatches and worked out plans for speedy movement between them of both messages and troops.[39]

That very night Wallace's nerves were tested when skirmishing flared up on the front of Sherman's division, the most outlying of the main camps, several miles inland from Pittsburg Landing. It was dark and rainy, and the sound of firing brought "a good deal of excitement" to the Union camps. "Several divisions formed in line," Wallace wrote Ann the next morning. "I had my division ready, but did not turn out." It was not unnecessary. Sherman's forces easily drove the rebels back, pursuing them some distance until they received artillery support. Casualties were a dozen or two on each side. Wallace mounted and rode the three miles through the black night to Sherman's headquarters, accompanied by Col. James B. McPherson of Grant's staff. They arrived there to find all quiet in front and General Sherman in high spirits, confident in his ability to deal with whatever Confederate rabble might be in the woods. As Wallace and McPherson rode back toward the former's camp, they met Grant riding up from Pittsburg Landing. The sound of the firing had drawn him from his headquarters in Savannah to learn the situation of his army. Wallace and McPherson, two officers in whom he was coming to have great confidence, assured him that all was well. In his memoirs, Grant implies that their word was sufficient to reassure him and that he did not proceed to Sherman's headquarters. While riding back to the landing, he suffered injury when his horse missed the path in the opaque rain and darkness and fell, landing on his leg and injuring his ankle. For the next two or three days Grant could walk only with crutches.[40]

The next morning Will wrote Ann, noting that command of a full division was "a great responsibility & does not set easy on me yet."[41] The tide of events did not give him the chance to grow accustomed to the job. Though Sherman and Grant dismissed the possibility of a full-scale rebel attack on the army around Pittsburg Landing, that was of course exactly what lay in the offing. The skirmish on Friday night, April 4, as well as other, smaller, skirmishes on the day before and the day after were the result of the growing Confederate force gathering in the vicinity with the purpose of crushing Grant's army.

On Sunday morning, April 6, the rebels struck. Because of the past three days of skirmishing, Wallace was alert. He had ordered that he and his staff should have their breakfast "at an early hour" and have horses saddled, ready for whatever might come. Shortly before

7:00 A.M. word arrived that full-scale battle had broken out at the positions of Sherman's and Prentiss's divisions, farthest from the landing. Besides getting his division up and in line, Wallace also dispatched a courier by steamboat to notify Grant in Savannah. By 7:30 Wallace marched his division away from its camps to reinforce the hard-pressed fighting line. On the way to the front, he met Grant, who had heard the sound of the guns even before Wallace's message arrived and had once again rushed to Pittsburg Landing by steamboat and ridden inland on horseback. As had been the case Friday evening, Grant again appeared satisfied with Wallace's report of the situation—a major battle this time—and immediately gave orders to bring Lew Wallace's division up from Crump's Landing.[42]

Grant went on his way to visit Sherman's front and left Wallace to lead his division to reinforce the center of the Union line. Shortly after nine o'clock his division reached the front—or the front reached it—and rather than reinforcing the center, the division became the center. The battered divisions of Sherman and Prentiss fell back on either side of it. Prentiss's remnant took up a position immediately adjoining Wallace's left. McClernand's moved up to fill the gap between Wallace's right and Sherman's division. Brig. Gen. Stephen A. Hurlbut's division moved up on the far side of Prentiss, along with some detached troops, to anchor the left of the Union line.

About ten o'clock the rebels came on again, and for the next several hours the battle raged intensely as wave after wave of Confederate troops hurled themselves at the Union position. In the center, Wallace's and Prentiss's commands clung doggedly to a stretch of country lane, in places eroded slightly below ground level, and refused to give up an inch of ground. When Prentiss's division, battered from its early morning fight, appeared ready to give way, Wallace alertly responded to his request for help by sending over the Eighth Iowa to bolster his line.[43]

Grant visited that sector at one point during the day and urged his commanders to hold the position at all costs. Still, as the afternoon wore on, the rebels gradually drove back the Union line on either side of the Wallace-Prentiss position, which in turn became the focal point of the Confederate offensive effort. In Wallace's front a Southern officer massed some forty cannon, the largest collection of artillery yet seen on the continent, and blasted away at the Union position in the farm lane. On Prentiss's left, Confederate army commander Albert Sidney Johnston received his death wound as he personally led a charge that finally pushed back Hurlbut's division, forcing it to drop its grip on the left of Prentiss's line. At almost the same time, Sherman and McClernand also gave way, breaking contact with Wallace's right.

This placed Prentiss and Wallace in extreme danger of being attacked in flank and even in rear. Prentiss understood Grant's orders as being imperative, regardless of circumstances, and took literally the injunction to hold at all hazards. About this time Prentiss and Wallace held a hurried battlefield conference. As Prentiss remembered it, they "agreed to hold our positions at all hazards." The situation was changing rapidly, however, and although Prentiss may have been willing to let his command become surrounded in order to go on holding his ground, Wallace was not. Within a very short time after this discussion must have taken place, he had decided to extract his division from its increasingly hopeless situation. As at Fort Donelson, he had held his position until the danger of encirclement had become acute. Now he gave the order to withdraw and, perhaps thinking of how the Eleventh Illinois had not gotten the word at Fort Donelson, he set out to supervise the withdrawal in person. The situation to the rear of his battle line was by then extremely fluid and deteriorating by the moment. Confederate troops were cropping up in places where none but friendly units should have been. As he directed the first part of the withdrawal, Wallace came under fire from Confederates in a nearby patch of woods. Rising in the stirrups to try to identify more closely the source of the firing, Wallace took a bullet in the head and fell to the ground.[44]

Most of his troops did get out of the rapidly closing trap, though a couple of regiments remained with what was left of Prentiss's command and surrendered along with him an hour or so later. The portion of the division that escaped was nevertheless badly thinned by the day's furious fighting and disorganized by the desperate retreat and the shift in command from the fallen Wallace to his senior brigade commander. Its remnants were regrouping behind the final Union defense line that evening when the Confederate assault ceased shortly before sunset. Wallace's stubborn stand had pressed to almost the precise maximum of the time that could be won without the annihilation of his command. Other divisions had fallen back earlier; Prentiss's had stayed and suffered capture. Wallace had fought on until the last possible moment and then given the order to withdraw in time to extract most of a division that, after resting and regrouping, lived to fight another day.

Wallace himself was left for dead on the battlefield during the desperate struggle of the division to escape encirclement. There he lay through a night of thunder, lightning, and cold rain. The next day Grant struck back at his assailants and drove the rebels back across the ground they had taken on Sunday. Wallace was taken up from the battlefield by his friends and found to be still breathing. They carried him to the landing, where Ann was aboard one of the steamboats, having arrived Sunday morning, just as fighting broke out, for the purpose of paying him a surprise visit. She found quarters for them in Savannah and did her best to nurse her husband back to health. In the days that followed he regained consciousness, and his friends entertained hopes for his recovery, but it was not to be. On April 10 he finally succumbed to the effects of his wound. "We have lost a great and good man," wrote the Eleventh Illinois's Lt. Douglas Hapeman in his diary that day.[45]

William Harvey Lamb Wallace did not live long enough to become a "Grant man," or one of Grant's chief lieutenants. His career was brief, his rank relatively low, and his impact limited. Yet he did have an impact on Grant and on the war, and Grant's treatment of him revealed something about the man from Galena as well. Wallace was no military professional, but he showed an aptitude for the business. His talent was not that of a natural genius for war such as Nathan Bedford Forrest but of a diligent, intelligent man who was willing to learn and knew when to keep his mouth shut. Grant was a military professional with a military professional's preference for others of his own sort—a preference that usually proved to be justified by events. Yet he was also unusual among professional officers in his relative willingness to promote and rely on capable citizen-generals. The case of W. H. L. Wallace both demonstrates that characteristic of Grant and may perhaps, to a small extent, have helped to develop it further.

Wallace's qualifications as a successful officer began with his experience in the Mexican War. That brief tour of duty was a far cry from a West Point education, but he profited from it more than most. That he did so was a factor of his own character qualities. First of all, he was a diligent officer. He devoted abundant time, energy, and personal attention to seeing that his men were equipped, fed, trained, and as healthy and comfortable as possible. Second, he had a relatively healthy concept of military authority. He expected his troops to obey orders, and he enforced discipline within his command. He also took seriously the orders of his superiors, carrying them out faithfully even when he could see little point in them.

A corollary of Wallace's respect for military authority was his reticence about public denunciations of his commanding officer. Throughout his career in the army, he seems to have had less confidence in Grant than Grant had in him, but he kept his mouth shut where and when it was important to do so. Neither to the papers, nor to the politicians, nor to his fellow officers, nor to anyone besides his beloved confidante Ann did he reveal his doubts and criticisms of his commander. This reticence prevented his becoming the sort of unusable officer and all-around disruptive influence that some other civilian generals became.

These traits were inseparable from Wallace's character as a man. His performance as a general was a product of the sum total of his life. He could refrain from criticizing his superior to his fellow officers in part because his close and loving marriage allowed him to confide such concerns in his wife. He could carry out orders, do his duty, and always try to do his best, because—even if he did not necessarily trust his commander—he could unreservedly trust his God for the outcome.

For Grant, Wallace was the best sort of citizen-general. His loyalty, discipline, diligence, and attention to detail made him one of the most usable of the breed. Grant not only entrusted him with increasingly important assignments but also showed a personal regard for him by inviting him on several occasions to share his steamboat and by confiding at least some of his plans and intentions to the former Ottawa lawyer. Moreover, Wallace's rise in rank was gradual, with opportunity to demonstrate to Grant his competence at regimental and brigade command. Grant then could promote him rapidly to levels of command for which he believed him well qualified. The acid test for Grant seems to have been Wallace's performance on the battlefield of Fort Donelson. There he demonstrated that he combined with his careful administration and amiable nature the qualities of a skillful and determined combat commander. In Grant's eyes, therefore, Wallace, and others like him, belonged to an entirely different class from that of the political general who gained his rank by pulling wires in the state or national capital. Instead, Wallace shared with the regulars the right to command, because he had "earned the position on the field of battle."

The Reliable First Team

Grant and Charles Ferguson Smith

Ꮽ *Benjamin Franklin Cooling*

February afternoon shadows had just begun to lengthen when Sam Grant found his former West Point mentor sitting calmly on a log whittling at a stick. Sounds of battle echoed across the hills and ravines behind Confederate Fort Donelson. Snow covered the ground, and Brig. Gen. Charles Ferguson Smith, commandant of cadets at the Military Academy when Grant had been an underclassman there two decades before, looked up from his reveries to see what his former charge, now his commanding officer, had to say. Grant, briefed by staffers that his capture of the rebel position now seemed in doubt due to a surprise counterattack that Saturday morning, addressed the older man. "All has failed on the right. You must take Fort Donelson." Smith pulled his six-foot frame to full height, brushed a flowing white mustache, and replied, "I will do it." Grant needed no clarification and Smith gave none. The two saluted and within hours, the deed was done.[1]

Indeed, Smith on horseback, leading overcoated and panting soldiers of his division up a steep slope, accomplished the first breach of Confederate lines, leading to a midnight request for an armistice by the fort's commander, Brig. Gen. Simon Bolivar Buckner. Receiving the request, Smith exclaimed, "I make no terms with rebels with arms in their hands—my terms are immediate and unconditional surrender!" But he took the request to Grant, rousting the army commander from a much-needed sleep with the comment, "There's something for you to read, General." Sleepily, in reply, Grant asked, "What answer should I send?" "No terms to the damned rebels!" boomed Smith, to Grant's amusement. Back went the note with the courier, stating unequivocally, "No terms except unconditional and immediate surrender can be accepted." The phrase and attitude were clearly Smith's although Grant polished the wording and added a final sentence apropos of both their styles: "I propose to move immediately upon your works."[2]

Born in Philadelphia on April 24, 1807, Smith came from a military family. His father was Samuel Blair Smith, an army surgeon; his grandfather had been a colonel in the Continental army. He graduated from West Point in 1825 and was commissioned in the artillery. After four years of garrison duty he returned to the Military Academy, where for thirteen years he served as assistant instructor of infantry tactics, adjutant, and finally commandant of cadets. It was during this period that Grant first encountered the tall, erect model young officer who inspired a coterie of impressionable young cadets with his military demeanor, strict adherence to duty, and firm but fair discipline. Grant, for one, never forgot his mentor, and for the rest of his life stood somewhat in awe of the older man.[3]

Smith, like Grant, rose to fame in the Mexican War, serving with distinction under both Zachary Taylor and Winfield Scott while commanding both artillery and light infantry units. He saw action at Palo Alto, Resaca de la Palma, Monterrey, Contreras, and Churubusco. He subsequently commanded a military police contingent in occupied Mexico City. Citizens of his native Philadelphia subscribed to present him with a sword of honor for his skillful leadership. Moreover, he earned brevet ranks up to colonelcy, although not gaining permanent promotion to major until 1854. But it was in Mexico that the paths of Grant and Smith crossed once more. Smith was among the constitutional officers of the Aztec Club (a social organization established by U.S. Army officers in Mexico City in 1847) who elected Lt. U. S. Grant, Fourth Infantry, to their membership.[4]

Smith went on to lead an exploratory expedition up the Red River in Minnesota in 1856 and the following year participated in the campaign against the Mormons in Utah, taking command of the Department of Utah in 1860. He was briefly involved with defending the national capital in the early days of the Civil War before departing for recruiting duty in New York City. His brusque, stiff demeanor and his aloofness toward politicians, rather typical of regular army men, cast doubt on his enthusiasm for the Union cause in certain Washington circles. For a time, his potential and services languished, until finally on August 31, 1861, he was commissioned a brigadier general of volunteers and sent to Maj. Gen. John C. Frémont's Department of the West for assignment.[5]

In the flurry of Union and Confederate activity that ended Kentucky's neutrality in early September, Grant moved quickly (while awaiting Frémont's sanction) to occupy the strategic town of Paducah, where the Tennessee River empties into the Ohio. He then returned to Cairo, all in the space of the same day. On September 5 Frémont ordered Smith to take over at Paducah, fortify the place, and to make no further advance. Grant was relegated to actions in the Cairo–northeast Missouri area. But from that time forward, the lives of Grant and Smith were once again intertwined. At this point, however, they functioned as equals, not as hierarchical senior and junior.[6]

At first, it may have seemed that Frémont had sent Smith to Paducah as a sort of rebuke to Grant for his independent, even precipitous intrusion onto Kentucky soil, as the Grant scholars Bruce Catton and John Y. Simon have suggested. No matter, for neither brigadier was self-serving, and Grant's biographer Geoffrey Perret is merely speculating when he contends that their relationship "was slightly uncomfortable for both of them," or that Grant was "uneasy when he met up with Smith in 1861." As was the case with the naval captain Andrew Hull Foote, into whose cooperative partnership Grant was also thrown at this time, the general and his former mentor had enough to do fighting the war not to worry about seniority and age. Continuing threats from Confederate forces in western Kentucky dictated cooperation and coordination in order to get the job done. In Frémont's eyes, as his adjutant wrote Grant on September 16, reinforcements in men and arms would provide the means whereby "you will be enabled in concert with Brig. Gen. Smith to control the rebel forces on both the Kentucky and Missouri shores." This was a simple fact of life at the time on the western rivers.[7]

Thus began the second of Grant's early war partnerships with men who would both befriend him as well as advance his career and fame, possibly at the expense of their own. By mid-October, a pattern of phrase was set in the correspondence between Grant at Cairo and Smith at Paducah. Perhaps Grant's words, "I am ready to cooperate to the extent of my limited means," did betray a certain uneasiness in the younger officer toward the parade-ground old-timer like Smith. Nonetheless, cooperation entailed not merely operational demonstrations against the rebels but also sharing of intelligence and interdiction of illegal trade, leading to a consequent buildup of trust and confidence. This reliance was also developing at the time between Grant and Foote as well as between Smith and the gunboat commander Lt. Ledyard Phelps. Grant, at least, was already thinking that he and Foote might start a general advance to clean out Columbus—that freshly established Confederate defensive bastion on the Mississippi River just north of the Tennessee line. By November, Grant's idea had more clearly crystallized and also embraced Smith.[8]

Frémont, it seems, had been scheming for several months to position Grant and Smith in order to advance his own cause, with wider command in the Kentucky theater. But Pres. Abraham Lincoln was tired of such importuning and of the Pathfinder's attempts to set policy concerning slave emancipation. He had been replaced with a new man, Maj. Gen. Henry Halleck, by November. Halleck, who thought little more of Grant than had Frémont, had greater respect for the old army man Smith. He stood by him when ugly rumors circulated from a Paducah citizen as well as from a fractious Illinois brigadier concerning Smith's avowed softness toward rebels. And learning of such a minor success as Smith's dispatch of a small force to chase rebels from the neighborhood of Eddyville, Kentucky, on October 26, Halleck was amenable to a sort of coordinated operation two weeks later that saw Grant's waterborne force touch down at Belmont, Missouri, opposite Columbus, while a land column from Paducah demonstrated against that bastion from the rear. Nothing much came of either move, except a rebuff to Grant's reputation, perhaps, mystification on the part of the Confederates as to what both Federal columns were all about, and further correspondence between Grant and Smith.[9]

Neither of the brigadiers properly maintained control over subordinates either on the field of battle or on the demonstration march. Much has been made of the breakdown in Grant's command at Belmont, but overlooked was Smith's poor supervision of the reinforced brigade that he entrusted to the Columbus land demonstration. But this was a time of learning and education for leaders and soldiery alike. The greatest result of the shadowboxing that took place that fall in western Kentucky stemmed from intelligence gleaned from naval and land reconnaissance, in which Grant's colleagues Foote and Smith played a prominent role. Both senior officers passed along data from subordinates that detailed conditions among their opponents, with great portent for the future.[10]

Involved was not the Confederacy's Gibraltar at Columbus but two forlorn, isolated and neglected posts on the Tennessee and Cumberland Rivers. On October 16, Smith sent information to the St. Louis headquarters that had been gathered by Phelps and his gunboat *Cones-*

toga concerning Fort Henry on the Tennessee. On November 8, Smith wrote army headquarters in Washington that Phelps "is constantly moving his vessel up and down the Tennessee and Cumberland" and added data concerning a similar Confederate fort on the Cumberland. Smith was anxious to pass this information on because of his own relatively undermanned position at Paducah and "because it is a favorite idea announced on the other side that Paducah is to be attacked from three quarters at once, one quarter being by one or both rivers." Later that month, Halleck advised Smith to be alert to rumors that Maj. Gen. Leonidas Polk was reinforced at Columbus and would soon strike for Paducah while Maj. Gen. William S. Hardee would move north from Bowling Green, Kentucky, and cross the Ohio between the Wabash and Cumberland Rivers "to destroy the Ohio and Mississippi and the Illinois Central Railroad." There was also great concern by all parties that Confederate gunboats would descend the Tennessee and attack Smith at Paducah. Thus, there was an offensive-defense complexion to Union concerns about military activities in the region by the end of the year.[11]

The unflappable Smith merely reported back that marauding parties, not a whole rebel army, were the cause of such rumors. Still, both sides were spooked by one another's possible moves and intentions and because of the relatively disorganized arrangement of Federal army jurisdictions in the region in late 1861; Grant's orientation to the axis of the Mississippi and Columbus permitted Smith at Paducah the luxury of concentrating attention on the twin rivers invasion route into Kentucky and Tennessee. True, Grant necessarily retained a healthy interest in affairs affecting Smith—especially reports from Unionist Kentucky citizens about the marauding rebels impressing horses, produce, salt, powder, and all manner of war-supporting material. Yet during the continuing shadowboxing and demonstrations in western Kentucky in December and January, it was Smith who steadily plied St. Louis and Washington with information that enabled Halleck, Gen. D. C. Buell (in charge of the Department of the Ohio at Louisville), and Maj. Gen. George B. McClellan, the army's general-in-chief, to develop plans for the general offensive slated for spring. The interregnum of command between Frémont and Halleck in St. Louis (who took over only on November 19) resulted in Smith's reporting directly to Washington, causing yet another cook to enter the kitchen.[12]

Indeed, the confusion that seemed to attend Union military correspondence during this period was occasioned greatly by Lincoln's concern for the plight of Unionists in Appalachia from eastern Kentucky to north Alabama (especially those in East Tennessee). McClellan continually pressed Buell for action, including some form of waterborne movement to be commanded by Smith. He also urged Halleck to cooperate with Buell on such a movement using the Tennessee and Cumberland, since the latter river formed the boundary for their jurisdictions in Kentucky. Halleck, preoccupied with sorting out affairs both at departmental headquarters and in the field had little time for concrete coordination with Buell, for helping Foote build his gunboats, or to follow events closely with Grant and Smith in Kentucky, it seemed.[13]

Such circumstances permitted each of Halleck's subordinates some freedom of action. Two days before Christmas, Grant issued orders reflecting a change in his jurisdiction's name from the District of Southeast Missouri to a new District of Cairo and now including Smith's forces, controlling the mouths of the Tennessee and Cumberland Rivers. From this date, notwithstanding Grant's near deference toward his old mentor from West Point, the irony of the juxtaposition of their two positions could not be overlooked. Toward the end of the month, Smith sent Brig. Gen. Lewis Wallace of his Second Brigade with a tiny force to reconnoiter Camp Beauregard and to ascertain whether or not reinforcements had left there for the principal Confederate army at Bowling Green. Meanwhile, the New Year had opened with a flurry of communication among Lincoln, McClellan, Buell, and Halleck about coordinating their efforts in the West, movement into Appalachia, breaching the rebel defense line by way of the twin rivers, and outflanking (thus forcing evacuation of) both Columbus and Bowling Green. Time passed as the four principals wrangled over readiness, the nature of cooperation, timing, and other details. Halleck, for one, whined, "I am satisfied that the authorities at Washington do not appreciate the difficulties with which we have to contend here." It was apparent that something was afoot.[14]

Of course, it was winter and hardly conducive to active campaigning, according to conventional wisdom—better to continue to muster strength and carefully hone the instruments for the spring campaign. McClellan had suggested to Buell that since Halleck seemed unready for cooperation, perhaps the Louisville general himself should advance by the twin rivers. But then on January 6 he reversed course, offering the enlightening view that his eastern armies could not themselves move forward to take Richmond until Buell had captured East Tennes-

see, so as to interdict the railroad that allowed the Confederates later-
ally to reinforce threatened theaters of operations. Bowling Green and
Nashville were "of very secondary importance at the present moment," stated the general in chief. "Interesting as Nashville may be to
the Louisville interests, it strikes me that its possession is of very secondary importance in comparison with the immense results that would
arise from the adherence to our cause of the masses in East Tennessee,
West North Carolina, South Carolina, North Georgia, and Alabama, results that I feel assured would ere long flow from the movement I allude
to," he opined. Here was the Washington viewpoint set against those
of the western generals on the ground. Yet Halleck, for one, had just
told the president by telegram that any thought of advance by separate
armies on exterior lines against the Confederate defense system in the
West (blessed with interior lines of communication) would simply rep-
licate the disastrous Bull Run operation of the previous summer. The
long-suffering chief executive wrote on the bottom of Halleck's missive: "It is exceedingly discouraging. As everywhere else, nothing can
be done."[15]

Nevertheless, there were men of action in the West—limited at
best, perhaps, but proactive at least. Sensing both the need to support
Buell and perhaps to garner glories for himself, and just such a man of
action, Halleck directed Grant on January 6 to mount a demonstration
from Cairo and Paducah into what was styled "the Purchase" area of
western Kentucky between the Tennessee and Mississippi Rivers. Even
here, Halleck's guidance was fuzzy. Ostensibly, the idea was somehow
to help Buell by preventing Confederate transfer of reinforcements
from Columbus to Bowling Green. Grant was to "make a great fuss
about moving all your forces towards Nashville, and let it be so reported by the newspapers." The object of the attack (Halleck's words)
was to be Dover, that is, Fort Donelson on the Cumberland, using roads
through Mayfield and Murray. But "Do not advance far enough to ex-
pose your flank and rear to an attack from Columbus, and by all means
avoid a serious engagement," he was told. It was typically Halleck/
Buell in tone—probing, hesitant, slightly unready for crisp implemen-
tation. Still, it would get the men out of camp, give them some condi-
tioning, uncover Confederate strength and intentions, and at least temporarily show Washington that somebody in the Mississippi Valley was
doing something. As Halleck wired McClellan on January 14: "The
demonstrations which General Grant is now making I have no doubt

will keep [the Confederates] in check till preparations can be made for operations on the Tennessee and Cumberland." Old Brains, as Halleck was known, had grander plans in mind, but a Grant/Smith demonstration would do for the moment.[16]

Fog and delay in receiving reinforcements caused the venture to languish for several days. But by January 10 the demonstration went forward on two avenues of advance—Brig. Gen. John McClernand's march from Cairo and that of Smith from Paducah. Grant issued stern orders against pillaging and confiscation of private property although "it is a fair inference that every stranger met is our enemy." But weather conditions were wretched, and once again Smith lost control of his men, there being great liberation of hogs and poultry by the marching column. Eight days later, Grant decided to break off the operation, having accomplished its object (although the Confederates were once more baffled by what seemed to them an aimless thrashing about in the rain, sleet, and slop of intolerable western Kentucky roads). Smith came out of it suggesting to his young chief that although "I know nothing about the course of operations to be pursued," in the future, thought should be given to targeting Union City behind the Confederate defense perimeter in northwest Tennessee and accessible by rail and road from both Cairo and Paducah. But Smith soon had even more important advice for his superiors.[17]

Actually, the proud professional soldier was as restless as Grant about getting on with a major thrust to crack the Confederate defense line. At one point, such impatience caused Smith to board the *Lexington* for a look at Fort Henry. The reconnaissance confirmed the suspected weakness and poor position of the post. "I think two iron-clad gunboats would make short work of Fort Henry," he apprised Grant on January 22. He knew that Grant was familiar with Fort Henry, having seen a rough sketch of the position in Smith's Paducah quarters during his November visit there. While Halleck contentedly built up strength and played with operations on paper, Grant, Smith, and Foote plotted a more aggressive move. It wasn't long before Grant was able to get permission to approach Halleck in St. Louis about further action.[18]

Grant finally got a chance to make his case to Halleck on January 24, and he bungled the opportunity miserably, suffering a rebuff from his superior. Halleck already knew the details behind what Grant wanted to tell him. Frankly, just about everyone in the theater—on either side—did. It was patently obvious by simply staring at a map. But four days later, separate (yet collaborative) telegrams from both Grant and Foote reiterated the desirability and feasibility of immediately moving to capture Fort Henry. This time, they were more successful. Halleck listened to Foote, it seemed; in Grant, he had little faith. Still, the various reconnaissance trips by Smith, Phelps, and more lately Lt. James W. Shirk aboard the USS *Lexington* more than likely had paved the way for the department commander. Looking for someone like Maj. Gen. Ethan Allan Hitchcock to come out of retirement and take charge of such an offensive, Halleck had delayed also because of the repeated warnings from Foote about the unreadiness of his gun- and mortarboats and the dearth of crews to man them. Finally, Halleck told Foote on the twenty-ninth that once he had Smith's judgment about road conditions between Smithland and Fort Henry, he would give the order to advance (to which Foote quickly rejoined that the road was reportedly in good shape). Then, suddenly, that same day, intelligence from Virginia suggested that the vaunted Confederate general P. G. T. Beauregard was bringing fifteen regiments west to reinforce Gen. Albert Sidney Johnston. The next day Halleck abruptly wired Grant: "Make your preparations to take and hold Fort Henry." Further instructions would come by mail.[19]

Indeed, these instructions, sent later that same day, clarified that Grant would take forward all available forces (except garrisons for his rear bases). He would be supported by Foote's gunboats, and he was to construct a telegraph line from Paducah to Fort Henry "as rapidly as possible." This was designed to keep Halleck informed almost from the battlefield. Once the excitement of the go-ahead telegram wore off at his headquarters in Cairo, Grant instructed McClernand and Smith to prepare their forces. There would be little cavalry or wagon transport; everything would move by steamboat. Smith would command the Second Division of the expedition, and it was determined that his particular mission, once they landed before Fort Henry, would entail marching up the west bank (while McClernand covered the east bank approach) and taking an ill-defined Fort Heiman across the river from the main bastion. By February 5, Grant had his land force in position to attack the rather unsuspecting Confederates.[20]

Smith took his men ashore at the Pine Bluff landing and, like McClernand, eventually attained his object of capturing what turned out to be an abandoned and incomplete Confederate battery position. But McClernand's men were similarly delayed in crossing flooded sloughs en route to Fort Henry, and the battle proved to be an all-navy show. Only Foote's gunboats quickly dispatched the token Confederate defenders left to combat the Yankee thrust. One of Smith's subordinates, Lew Wallace, wondered aloud to his chief what kind of "a stiff fight" they all might have had if the Confederates had chosen to stay and really defend Fort Henry. But the point was moot; the victory was easily won; the mountain of abandoned stores and equipment proved most surprising but time-consuming to inventory. And for the next week, bad weather and roads kept Grant and his lieutenants from striking overland to complete the victory by taking Fort Donelson on the Cumberland.[21]

Fort Donelson proved to be a different experience from Fort Henry. There, some fifteen thousand to seventeen thousand Confederates had come prepared to fight. With McClernand in the lead, followed by Smith, the Federals finally completed the twelve-mile overland march on February 12 and 13 while Foote's gunboats made their way around by river (some stopping at Mound City for repairs). Smith left Wallace behind, guarding the advance base at Fort Henry—much to the Hoosier's consternation. Grant told both his division commanders not to bring on any general action, pending Foote's arrival. McClernand would move to his right to complete investment of the Confederate position, encompassing Fort Donelson and the little county seat of Dover. Smith would occupy high ground on the left, facing rebel outworks closest to the main fort itself. But in taking position on February 13, both McClernand and Smith provoked sharp skirmishing in violation of Grant's instructions. The result was several bloody repulses and wiser heads among Grant's lieutenants. Since Foote had largely promised to repeat his Fort Henry success, the Federal army awaited repetition once the gunboats arrived and attacked Fort Donelson's water batteries on Valentine's Day. When that attack failed so miserably, Grant determined that only a siege would force his opponents to surrender the fort.[22]

Grant and his army had simply become overconfident. Granted, the Confederate high command in the West—Albert Sidney Johnston and his principal subordinates like Beauregard (without the fifteen regiments of reinforcements) and Gen. Leonidas Polk, an Episcopal bishop, at Columbus—had reacted haltingly to the Federal threat. They could not be sure that Grant's move wasn't a feint, while Halleck and Buell coordinated major moves down the Mississippi and the Louisville-Nashville axis. Too late, the Grant–Foote operation caught them flat-footed, and their response was less than vigorous. Still, Johnston sent reinforcements to the Cumberland while four separate brigadiers (hardly unity of command) were instructed to hold the fort long enough for Confederate forces elsewhere to retreat from their advanced positions in Kentucky. Then these generals were to disengage and save their army. Brigadiers John B. Floyd, Gideon Pillow, Simon B. Buckner, and Bushrod Johnson determined to do just that. Yet the devil lay in the details. Imprecise orders but a willingness to stand and fight counted for something during those February 13 actions as well as the unexpected success against Foote's gunboats. Such intent then transferred to a spirited breakout attempt on the morning of February 15. Suddenly, Grant and his lieutenants no longer held the initiative.[23]

Grant and his subordinates were put to the test that morning. The sharp yips of the Confederate rebel yell caught everyone, including Grant and Smith, off guard that snowy morning in mid-February. Grant had gone to confer with an injured Foote aboard his gunboat, leaving nobody in charge since he expected that the Confederates would remain inactive. McClernand's people were just emerging from makeshift bivouacs when the Confederate attack hit them, rolling up their line steadily all morning. Smith, for some reason, heard little of the combat to his far right and remained passive, failing to sense that the Confederate earthworks to his front had been stripped of men to send to the attack force. Here was a stolid professional who was wedded to obedience and discipline. He simply awaited orders. Not so the newly arrived Lew Wallace (now commanding reinforcements making up a Third Division): he had seen the flotsam of McClernand's destroyed division and moved quickly to blunt the thrust. Smith had done nothing to help thus far. Such was the state of things when Grant, returning in haste early that afternoon, rode to the point of danger. Passing Smith's command post, he spotted his old friend calmly sitting under a tree, an aide nearby.[24]

Grant was blunt. Orders were snapped and men moved as the aide went off to muster the division into line. Within minutes, Smith, astride his horse, sword held aloft, addressed the leading regiment. "Second Iowa, you must take that fort. Take the caps off your guns, fix bayonets, and I will support you." Four other regiments followed their lead, but Smith did more than merely support—he led them in person (inspiring Grant to mention just that in his dispatches). Down the hill across the ravine and up the slope toward Confederate abatis and earthworks they went behind the old man. The works in this sector were weakly held by a shotgun-wielding Thirtieth Tennessee, unsupported by artillery. "Damn you, gentlemen, I see skulkers. I'll have none here. Come on, you volunteers, come on," he shouted, mixing oaths with other comments: "This is your chance. You volunteered to be killed for love of your country and now you can be." He did not want to be killed, Smith yelled at them, "but you are only damned volunteers, you came to be killed and now you can be." Very few were, however, for the undermanned line of rebels fled at their approach. Smith was supposedly among the first into those trenches and "by his presence and heroic conduct he led the green men to do things that no other man could have done."[25]

Perhaps this was what he had meant when he had instructed Wallace the previous September: "In battle, a general's duties insofar as they are reducible to rule, are—first, to fight; second, to fight to the best advantage." Smith's actions cracked the Confederate's outer defense line. As Grant phrased it in the victory dispatch, Smith's charge "was most brilliantly executed and gave to our arms full assurance of victory." Yet Smith did not capture the fort itself. As Wallace and McClernand (under Grant's supervision) pushed the sortie force back into the outer works on the right of the line, Buckner's returning legion erected a second line of entrenchments on a ridge adjacent to the ones Smith had taken. Another dark, cold night settled over the dead, the dying, and the cheerless living of the two confronting armies. It was then that the full impact of Smith's success gave Grant the ultimate victory. In an opéra bouffe of changing command and failing willpower, the Confederate brigadiers sacrificed victory and their army largely because Buckner felt that Smith's achievement doomed his position for the next day. About 3:00 A.M. on February 16, a flag of truce came through Smith's lines with a message for Grant; the Confederates wanted to negotiate terms for surrender. "I make no terms with Rebels with arms in their hands," Smith declared to the distressed Southerner; "my terms are unconditional and immediate surrender" (echoing Foote's conditions at Fort Henry and presaging what Grant would ultimately tell the rebel brigadiers at Donelson). Grasping the courier's missive, he set off for Grant's headquarters, not far away.[26]

Smith strode into the Widow Crisp's little cabin, waking Grant and thrusting the communiqué at him: "There's something for you to read, General." The army commander pulled himself together and took the letter, which was from another old army comrade, Buckner, upon whom had descended the mantle of command inside the trenches. "What answer shall I send to this?" Grant asked Smith. "No terms to the damned Rebels!" he replied, at which Grant chuckled. But "no terms" it was ("the same thing in smoother words," was Smith's conclusion) that Grant sent back to Buckner, and Smith handed over the message to the Confederate courier. Plans were already afoot for a general attack by the Federals at daybreak, so Buckner's capitulation saved time and lives on both sides. Before that day was out, Smith and his division had indeed marched into Fort Donelson. But significantly, it was the crisp old regular who had used the phrase "unconditional surrender," for which Grant subsequently garnered all the fame.[27]

Smith had also instructed Wallace in September that genius was determinable by the manner of obedience. "A fort is to be taken; genius consists in finding a way to take it with the least appreciable loss," he had proclaimed. But in Grant's case it had been more luck than genius, closely helped by an absence of Confederate leadership and resolve as well as by Smith's keen sense of duty. "Obedience being the soul of military organization," claimed Smith in that same instruction to Wallace, "I hold it the beginning and end of duty. It is the rein in hand by which the superior does his driving." Perhaps that sense was what had held Smith back from rushing to McClernand's aid—absent instructions from his commanding officer, no matter that the officer was junior in age and expertise. The day after Buckner's surrender of Fort Donelson, the Confederate remarked to Smith, "You made a brilliant charge and terribly surprised us on our right yesterday afternoon, General Smith. It decided the day against us." "I simply obeyed orders, nothing more, sir," Grant's loyal subordinate replied.[28]

Smith very truly became Grant's right arm from this point, if he had not been so even before. On February 19, Grant told him to go upriver and capture Clarksville but under no circumstances to go any farther. Actually, Foote and some of Grant's staff had taken possession of the city the day before, finding the Confederates gone and the railroad bridge but lightly damaged. Smith's men had an easy job of temporary occupation when they arrived there later. By this time, however, Grant and Foote were chafing to get on and capture Nashville, while Halleck prodded his colleague Buell to do just that since the city really lay within his jurisdiction. By then, however, there were bigger things at stake in the West.[29]

Halleck was hoping for overall command of the Western Theater. He wired McClellan enthusiastically at 1:00 P.M. on February 17, asking him to make Buell, Grant, and John Pope major generals and himself commander in the West—"I ask this in return for Forts Henry and Donelson." Two days later, he even more enthusiastically urged McClellan to make Smith a major general. "You can't get a better one." "By his coolness and bravery at Fort Donelson when the battle was against us, [he] turned the tide and carried the enemy's outworks." So, suggested Halleck, honor him for this victory and "the whole country will applaud." As for Grant, one of Halleck's staffers sent a general order congratulating the general and Foote "on the recent brilliant victories on the Tennessee and Cumberland" but enjoining them that "the war is not yet ended. Prepare for new conflicts and new victories. Victory and glory await the brave." The words were Halleck's, the messenger but an aide. As for the scheme to bring Hitchcock aboard, the retiree did not want active service anymore. And Halleck could not get Buell to accept his halfhearted offer to take personal charge on the twin rivers. In fact, by remaining in St. Louis, Halleck soon found himself out of touch with affairs in Tennessee.[30]

Part of the trouble stemmed from the fact that when Buell himself finally moved forward in the wake of the Confederate retreat from central Kentucky, it brought him in range of the Grant/Foote team on the Cumberland. Buell, thinking he needed reinforcement against an imagined Confederate counteroffensive to retake Nashville, tried to tap Smith at Clarksville for manpower. This, of course, led a newly frocked two-star Ulysses S. Grant to travel upriver to set Buell straight, thereby disobeying Halleck's orders not to go beyond Clarksville. Then the breakdown in telegraphic communications between the pair allowed Halleck to wire Washington that Grant needed a good disciplining as much as the soldiery. With McClellan's blessing, Halleck removed Grant from command of the new Tennessee River expedition, replacing him with Smith. As Bruce Catton has noted, all of this occurred "just sixteen days after the unconditional surrender of Fort Donelson." Frankly, it looked as if the subordinates had moved too fast and too successfully for the lockstep, orderly offensive planned by Halleck, Buell, and McClellan. Grant became the scapegoat, despite the victories; Smith became the convenient and obedient substitute.[31]

Such machinations and misunderstandings kept the Federal advance stymied for much of the next month. While Leonidas Polk evacuated Columbus in early March and retreated south to regroup with Johnston in northern Mississippi, Grant remained at Fort Henry supporting Smith as he took the army upriver by steamboat to the vicinity of Savannah, Tennessee, and slightly above to a spot called Pittsburg Landing. A peeved, even chagrined Grant explained his post-Donelson actions to Halleck, and the pair settled into a round of discourse that ultimately resulted in Grant's restoration to command. By this time, the high command situation had also changed, as Halleck vaulted into overall command in the West and McClellan found himself demoted from supreme commander to mere army command in Virginia. Meanwhile, Smith had concentrated his expanding expeditionary force at Pittsburg Landing, where they could begin antirailroad operations that Halleck wanted carried out along the Memphis and Charleston line at Corinth, some twenty miles distant. Grant, from his supporting role, on March 5 warned Smith about Corinth as a possible rebel concentration point of its own.[32]

Halleck directed Grant on March 10 to take charge of reinforcements coming from Missouri "and be ready yourself to take the general command" once again. Smith wrote him four days later expressing his pleasure "that you were to resume your old command from which you were so unceremoniously and (as I think) improperly stricken down." By this point, the old brigadier was laid up in a cabin on board a steamer off Pittsburg Landing, suffering from a leg injury incurred by jumping into a yawl on the river. A head cold that he had contracted at Fort Donelson hardly helped his frame of mind, either. Smith realized well the hurt that Grant felt at his sacking and that "from old awe of me . . . he dislikes to give me an order and says I ought to be in his place." Foote had gone from the rivers team (transferred to the Mississippi advance), and Grant undoubtedly looked to Smith as his new soul mate. He had, until hearing of Smith's injury, intended him to control the advance. But both generals were of one mind. The advance had been too long delayed just because Halleck wanted all possible strength concentrated. The Confederates had entirely too much time to regroup, mobilize, and prepare a counteroffensive, although the two Federal generals placed little stock in the "temper" of the rebel troops around Corinth, something of a miscalculation as it turned out.[33]

Grant arrived in Savannah on March 15, still suffering lingering symptoms of his own head cold. In fact, it was the cough medicine that he was consuming that led to renewed rumors of liquor abuse. In any event, the limited carrying capacity of the steamboats delayed the Grant/Smith concentration, and Buell's overland march from Nashville was also dilatory. Intelligence reports increasingly suggested a Confederate buildup, causing Grant to tell Smith on March 23, "I am clearly of the opinion that the enemy are gathering strength at Corinth quite as rapidly as we are here and the sooner we attack the easier will be the task of taking the place." It was the Fort Henry–Donelson business all over again, and once more St. Louis seemed lethargic. While Grant pushed forward all the arriving contingents so that they could be directly under Smith's supervision at Pittsburg Landing, the continuing inability of his old commandant to leave quarters and mount a horse to inspect positions ashore certainly hampered preparations. Once again, the Confederates were about to steal a march on Grant.[34]

It did not help that McClernand and Smith were also uncertain as to relative rank and precedence. Both (along with Lew Wallace) had been promoted to major general on March 21. But it was McClernand who pointedly suggested on the twenty-seventh that Grant's presence was needed at the landing, not only to clarify command and control but also to better lay out "some general and connected plan" for the various army camps, due to "our proximity to the enemy." Neither Grant nor Smith was truly watchful; both were against entrenching (Smith said it was bad for morale and might suggest to the young volunteers that their generals feared the enemy). Besides, contended Smith's comrade William T. Sherman (and historian Kenneth P. Williams a century later), the Federal position around Pittsburg Landing had been chosen by Smith. Sherman, in fact, commanded the point with "the object indicated by General Smith" of cutting "the Charleston and Memphis road, without a general or serious engagement." Memories of getting temporarily sacked six months earlier for crying wolf about Confederates in Kentucky made Sherman skittish at taking undue fright merely because skirmishing had increased in the neighborhood by early April. The high ground, ravines, and creeks protecting their flanks and the whole offensive demeanor of Union arms belied their watchfulness. The fact is that the Federals were simply overconfident, even cocky. Johnston was able to position his whole attacking army on the outskirts of Grant's unwary camps.[35]

It fell to others to pull Grant's chestnuts from the resulting Shiloh inferno. Smith could do little more than listen to the sounds of distant gunfire from his sickroom, upstairs in the Cherry Mansion headquarters in Savannah. Grant had seen to it that he had been transferred from a cramped steamboat cabin to a white-sheeted bed ashore. When another old friend, Col. Jacob Ammen, commanding the Tenth Brigade of the Fourth Division in Buell's army visited Smith while passing through Savannah on April 6, he found the old soldier in "fine spirits." In fact, the sick man laughed at Ammen "for thinking that a great battle was raging" at that very moment. Smith declared it was only a skirmish of pickets "and that I was accustomed to small affairs," noted Ammen. Smith thought "it was a large and hot picket skirmish." When there was no cessation to the distant firing, "no diminution, and the sounds appeared to be coming nearer and growing more distinct, he said a part of the army might be engaged." He desperately wanted to be with his men. Had he been, perhaps Smith, not his successor in command of the Second Division, Brig. Gen. W. H. L. Wallace, might have been mortally wounded at the Hornet's Nest. One might only speculate whether the old fighter could have done any more to rally Grant's beaten army on Shiloh's first day. Since he had argued previously against having the men simply dig in on the defensive, there can be little doubt, however, as to what he would have advised his former pupil to do on the second day.[36]

Smith's leg never healed, and infection soon ravaged his whole body. George Cullum declared in a later tribute, "This, with his debility caused by a cold taken at Donelson, continued harassing exertion, bad climate, supervening erysipelas, and poisonous drugs, completely sapped his vital energy." Twenty days later Smith was dead, mourned in the wake of Shiloh as Cullum likened him to "a brave and noble paladin" who was "as intrepid as Ney, as chivalric as Murat, and as rock-fast as Macdonald," warrior-leaders all. Grant's aide, Lt. Col. John A. Rawlins, referred to Smith as "that best soldier of the Republic," and Halleck, in publishing Smith's army obituary order from Pittsburg Landing (where he had gone to take field command for the final triumphal march on Corinth), said that he combined "the qualities of a faithful officer, an excellent disciplinarian, an able commander, and a modest and courteous gentleman. . . . In his death the Army has lost one of its brightest ornaments and the country a general whose place it will be difficult to supply."

Three days later, at Secretary of War Edwin Stanton's direction,

Halleck ordered all department posts and naval craft to fire thirteen-minute guns beginning at noon and flags to fly at half-staff until sunset. "The flag of his division will be draped in mourning and the officers of the division will wear the usual badge for thirty days," read the general order.[37]

Smith's body was sent to St. Louis en route to burial in his native Philadelphia. Perhaps only Lew Wallace retained a somewhat begrudging feeling toward Smith. Wallace, a volunteer or citizen-soldier, maintained public respect for the professional officer but privately bridled that West Pointers by right outranked any and all volunteers. After Shiloh, his own difficulties with Grant's interpretation of his performance in that battle kept him silent about Smith, his erstwhile competitor. But certainly no one felt more saddened at Smith's passing than Ulysses Grant himself. In a letter to Smith's widow in New York City on April 26, Grant wrote, "In his death the nation has lost one of its most gallant and most able defenders." Referring to his service with Smith dating from the Academy and "in all his battles in Mexico," Grant bore honest testimony to his great worth as a soldier and friend. "Where an entire nation condoles with you in your bereavement," he concluded, "no one can do so with more heartfelt grief than myself." Indeed, Grant's caring did not stop there.[38]

In the first autumn after the war, Grant wrote in behalf of Smith's wife and family, "In time of peace he was regarded as about the best, if not the very best, soldier in the army," the hero of Donelson, Vicksburg, and Appomattox told the Hon. John Tucker of Philadelphia, concluding that in war "he sustained the reputation made in time of peace." Tucker was attempting to raise an endowment for Smith's survivors, and Grant wished him the best. "The family of such a man [as Smith] have a claim upon the gratitude of their country," declared the Union's top general. In July 1866, Grant also wrote Stanton requesting a second lieutenancy for Smith's son Allen and asking "this as due to the memory of his father." The general's widow had just died, leaving young Smith and a sister, Henrietta, "full orphans to get through the world almost destitute of means," he noted. Three days later, an elated Grant wrote to Henrietta Smith: "I need scarcely assure you of the great pleasure it affords me to be able to serve in any way within my power the family of one who I so highly respected." Allen Smith got the commission but died the next year in the New Orleans yellow fever epidemic. Still a decade later, the outgoing President Grant wrote to

James Pollock, director of the Mint of the United States, in Henrietta's behalf in her quest for a position in the Philadelphia mint: "There is nothing that I would not do to aid the children of my once old chief and afterwards subordinate in their life struggles." It seems that Grant never lost the respect, even the awe, that Smith had induced in him as a young cadet.[39]

Charles Ferguson Smith's character and bearing as a professional soldier prompted such veneration. He truly breathed the qualities of duty, honor, country. "As the preacher knows his Bible, as the lawyer knows his statutes, every general should know the regulations and articles of war," he had told Lew Wallace in the first autumn of the Civil War. "The chief duties of a general to his command may be classified—the enforcement of discipline—tactical instruction—care of the health of his men—and they are all important because tending to efficiency, the measure of which is the exact measure of his own efficiency." Finally, he suggested that battle was the ultimate to which an officer's whole life's labor should be directed. That officer might live to retirement age without seeing a battle: "Still he must always be getting ready for it." Then, whether it comes late or early, "he must be willing to fight—and he *must* fight."[40]

If those were the principles that Smith transmitted to Grant, even at an early and impressionable cadet's age, then the older man must surely have been proud to see them borne out when his pupil subsequently became his superior officer. True, Sherman wrote Prof. Henry Coppee in June 1864, it was Smith who had selected the battlefield of Shiloh, and it was he who had arranged the divisions in the order as encamped when Johnston attacked. "All those subordinate dispositions were made by the order of Genl. Smith," noted Sherman, "before Genl. Grant succeeded him to the Command of all the forces up the Tennessee, Head Qrs. Savannah." Thus, "If there was any error in putting that Army on the west side of the Tennessee, exposed to the superior force of the enemy also assembling at Corinth, the mistake was not Genl. Grants." By implication, said Sherman, Smith, not Grant, was the culprit of the near disaster at Shiloh. Yet Sherman, in his support for both former chiefs, was the one who opined in his memoirs, "Had C. F. Smith lived, Grant would have disappeared to history after Fort Donelson." Overstated, perhaps, but one suspects that even "Unconditional Surrender" Grant would have muttered, "Indeed I was rather inclined to this opinion myself at that time, and would have served as faithfully under Smith as he had done under me."[41]

"If He Had Less Rank"

Lewis Wallace

⌁ Stacy D. Allen

"Every life has its ups and downs," wrote Lew Wallace in 1906. "There is a difference however," he added. "Some, once down, stay down."[1] General Lewis (Lew) Wallace was no stranger to danger and battle. By summer 1862, he had fought in two battles, three campaigns, and numerous skirmishes in western Virginia, Kentucky, Tennessee, and northern Mississippi. His military career seemed extraordinarily promising. At thirty-four he became the youngest major general in the U.S. Army. A War Democrat, Wallace's initial commission to brigadier had been granted by political appointment. Although he clearly earned his second star on the merits of nearly twelve months of honorable military service, members of the professional officer corps considered the Indiana native a "mushroom general," the term applied to similar political generals in the Mexican War. Wallace's volunteer military service in the Western Theater, from the occupation of Paducah, Kentucky, through the capture of Vicksburg, Mississippi, reveals the general hostility that overshadowed civil-military relations in the United States. It also reveals that military history is relevant, "not because of maneuvers, campaigns or even the reconstruction of battle details on maps or the actual ground, but because of seeing how men reacted to the sort of stress that could bring out the best or the worst in them."[2]

Indiana had been a state for eleven years when Lewis Wallace was born in Brookville, Franklin County, on April 10, 1827. His father, David Wallace, was a graduate of West Point, where he taught mathematics, and in 1837 he had been elected governor of Indiana. Lew was a precocious boy who hated school. Tired of his constant truancy, his mother discovered that a book would hold her son in bounds, and soon Lew became a voracious reader and loved learning about exotic locations, people, and times. From an early age a passionate quest for martial glory became part of his character. He was studying law when war with Mexico erupted in 1846. After raising a company of militia, Wallace was elected second lieutenant of the First Indiana Volunteers. He served nearly a year along the Rio Grande River but fought no action. After the war, he completed his law studies, passed the bar, and married Susan A. Elston. From their home in Crawfordsville, Wallace practiced law and entered politics, winning election to the state senate in 1856. That same year he organized a militia company. After studying about the French Algerian Zouaves, he adopted their theatrical drill, colorful uniforms, and light infantry tactics for use by his Montgomery (County) Guards.[3]

When civil war erupted on April 12, 1861, with the Confederate bombardment on Fort Sumter, Lew Wallace appeared ready to assume an important role in the conflict. Called to Indianapolis to report to Gov. Oliver P. Morton, Wallace left immediately. "The combination of pride, courage, and endurance had always made wars long and bloody," he wrote later of his motivation to offer service to his country; "I was not going to engage . . . in old arguments; . . . I was going simply to become a soldier for the Union." To deliver Pres. Abraham Lincoln's appeal to the nation for seventy-five thousand militia to put down the insurrection, Morton appointed Wallace adjutant general of the state and put him to work on enlisting Indiana's quota of volunteers. Within four days, he had delivered nearly nine thousand men—twice the number the state was asked to contribute. His task complete, he resigned as adjutant general and on April 25 received a commission to colonel and command of the Eleventh Indiana (Zouave) Regiment. His romantic and dramatic nature surfaced during ceremonies marking the regiment's departure from Indianapolis for the front. The young colonel marched his men to the statehouse, where the entire regiment knelt and swore an oath to avenge the Indiana volunteers, whom they felt had been unjustly accused of cowardice by Gen. Zachary Taylor after the battle of Buena Vista in the Mexican War. The emotional scene made national news when the influential publication, *Harper's Weekly*, ran a full-page illustration of the event for its readers.

Wallace's Zouaves fought their first action on June 13, at Romney in western Virginia. Over the next month, the regiment participated in operations to defend the vital Baltimore and Ohio Railroad. In recognition of the bravery and vigilance he displayed in carrying out his duties, Wallace received commendation from General in Chief Winfield Scott and Maj. Gen. George B. McClellan. Transferred home for mustering-out in August, Colonel Wallace and his three-month regiment reenlisted for three more years of service and after reorganization were assigned to serve in the West, stationed in Paducah, Kentucky. Several days after reaching his new post, he learned he had received appointment to the rank of brigadier general.[4]

As a junior member of a highly motivated circle of Western Theater Union generals, Wallace seemed unable to shake off the cloud of antebellum Democratic affiliation and militia service he carried into the war. The Civil War was a war of peoples, not professional armies, and politics weighed heavily in the selection of commanders and war strategy. In the U.S. Army, to a greater extent than in Confederate service, command was often entrusted to men whose claim for preferment rested primarily on political considerations. President Lincoln struggled to reconcile conflicting interests among diametrically opposed factions, such as "hard-core abolitionists, high tariff protectionists, foreign language immigrant populations, and War Democrats," to enlist support for the war. In addition to professional officers, these four factions provided most of Lincoln's political appointments.[5]

Despite his passion to preserve the Union, Lew Wallace clearly had military acclaim as a goal in the war. He believed he possessed the necessary skills to command troops and implement strategy. "There was a romantic element to Wallace's nature—later exhibited in his books, but revealed during the war in colorful battle reports—which led him to view battles in terms of [courage] and glory." Scholars believe that he suffered under the "the misguided concept of knight-errantry," which Mark Twain called "the Walter Scott disease." Thus, his heart and emotions often guided his actions. Wallace believed that professional officers discriminated against political appointees, and he "resented and called villainous the unwritten regulation that regulars (West Pointers) by right outranked any and all volunteers." His feelings on this issue were shared by the vast majority of civilians in uniform, who often displayed open hostility toward West Point officers and their closed society. Conversely, professional soldiers were unanimous in their contempt for citizen-soldiers. The traditional public adulation of "militia" appeared as an affront to the West Point officer corps and challenged their claims to special expertise. Volunteers were denounced as being "motivated by political ambition, undisciplined, ineffective in combat, extravagantly expensive, and brutal in their conduct of warfare." The friction resulting from this general hostility often hampered efficient unity of command.[6]

In his relationships with superiors, Wallace was too outspoken. Many of his critical remarks made it back to those he criticized. In an army of professionals, he risked alienating higher authority, and only later in life did he learn to curb his tongue. On the whole, however, he labored to sustain a positive association with the professionals and managed to avoid the intrigue practiced by many political generals.[7]

At his new post in Paducah, Wallace commanded a brigade under post commander Brig. Gen. Charles F. Smith. Smith was Old Army and tough as nails. The crusty old warrior, however, soon took Wallace under his wing. Initially, Wallace appeared captivated by his new mentor. "By reputation he was the best all-around officer in the regular army," he noted, "a disciplinarian, stern, unsympathetic, an ogre to volunteers, but withal a magnificent soldier of the old school of Winfield Scott." After a recent tour of Union garrisons, an army inspector reported that Smith commanded the most soldierly and disciplined post in the West. Yet, Smith soon became embroiled in public controversy when some of Wallace's men attacked a local secession sympathizer who had attempted to raise a Confederate flag over his house. Smith promptly punished the unruly volunteers for their undisciplined behavior. As a result, Northern journalists accused him of harboring Confederate sympathies but praised Wallace's patriotism in the incident. They alleged that Smith permitted trade with Confederates but interfered with the trade of loyalists. In a letter to Secretary of War Simon Cameron, the editor of the *Chicago Tribune* declared, "This man Smith is doubtlessly a secession sympathizer—if not worse." Pressure mounted to have him removed.[8]

In late October 1861, U. S. Grant arrived in Paducah to visit Smith, his old West Point commandant. The visit marked the first encounter between Grant and his future lieutenant—Lew Wallace. Grant commanded a district within the Western Department, with headquarters at Cairo, Illinois—a geographically important port facility situated on the confluence of the Ohio and Mississippi Rivers. Comparatively unknown, the thirty-nine-year-old Grant, a graduate of West Point and veteran of the Mexican War and frontier duty in the West, had already rendered valuable service to the Union. When Confederates invaded Kentucky earlier in September, he seized Paducah. His prompt action was one of the decisive moves of the war and secured the Tennessee and Cumberland Rivers as routes of invasion into the Confederacy. Grant boarded with Wallace while in Paducah. From their initial encounter, Wallace studied his future commander, whom he "received . . . as I would any other undistinguished officer of his rank." He noted the details of Grant's appearance and behavior: "one, [that he wore] a uniform coat off-color and the worse for tarnished brass buttons; another, that there was nothing about [Grant] suggestive of greatness, nothing heroic." He remembered that Grant "smoked incessantly and talked freely." Grant's ability to narrate struck a cord with the literary-minded Wallace. "General Grant could not make a (public) speech," Wallace noted, but "in amends for that, . . . he was really a fine talker, and particularly excellent in description." After a private conference with Smith on military issues, Grant departed the next day. When Wallace next encountered him, in February 1862, they would have a more important association.[9]

The newspaper criticism and agitation against Smith eventually led to his being superseded by Grant for district command and also brought pressure on Gen. Henry Halleck, the department commander, to remove Smith entirely. He was a rigid disciplinarian, and this behavior had created the recent political unrest. Halleck sent two generals and a colonel to Paducah to investigate, and they reported that the fault in the controversies between Smith and subordinates lay with the latter. Halleck agreed and stated that Grant shared the same opinion. Talk at Grant's headquarters blamed Wallace for inciting the affair over the flag. Moreover, Grant's aides still fumed about earlier sensationalized newspaper reports about his recent visit to Paducah. The journalists charged that there had been "an orgy, a beastly drunken revel led by both Grant and Smith," at Wallace's headquarters. Grant's reputation for drinking was common knowledge within the Old Army, but following his stay with Wallace, rumors quickly spread that he was a habitual drunkard. Wallace admitted that there were cigars, liquor, and some singing but insisted there was neither intoxication nor revelry. Grant's staff, however, may have held Wallace responsible for the sensationalized rumors. Gossip at both district and departmental headquarters labeled Lew Wallace a political demagogue.[10]

From mid-November through January 1862, no significant action occurred in the West, and Wallace began fretting about the inactivity. He became a malcontent and fell into an "unfortunate pattern of chafing with impatience." Despite Smith's friendliness, he complained of his commander's lack of initiative, and in letters to friends and family, he suggested ways Smith could do better. "This lying here," he wrote Governor Morton, "while work is doing everywhere, and while we are everywhere unlucky, is intolerable." "Nothing to do but grin and bear it," he wrote his wife, "Defeat follows defeat—mismanagement after mismanagement." Isaac Elston Jr., Wallace's brother-in-law and a member of his military staff, mentioned in a letter home that "Lew is full of complaints because he has no brigade assigned him commensurate with his abilities." Publicly, Wallace expressed only the highest respect for Smith, but some friction had developed after the flag incident, and he was counted among Smith's detractors. In January 1862, Susan Wallace's brother-in-law, Sen. Henry S. Lane, petitioned for Smith's removal. Wallace may have been a factor in that petition. In a letter to Susan written February 19, 1862, he claimed satisfaction at "the happy riddance of Gen. Smith, which is at last accomplished. He left me behind . . . thro' jealousy." The record is not conclusive, but Wallace's "resentment of Smith" may have only been "his customary sense of feeling slighted" when not allowed a personal role in the forefront of military action.[11]

As February approached, Lewis Wallace came under the direct command of Ulysses S. Grant. The relationship that developed illustrates the traditional prejudice that existed in civil-military relations in the United States, a prejudice marked by the nonpartisan, nonemotional solidarity of service and professional ethic of the regulars as opposed to the emotional partisanship found in the larger society of citizen-soldiers. From Grant's viewpoint, the regular army represented all that citizen-soldiers like Lew Wallace did not: "cohesion, expertise, devotion to duty, and professional neutrality and restraint." The failure of Wallace to become a "Grant Man" had little foundation in his ability to command, obey orders, or act under stress in combat. Instead, Grant's judgment of Wallace, yet to surface, was influenced by other criteria. It is remarkable that during the five-month period (February–June 1862) that Grant and Wallace actively served together in the West, each was at most in the physical presence of the other for only several dozen hours.[12]

The 1862 campaign began with General Halleck authorizing a joint Union army/navy attack up the Tennessee River against Fort Henry, located just south of the Kentucky state line. On February 6, while Grant's fifteen thousand men slogged south to position themselves for the attack on Henry, a naval flotilla of four ironclads and three wooden gunboats under Flag Officer Andrew H. Foote steamed forward and bombarded the partially flooded fort into submission, thus opening the lower Tennessee River to Union control. In the attack, Wallace commanded his brigade in Smith's column, which advanced on Fort Heiman, an unfinished fortification located west of the river opposite Fort Henry. Like the rest of the army, Wallace saw no fighting.[13]

Within the week, Grant moved on Fort Donelson, eleven miles to the east near Dover, Tennessee, on the Cumberland River. Grant's troops quickly invested the Confederate installation and minor engagements broke out along the lines. Donelson proved a more formidable bastion than Fort Henry. Behind its entrenchments served a reinforced Southern garrison of 17,500 men. On February 14 an attack by Foote's gunboats was severely repulsed by Confederate river batteries. As a fierce winter storm gripped the region, Grant was forced to tighten the investment and call for reinforcements.

Initially left behind to garrison Fort Henry, Lew Wallace was soon called up and given command of a newly organized Third Division. He deployed in the center of the encircling Union line, with C. F. Smith's division on the left and John A. McClernand's on the right. At dawn, February 15, the Confederate army stormed out from behind their entrenchments in a massive assault against the Union right flank. In heavy fighting, the determined Confederates drove McClernand's outnumbered division back toward Wallace. McClernand sent word he needed assistance. Wallace, however, was prohibited by standing orders from Grant to hold his position. He attempted to communicate with his commander, but before dawn Grant had left the field and was six miles downstream in conference with Flag Officer Foote. When McClernand again pleaded for assistance, Wallace seized the initiative. On his own authority, and in disobedience to orders, Wallace reinforced McClernand's crippled and routed division and mounted a determined defensive stand that checked further Confederate advance. In the early afternoon, Grant arrived on the battlefield. Realizing the rebel attack was an attempt to escape, he ordered all commands to counterattack. By nightfall the Confederates had been driven back into their entrenchments. Wallace's decision to move and engage the enemy, when for some reason the trained professional Smith sat idle, materially led to the surrender of the Confederate garrison the next day. Capt. William S. Hillyer, a member of Grant's staff, considered Wallace's action decisive and sent him a note: "I speak advisedly. God bless you—you did save the day on the right."[14]

The surrender of Donelson, with 13,500 Confederate troops, heavy and light cannon, and equipment, resulted in the capture of Nashville and proved the most successful achievement by U.S. forces thus far in the war. The victory clearly launched Grant, now known as "Unconditional Surrender" Grant, on the eventual road to command of all U.S. armies by 1864. Wallace's performance proved a major element in the outcome and preserved for Grant the chance to obtain unconditional victory. Grant, however, took little notice of Wallace's contribution and in his battle report made no mention of his initiative. True, neither Wallace nor McClernand had proceeded beyond the defensive roadblock that Wallace had established on the Wynn's Ferry road. Grant appears to have been angry with McClernand and Wallace for not having reorganized the masses of panicked national troops, resupplied them with ammunition, and counterattacked. It took Grant's presence to generate the counterattack, and he always remembered that important fact. It should be noted that, unlike Wallace, who advanced before Grant arrived, the division under the old regular C. F. Smith remained stationary until Grant issued orders for the counterattack. In his report, Grant extended the customary professional acknowledgment that Generals McClernand and Wallace "were with their commands in the midst of danger, and were always ready to execute all orders, no matter what the exposure to themselves." In comparison, he spoke in high praise of Smith's attack, "which was most brilliantly executed, and gave to our arms full assurance of victory."[15]

Examination of Grant's and Wallace's written observations of the Henry and Donelson campaign illustrates the different perspectives from which each viewed his world. The literary-minded Wallace, in his report and *Autobiography*, describes in illustrative and colorful prose detailed observations of troops, artillery, dead soldiers, and the winter landscape and notes every sequential phase of battle precisely. Grant, however, in his report and later in his *Memoirs*, describes the panorama of the event. He examines the big picture and selects only the most critical details (e.g., the Confederates carried several days' rations in their haversacks, signaling the sortie was an attempt to escape) to interpret the scope and direction of battle. Donelson gave Wallace confidence in his abilities to command men in battle and permitted the opportunity to work with Grant under combat conditions. The initiative he displayed illustrated that Wallace was an officer with tactical instinct and intelligence and, as one student of the battle has written, he "saved the budding career" of Ulysses S. Grant. Wallace earned promotion to the rank of major general of volunteers after Donelson, and his future in the army showed promise.[16]

Fresh from their capture of Fort Donelson, the Union commanders optimistically prepared another offensive, which they believed (Grant especially) would decide the fate of the war in the West. What the Federal leaders did not take into account was that western Confederate forces, far from collapse, might seek to regain their losses. General Halleck, now commander of all western Union forces, decided to sever east-west Confederate rail communications in northern Alabama and Mississippi, which would isolate Southern defenses in the Mississippi Valley. Grant was ordered to ascend the Tennessee River to Savannah, Tennessee, while Maj. Gen. Don Carlos Buell, with the Army of the Ohio, was ordered to march overland from Nashville to join Grant on the river. When the two armies combined, Halleck would lead the campaign against the Confederates. On March 17, Grant reached Savannah, where the decision was finalized to establish the forward base of operations further upstream at Pittsburg Landing, on the west side of the river, twenty-two miles northeast of the Confederate base at Corinth. Grant disembarked five divisions and made camp. The Union front rested two miles southwest of the landing near a small wilderness church, Shiloh Meetinghouse. Grant posted headquarters in Savannah and waited for Buell. He made daily trips to Pittsburg to supervise training and to stockpile supplies for the campaign. He had orders not to bring on an engagement before Buell arrived.[17]

On April 5, Brig. Gen. William Nelson reached Savannah with the advance division of Buell's army. Grant learned that Buell himself planned to arrive the next day. Although several skirmishes had occurred during the last two days, Grant stated there was no need for haste and informed Nelson, "There will be no fight at Pittsburg Landing, we will have to go to Corinth, where the rebels are fortified." The Union plan had a serious flaw, however—Gen. Albert Sidney Johnston, supreme Confederate commander in the West, refused to remain at Corinth. At dawn on April 6, 1862, Johnston hurled nearly forty-four thousand men in a surprise attack on Pittsburg Landing. Around Shiloh Church, the forward Union divisions, mostly raw recruits, stubbornly resisted the savage onslaught, while their commanders called for reinforcements. By 9:00 A.M., the five Union divisions (forty thousand men) were either engaged or in motion to the front.[18]

Six miles away, posted at Crump's Landing, was the Third Division under Lew Wallace. The veteran general heard the roar of battle to the south and interpreted it as a general Confederate attack. He ordered the division alerted and under arms. Realizing that Grant, by boat, would soon pass upstream from Savannah, Wallace went to the river and boarded a steamboat to await orders. About eight o'clock Grant arrived. Uncertain whether the attack was a general one, Grant directed Wallace to "hold his division ready to march in any direction." The conference lasted only a few minutes, before Grant steamed for Pittsburg Landing, reaching it about nine o'clock.[19]

Earlier, Wallace had issued orders to concentrate his three brigades, which were scattered for five miles along the Purdy Road to Adamsville. He ordered the First Brigade, encamped at Crump's, and the Third Brigade, posted at Adamsville, to converge on the Second Brigade, deployed at Stoney Lonesome, two and a half miles inland. Wallace ordered a horse be saddled for the expected courier from Grant. Later in the morning, when the courier had not yet appeared, Wallace instructed Capt. James Ross to return to Crump's and provide escort for the messenger to Wallace's command post. Wallace then rode inland to Stoney Lonesome.[20]

At Pittsburg Landing, Grant learned from Brig. Gen. William H. L. Wallace that the attack was a general Confederate offensive and that the entire army was engaged. Grant realized the disposition of forces had to be changed. It was imperative that Lew Wallace reinforce the main army immediately, and Grant dispatched his quartermaster, Capt. A. S. Baxter, to order him to move up. Baxter departed around 10:00 A.M. Grant's order was verbal, but Baxter made a written copy of the instructions while he steamed downriver to Crump's Landing. When he reached Crump's, he met Captain Ross, who guided him to Stoney Lonesome, reaching Wallace at 11:30 A.M. Wallace reported that Baxter handed him a ruled half-sheet of tobacco-stained foolscap with an unsigned, unaddressed scrawl in pencil: "You will leave a sufficient force at Crump's Landing to guard the public property there; with the rest of the division march and form junction with the right of the army. Form line of battle at right angle with the river, and be governed by circumstances." "Whose order is this?" Wallace asked. Baxter responded it was Grant's. Wallace asked why it was not signed, and

Baxter explained the initial orders had been verbal, and "fearing a mistake in the delivery," he had written them down while aboard the boat, using paper he picked up from the floor of the ladies' cabin. Wallace accepted the orders and told Baxter to report so to General Grant. According to Wallace, he then asked Baxter about the battle. "We are repulsing the enemy!" came the reply. Baxter was with Wallace for about three to four minutes, then departed.[21]

Wallace left infantry, cavalry, and one cannon, a total of 1,727 men, to guard Crump's Landing. At noon, after giving the troops thirty minutes to eat rations and make final preparations, he marched from Stoney Lonesome on a route known as the Shunpike Road to join the right of the main army, as he understood division alignments existed before the attack. He was already familiar with the route he followed. Toward the end of March, Grant had developed concern for the security of the Third Division. Wallace's camps lay north of the flooded valley of Snake Creek, isolated from the main force at Camp Shiloh. Grant wished to keep Wallace north of Snake Creek, where he could threaten the Mobile and Ohio Railroad, located eighteen miles west of Crump's Landing. Wallace's presence also denied Confederate access to Crump's, from where rebel artillery might threaten river navigation and communications. Thus, a contingency plan was devised to reinforce Wallace with troops from Camp Shiloh, should the need arise.[22]

The direct route to Crump's Landing from Camp Shiloh was the River Road, or Hamburg-Savannah Road, which road crossed Snake Creek two miles west-northwest of Pittsburg Landing. With the Tennessee River in flood, the Snake Creek bottoms were inundated, the bridge itself recently submerged. Gen. William Wallace was assigned the task to open that route. Until these road repairs were finished, an alternative route was required to pass troops from Camp Shiloh north across Snake Creek. Lew Wallace ordered his cavalry to scout the Shunpike Road to establish a point where juncture with Camp Shiloh could be made. On April 4 he wrote to William Wallace with a recommendation that they pass cavalry across this route so that the troopers can "act promptly in case of emergency as guides to and from the different camps." The letter that passed between the two generals survived the war and was provided to Grant in 1884 by Ann Wallace, the widow of William Wallace, who died of wounds received at Shiloh. The letter confirms that Grant's lieutenants made prebattle preparations to use the Shunpike Road to pass reinforcements from Pittsburg Landing to Lew Wallace. From Camp Shiloh, the contingency route was attainable by passing troops west on the Hamburg-Purdy Road, from Sherman's camps near Shiloh Church, to a bridge across Owl Creek. A short distance west of the Owl Creek bridge, another road, the Shunpike, proceeded north to another crossing of Snake Creek, near the Overshot Mill, two miles south of Adamsville, the location where Wallace's Third Brigade was encamped. Grant left the arrangements of this scheme to his lieutenants, and he and his staff apparently were ignorant of its details. The failure to keep abreast of these prebattle decisions embarrassed Grant on April 6.[23]

Thus, while Wallace followed the contingency plan in reverse, and marched southwest on the Shunpike toward the Overshot Mill, Grant observed the battle from behind the Federal lines. He had visited every division commander engaged on the field and ordered each to hold his ground, for reinforcements would soon arrive. Before noon, Grant learned his right flank was retreating north. Hours had passed since he issued the order for Wallace to move up, and there was still no contact with his column. The situation was fast getting out of control. The embattled Union army sorely needed Wallace's veteran division; their arrival might halt the Confederate advance and perhaps permit counterattack.[24]

About an hour after Captain Baxter departed with the first order, Grant sent a second courier to Lew Wallace. A cavalry officer familiar with the River Road was ordered to ride to Crump's Landing and hurry him forward. Shortly after noon, the second courier returned and told Grant that General Wallace "would only obey written orders." There is reason to believe the courier misinterpreted Wallace's asking if he "had written orders from Grant." In his previous military service, Wallace had never refused an order, whether verbal or written. In any event, Grant was angered by the courier's information, and at 12:30 P.M. dispatched Capt. William R. Rowley, guided by the same cavalry officer, with orders for Wallace to move. If he desired written orders, Rowley was to provide them, but by all means the Third Division was to move up immediately.[25]

Rowley galloped up the River Road to Crump's Landing. Informed that Wallace had gone to Stoney Lonesome, Rowley proceeded to that location, then southwest along the Shunpike. At a point five to six miles from Crump's Landing, near Snake Creek, he overtook the rear of Wallace's column. He wrote later that he found the entire division at rest (stopped along the road). Continuing, he located Wallace at the head of the division just north of Clear Creek, four miles short of the Owl Creek bridge. Rowley relayed Grant's order. Wallace said that he could not understand the need for two messages to prod him when the division was making remarkably good time. "Where are you going?" demanded Rowley. Wallace replied, "To join Sherman." Pulling Wallace aside, Rowley explained that the army "had been beaten back, that the right, to which [he] was proceeding, was then fighting closer to the river, and that the road [Wallace now] pursued would take [him] in the enemy's rear."[26]

Rowley's statement shocked Wallace, who recorded in his battle report that due to the "unfortunate condition of the battle, my command was in danger of being entirely cut off." He realized his troops were not where Grant wanted or needed them. Rowley informed him that Grant's orders had been to march by way of the River Road. Wallace replied that the current road he now marched "was the only road he knew anything about." Wallace's cavalry returned from a scout beyond Clear Creek with word that Confederate forces lay between the column and the Owl Creek bridge. On that news, Wallace ordered a countermarch. By midafternoon the column had recrossed Snake Creek, where it turned onto a crossover route—an old trace now known as Wallace's shortcut—and tramped southeast toward a junction with the River Road.[27]

About 3:30 P.M., Capt. John A. Rawlins and Lt. Col. James B. McPherson, of Grant's staff, overtook Wallace as the division marched along the shortcut. Grant had dispatched these two officers, as he had Rowley, to hasten Wallace forward. Six hours had passed since he had issued the first call for Wallace. The Third Division had been on the march for over three hours and was still four miles from the main army. Rawlins became agitated over the rate of progress and insisted the artillery be abandoned so that the infantry could press on more rapidly. When Wallace halted to allow the rear ranks to close up, an angry Rawlins pleaded that each regiment be pushed forward as it arrived. Wallace declined, on the tactical principle that "Grant . . . wanted the division, not a part of it." Rawlins suggested to McPherson that they arrest Wallace for dilatoriness, but McPherson, whom Wallace characterized as "more quiet and thoughtful," refused. The rear ranks having closed up, the march continued. When the column reached the River Road, Mc-

Pherson suggested that the artillery pull off the road so as not to impede the infantry any further. Wallace agreed.[28]

On the ridge north of Snake Creek, Wallace received word that Confederates held the bridge. The division halted while Rowley and McPherson, with the cavalry, rode ahead to check out the rumor. They sent back word the area was clear. A short time later, Grant's staff officers left Wallace and galloped off down the road, leaving him to push the last mile alone with his column. Darkness was at hand when, at 7:00 P.M., he rode across the wooden bridge spanning the flooded channel of Snake Creek, the same bridge he understood had been submerged only three days before.[29]

Earlier, the roar of battle that radiated from the Shiloh plateau had literally shaken the ground. Wallace remembered that the great battle seemed to pause, "and its fury underwent a noticeable lull." Behind him, the mud-covered division struggled through the final stretch of "dirty chocolate" swamp of the inundated creek bottom. "A fire of impatience burned the soul within me," he recalled years later, "and I kept my eyes on the sun, which seemed to go down with a leap of a diver, and still the old bridge rocked under the tread of companies in hurried passage. . . . In files of four, and feeling for the road, the brigades staggered on." When they finally came to high ground and he found "solid earth enough to accommodate the division," he ordered a halt, "and facing the column to the right (west), effected an alignment (on Sherman to the left). Pickets were sent at once." Nine hours had elapsed since Grant had issued his verbal order, seven since Wallace left Stoney Lonesome. The first day's fighting had already ended.

No member of Grant's staff, or courier, was present to guide Wallace's men. "Once more I was cast upon my own resources," stated Wallace, who believed it fortunate that "the fall of night put an end to the battle." He observed that both armies, "or the survivors of them, were seeking rest, each in the place it occupied when the light went out."[30]

News of Wallace's arrival was relayed to Grant at Pittsburg Landing. The absence of the Third Division that Sunday was a source of frustration and embarrassment to Grant, who later used the excuse of Wallace's tardiness to avert some of the blame leveled at him for the heavy casualties suffered at Shiloh. On the basis of a day of collective confusion in a battle in flux, Lew Wallace's military career suddenly turned sour. He never forgot the misfortune created by his failure to arrive in time to participate in the first day of fighting at Shiloh. In one of the hundreds of letters he wrote to defend his actions, he told Grant in 1884, "The terrible reflections in your indorsement on my official report of the battle [of Shiloh], and elsewhere, go to the world wholly unqualified. It is not possible to exaggerate the misfortune thus entailed upon me." Frustration probably accounts for why Wallace, years later, changed his mind on what might have happened had he been allowed to complete his original line of march. In 1862, he believed his division would be trapped behind Confederate lines if he continued. Years later, without the public exoneration from Grant that could have cleared his name, he began to speculate about what might have happened had he continued his march, to surprise Johnston's army and strike the rebel force in the rear.[31]

In early 1863 Wallace learned of Grant's negative endorsement of his original battle report. Although the statements are not harsh, they raised doubts about Wallace's conduct, questioned the accuracy of his report, and stated that Grant had tried to hurry Wallace to the scene of the battle. Grant finished his comments by adding, "This report in some other particulars I do not fully indorse." Believing these comments unfair, on March 14, 1863, Wallace wrote to General in Chief Halleck in Washington, stating that he knew a prejudice existed in Halleck's office because of his (Wallace's) failure to participate in fighting at Shiloh on April 6, 1862. That said, Wallace provided a detailed explanation of his actions, "to vindicate my conduct from unjust aspersions." Halleck sent the letter to Grant for remarks, who decided not to prepare a response but ordered Rowley, Rawlins, and McPherson, the staff officers dispatched that Sunday to hurry Wallace forward, to submit statements. Baxter, who carried the original order, was not asked to file a report. The statements from the three "Grant Men" proved damaging to Wallace. They charged that he failed to follow Grant's order, became lost, and responded slowly to the emergency, despite their repeated pleas for speed. With these statements in hand, Grant vouched for their accuracy and later used selected parts of them in his *Memoirs*.[32]

As his record shows elsewhere, Wallace was no dawdler. On the contrary, considering his zealous nature, he often had to be reined in like a young colt. "I was all eagerness to push on with my brigade," he wrote of his role in the capture of Forts Henry and Heiman on February 6, 1862, "but General Smith rode, like the veteran he was, laughing at my impatience, and refusing all my entreaties. He was too good a soldier *to divide his column* [italics added]." In remembering Fort Donelson, Wallace spoke of his frustration with inactivity as he stood listening to the terrible crash of battle that signaled McClernand's division was facing disaster. "The noise kept grinding on without lull or intermission," he wrote, "an hour—two hours—would it never end? The suspense became torturous." When McClernand called for assistance, Wallace obeyed Grant's prohibitive orders to hold his position and sent to his commander for instructions. No answer. Grant was absent from the field. When McClernand again cried for support, Wallace seized the initiative, violated orders, and dispatched reinforcements. Apparently, Lew Wallace understood his duty.[33]

What then about Wallace's conduct on the first day at Shiloh? The first issue of controversy to consider is the original order. Grant wrote in 1884 that his verbal order was for Wallace "to march immediately to Pittsburg [Landing], by the road nearest the river." If this was the order Wallace received, he failed to follow it. In his letter to Halleck, written in 1863, Wallace stated the order "directed me to leave a detachment to guard the public property at Crump's Landing, then march my division and form junction with the right of the army; after junction I was to form line of battle at a right angle with the river." This only differs slightly from Wallace's original report of April 12, 1862, when he wrote that the order directed him to "come up (move south) and take position on the right of the army and form my line of battle at a right angle with the river."[34]

Further documentation supports Wallace's recollections of the actual order as nearer the truth than Grant's version. The statements prepared in 1863 by Rowley, Rawlins, and McPherson provide three different versions of the original order. Although the three statements were not intended to exonerate Wallace, the staff officers' recollections are more consistent with Wallace's version than with Grant's recollections of the verbal order. In his account, Grant made no mention of the directive to join the right of the army; yet all three staff officers state that Wallace received orders to that effect (that is, the word "right" appears). Moreover, Rawlins, Grant's most devoted defender, stated that Wallace was to "form in line at right angles with the river," a point mentioned by Wallace but omitted from the Grant accounts. Rawlins also confirmed Wallace's statement that he received orders to leave a detachment to guard public property at Crump's Landing.

The actions Wallace took after he received the order from Baxter are consistent with the initial descriptions he wrote on the incident. He sent the detachment to Crump's Landing, then moved on a road that would take the division to the right of the army as it was positioned prior to the battle. Confusion over the order was Grant's error. Unfortunately, Capt. Frederick Knefler, Wallace's adjutant general, misplaced Baxter's written note. If it had survived, the note might have clarified the controversy. In his *Memoirs*, Grant wrote that the order was oral but that he understood Baxter had written it down, conceding that he did not know what order Baxter wrote, for he never saw the actual memorandum.[35]

Actually, Grant may not have issued the order to Baxter. Both Rawlins and Rowley provide conflicting stories on this matter. Rawlins wrote that Grant gave him the order and that he repeated it to Baxter; Rowley stated that Grant gave the order directly to Baxter. Grant knew by what route he wanted Wallace to proceed, but his verbal order was not explicit. In times of stress, oral commands invite misinterpretation. Before his death, Grant said he could not be certain what order Wallace actually received. In *The War in the West: The Mississippi Valley in the Civil War*, historian John Fiske has written, "The cause of [Wallace's] delay was a misunderstanding such as one is continually meeting with in every-day life." Fiske believes that it never occurred to Grant that Wallace would march by any route other than the River Road from Crump's Landing to the Snake Creek bridge. The entire controversy "might have been prevented," Fiske noted, "had Grant in the first place sent to Wallace a businesslike written order, specifying his line of march. It is in such minute attention to details that great generalship largely consists."[36]

When Wallace moved on a different route, Grant concluded he had made an error in judgment. Grant's biographer William S. McFeely notes that, in his relationships with his lieutenants, Grant *"measured details of personality in terms of expected responses to orders* [italics added]." McFeely believes Grant held reservations about his subordinates, and *"did not regard his generals as having the capacity for independent judgment* [italics added]." Thus, when the expected response failed to occur and Wallace marched by a different route, Grant associated his action in terms of Wallace's own personality and capacity for judgment. It never occurred to Grant that the crux of the problem existed with his verbal order, which was twice (perhaps three times) repeated and then written down, thereby creating a high probability of misinterpretation at some link in the chain of command.[37]

The historiography of the war characterizes Grant as a commander who routinely prepared his own written orders, an act that did not occur in the case of Lew Wallace at Shiloh. Perhaps the Grant so frequently observed drafting orders throughout the war is a general who does not trust the judgment of his own staff. To Halleck, on December 14, 1862, Grant revealed difficulties with his staff when he wrote, "My individual labors have been harder probably than that of any other general officer in the Army, except probably yours and McClellan. . . . Much of this was due to having an entire staff of inexperienced men in military matters." He achieved remarkable results with the methods he used to direct military operations. He understood that in an army, in contrast to civilian society, though orders might be badly carried out, they must be obeyed. "As long as Grant could sense the movement of battle he could give explicit orders and get from his officers their best." Grant appears to have possessed a remarkable sense of the whole of an event. He viewed battles in the dimension of time and space and sensed the continuity of motion on a battlefield. However, in the confusion at Shiloh, he failed to sense Wallace's response to his orders because Grant had already formed an expectation of what that response should be.[38]

There is no evidence to support the statements from Grant's aides that Wallace got lost. Like Grant, the aides assumed he had erred when he was discovered on a different road, which they interpreted as his being lost and wandering aimlessly. They believed he simply missed the River Road turnoff when he marched from Crump's Landing. In 1862 Wallace believed the need for his countermarch was due to a bad shift in the battle after he received Grant's original order, and he therefore assumed that Grant, and his aides, understood why he had originally marched down the Shunpike Road.[39]

The charges that the march was extremely slow are a different matter. The Third Division was stopped in column when Rowley arrived. Because he understood the seriousness of the situation, he naturally saw this as indifference on Wallace's part since it never occured to him that Wallace could not know the course of events on the battlefield. Both Rowley and Rawlins were critical of Wallace's decision to countermarch rather than reverse the order of brigade alignments. To countermarch the First Brigade, and the artillery, back through the length of the column would be difficult and time-consuming. However, the maneuver offers insight into Wallace's tactical thinking. The march began with proper displacement of personnel and equipment arranged in battle formation. By keeping the original alignment, Wallace would avoid confusion and delay when deploying the division for battle action.[40] Grant's aides were troubled by another element of Wallace's behavior: he frequently dismounted and sat down to rest, deliberate actions that seemed to prove that he was indifferent to the urgency of the situation. Rawlins testified that Wallace exhibited "the utmost coolness and indifference" during these pauses. Thus to him, Wallace seemed not to care about the plight of the army at Pittsburg Landing. Yet Rawlins and the other aides judged Wallace's deliberate march in comparison to the fluid dynamics they had recently experienced on the battlefield. Their conclusions appear inaccurate. The reports filed by the staff officers reveal that Wallace stopped periodically to permit the division to close ranks, halts that made tactical sense. A frequent concern among all field commanders in the Civil War was the problem with straggling on forced march. Remember Wallace's own impatience the previous February at Fort Henry, where General Smith reined him in so as not to divide the division. Wallace did not want the division to straggle into a pitched battle or become ambushed while entering a battle still in flux.[41]

The Third Division marched, and countermarched, for a total of seven hours. Part of the march was through inundated creek bottoms, a fact that Rowley, Rawlins, and McPherson ignored in their statements. From Stoney Lonesome the mud-covered division (5,837 men and eleven cannon) marched roughly fifteen miles. The First and Second Brigades marched the entire route and crossed the flooded bottoms of Snake Creek three times. Meanwhile, the Third Brigade, because the roads were blocked by the presence of the other two brigades, did not leave Adamsville until 2:00 P.M.; these 1,840 men covered eight miles in five hours.[42]

By comparison, during the battle of Antietam, on September 17, 1862, Maj. Gen. Ambrose P. Hill's famed Confederate Light Division of Stonewall Jackson's Corps covered the seventeen miles from Harpers Ferry, Virginia, to Sharpsburg, Maryland, in less than eight hours. Hill's division, numbering 3,300 men and including four batteries, encountered considerable straggling, with literally hundreds of men left by the roadside (Hill reported that only 2,000 men made it into the battle). Lew Wallace's march is a similar feat. The major difference was that Hill's men became significantly engaged in the climax of the battle, having arrived before the fighting ended that day; Wallace's did not.[43]

Grant stated in his *Memoirs* that Wallace erred by continuing his march even after the sounds of battle should have informed him that the Federal lines were being forced back. Battle sounds would have been hard to gauge from the angle of the march. At the battle of Iuka, Mississippi, in September 1862, due to the effects created by an acoustic shadow, Union forces commanded by Grant and Gen. Edward Ord, located roughly four miles from the battlefield, never heard the sounds of fighting. The route of Wallace's march and countermarch remained far north of the zone of battle at Shiloh. At no point along the way could he have interpreted by sound that Grant's lines were falling back.[44]

On April 7, reinforced with nearly 18,000 fresh troops under Buell and with Lew Wallace's division, Grant counterattacked. By nightfall, the outnumbered Confederate army had retreated from the field. Wallace's division fought on the extreme Federal right during the day (the heaviest fighting occurring during a four-hour span between 10:00 A.M. to 2:00 P.M.) and by nightfall had advanced nearly two miles. The division suffered light casualties, reporting 41 men killed, 251 wounded, and 4 men missing. The bitter struggle cost a combined total of 23,746 soldiers (Union and Confederate) killed, wounded, or missing. Both armies held the same ground they had possessed prior to the battle, and each stated victory had been won. The major difference was that the combined Union forces, heavily outnumbering the Confederates, remained in a strong position from which to sever Confederate rail communications and to thrust the invasion deeper into the South.

The American people, both Union and Confederate, were shocked by the immense loss of life. Leaders on both sides were bitterly assailed for blunders made in the confusion and flux of the battle. On April 11 General Halleck arrived and assumed command of field operations at Pittsburg Landing. Hearing stories that Grant was drunk during the battle, Secretary of War Stanton wrote Halleck and asked "whether any neglect or misconduct of . . . Grant or any officer contributed to the sad casualties that befell our forces." Halleck defiantly replied, "The sad casualties were due in part to the bad conduct of officers who were utterly unfit for their places, and in part to the numbers and bravery of the enemy." The unfit officers Halleck referred to were volunteers, not

West Pointers. Throughout the war, he targeted for removal many political soldiers whom he considered lacking in military education and military capacity—amateur generals who in the emergency of the Civil War invaded the private and professional domain of the regulars. To Sherman, in 1864, he further amplified his contempt for such men, stating, "It seems but little better than murder to give important commands to such men as Banks, Butler, McClernand, Sigel, and Lew Wallace." Later, as general in chief, Halleck actively labored, at times successfully, to eliminate political generals; and again as army chief of staff under Grant, from 1864 to 1865, he continued to use his position to hasten the removal of high-ranking citizen-soldiers he determined unfit for command.[45]

The Northern press corps bitterly attacked both Grant and Sherman for the surprise. The two generals also came under sharp criticism from their own troops. Numerous soldiers accused Grant of incompetence, imbecility, and irresponsibility. To date, there is no record of Wallace's troops having criticized their commander. Grant and Sherman did have their defenders, many in high places, and Halleck did his best to quash the matter of surprise. To Secretary Stanton, he boldly proclaimed, "The impression . . . that our forces were surprised in the morning of the 6th is entirely erroneous. Our troops were notified of the enemy's approach some time before the battle commenced." Halleck lied, but he also had a war to fight and acted decisively to eliminate any threat to his control of the army. As time passed, journalists eased off on cashiering Grant and Sherman. The "charges of negligence" heaped upon both officers rapidly disappeared from public attention, not to reappear until long after the war ended. Arriving at Shiloh, Halleck proclaimed Sherman the hero of the first day's fighting and asked that his friend be promoted to major general. The commission was approved.[46]

With Grant and Sherman supported by professional solidarity, many journalists shifted their attacks to Lew Wallace for "getting lost" and "arriving too late." In a letter dated April 17, 1862, Wallace told his wife not to believe the "several lies about me," including the report of his death. As for charges of "being lost from the scene of battle, and [getting] there too late," Wallace told Susan his version of what happened, and concluded, "Time will set everything right at last. It did so with the Donelson fight and will do so in this instance. I can afford to wait."[47]

It is simply ludicrous to blame Wallace for the carnage at Shiloh, as if the absence of his division somehow improved the accuracy of Confederate musketry and artillery fire. But it happened. Over time, Grant grew resentful of the attacks levied upon him concerning the heavy casualties, and he blamed Wallace's late arrival for the near defeat of the first day. When talk at Grant's headquarters turned to the subject of Shiloh, comments about Lew Wallace always entered the discussion. Cyrus B. Comstock, an engineer on Grant's staff, wrote in his diary on February 9, 1864, that after dinner in Nashville, "Gen. [Grant] got to talking about Shiloh & Lew Wallace. Wallace with 7,000 men & 4 miles distant got orders at 11 A.M. to move over a specified road to Sherman's left marched five of six miles from the fight & could only be got to his place at dark instead of 1 P.M. where his presence would have given us the day." Grant's later opinion seems clear: Lew Wallace had become the Shiloh scapegoat.[48]

At Pittsburg Landing, Halleck reorganized and called up heavy reinforcements. In the reorganization, Grant was elevated to second in command of the army group that Halleck concentrated to attack Corinth, Mississippi. Grant's army was placed under the command of Maj. Gen. George H. Thomas. Although both McClernand and Wallace were senior to Thomas, Halleck selected a professional. Stanton advised Halleck that Thomas was junior to other officers in his department, but Halleck did not alter the command assignments; regulars always outranked volunteers in his opinion. On April 29 the advance on Corinth began. At the conclusion of a hard month of maneuver and offensive entrenchment, on May 29 Confederate General P. G. T. Beauregard abandoned the position and retreated toward Tupelo. Halleck occupied the railroad junction the next day. After Union naval forces captured Memphis, on June 6, he decided to disperse Grant's troops throughout western Tennessee to police the region and to repair railroad facilities.[49]

On June 17 Wallace moved his division into Memphis, and as senior officer, he administered martial law over the twenty-three thousand inhabitants until Grant arrived on June 23. Wallace then asked for a two-week furlough. He had not been home since August 1861 and informed Grant he needed to close business matters with a law partner, see his dentist, and visit Susan. "On my arrival . . . Wallace applied for a leave of absence," Grant wired Halleck, "I granted it, . . . the command being left with General [Alvin P.] Hovey, who is fully qualified to fill the place of the former commander." Thus, Grant traded one volunteer Hoosier general for another, and Lew Wallace left the seat of war.[50]

In Indiana, Governor Morton summoned Wallace to Indianapolis and asked his friend to help recruit volunteers and to make public speeches in certain districts. From previous experience, Wallace disliked the role of recruitment officer and politely declined the governor's offer. Instead, he told Morton he wanted to resume command of his division. "There is nothing doing there," Morton bluntly replied. Confused, Wallace demanded that the governor explain his strange remark. He handed Wallace a telegram from Secretary Stanton that ordered him to report to the governor. Suddenly, Wallace realized with shock that without official notice or censure, "I stood actually relieved of my command. The division was no longer mine." Reluctantly, he made one of Morton's requested speeches and after returning home received formal instructions from Stanton to wait at Crawfordsville for orders. "The mischief was done," Wallace wrote later, "I was on the shelf; but for how long?" In Tennessee, Wallace's Third Division was broken up; only his staff remained with him. Troubled, he asked Morton to intercede for him with President Lincoln; but the governor refrained, and their friendship was never again the same. Lew Wallace stood relieved of his command—his military career seriously damaged. "Somebody in the dark gave me a push," Wallace wrote in his *Autobiography*, "and I fell, and fell so far that I could almost see bottom. Who did it? It took me a long time to find out."[51]

Although he had not been aware of a problem, Wallace's position in the army had grown precarious. Whether he deserved their animosity or not, he had angered both Grant and Halleck. Both considered him a political demagogue who thirsted for military glory, a militaristic amateur playing at war. It was also apparent that Halleck personally disliked Wallace, whom he considered a braggart. Wallace had repeatedly criticized Halleck during the advance on Corinth, and his ill-advised comments had made it back to the general with potential repercussions. Then came Shiloh, where Wallace did not respond as Grant had expected. He judged Wallace's personality, and his capacity for judgment, based on what Albert Sidney Johnston called "the test of merit." Before his death at Shiloh, Johnston wrote Jefferson Davis, "The test of merit in my profession with the people is success. It is a hard rule, but I think it right." At Shiloh, at least in Grant's estimation, Lew Wallace failed the exam.[52]

Removed from the war, Wallace found little to occupy his time but hunting and fishing on the Kankakee River. There were no formal charges against him and he did not lose his rank, but without orders he could do little but wait. In the panic brought about by the Confederate invasion of Kentucky during late summer 1862, he was ordered to duty. As military commander of Cincinnati, he mobilized thousands for the militia, declared martial law, and fortified the city and nearby Covington and Newport, Kentucky. His prompt action perhaps saved the communities from possible sacking by Confederate troops. When the emergency ended, Wallace was ordered home.[53]

On October 30, 1862, orders were issued calling Wallace to report to Grant at Corinth, Mississippi, where he would assume duties as post commander. While en route, however, new orders from Grant directed Wallace to Cincinnati, where he was appointed president of a military commission to investigate Gen. Don Carlos Buell, who stood accused of dilatory tactics for his response to the recent Confederate invasion of Kentucky. The tedious investigation lasted into May 1863, and once again, Wallace was sent home. On the Fourth of July, fortress Vicksburg fell to Grant; Lee retreated from Gettysburg; and Lew Wallace was still in Indiana.[54]

Why? What problem did Grant (and to a degree Halleck) have with Wallace that sound personnel management and the proper application of military discipline could not overcome? Ultimately, Grant clarified for the record, in clear language, his professional concerns with Lew Wallace. On December 14, 1862, while campaigning in northern Mississippi, Grant laid aside his customary reserve and wrote a long personal letter to Halleck in Washington. "I am now better situated with regard to wing and division commanders than I have ever been before," he confided to his chief, "and hope no officers will be sent into the department *who rank those who are now with me.* I am sorry to say it, but I would regard it as particularly unfortunate to have either McClernand or Wallace sent to me. *The latter I could manage if he had less rank,* but the former is unmanageable and incompetent [italics added]."[55]

Grant's acknowledged official concern with Wallace thus appears to be the question of military rank. His commission to major general of volunteers dated to March 21, 1862. On that day, he jumped seventy-two generals holding brigadier rank (volunteer and regular grade) in the Union army. After Shiloh, only Halleck, Grant, Buell, Pope, and

McClernand were senior to Wallace in West Tennessee. Within Grant's command, following the death of C. F. Smith on April 25, 1862, Wallace stood third behind McClernand. If either of the two political generals were to be assigned to Grant's command, they would outrank all other officers in the department except Grant. Their presence would displace his favorite professionals: Sherman and McPherson. One important fact about Grant's comments to Halleck is that he said McClernand was "unmanageable and incompetent," but not Lew Wallace. Apparently, Grant saw no difficulty in working with him, only the issue of rank, for he does not mention Wallace's performance at Shiloh. Unfortunately, the date of his commission was a matter that neither Grant nor Halleck (even if that officer had wanted to) could overcome. As early as September 1862, Wallace understood the true problem and in his *Autobiography* noted, "I was finding my rank a serious obstruction to getting back in active service."[56]

The blemish of Shiloh was still a painful memory, though. On July 18, 1863, Wallace wrote to Stanton and challenged the accuracy of Grant's comments concerning his official report of the battle. If the imputations were true, "I am unfit to hold a commission of any kind in the U.S. Army. The imputations can be easily shaped into charges of cowardice and treachery; and I regret to say such charges have been made." With his honor in question, Wallace asked for a court of inquiry to examine "my whole conduct in connection with the battle of Pittsburg Landing," and he believed that Judge Advocate General Joseph Holt should preside over the proceedings. On the reverse side of Wallace's letter is a scribbled comment from Halleck, "I do not think that Genl. Wallace is worth the trouble & expense of either a court of inquiry or a court martial. His only claim to consideration is that of gas."[57]

Wallace wrote an appeal to Sherman, in August 1863, asking if there was a possibility of obtaining a command under him. He was still Sherman's senior in rank, but he unselfishly acknowledged he would waive rank for the opportunity to again serve his country. Sherman returned a tactful response and spoke of Wallace's "delicate sense of honor," of Grant's esteem for him, and of his own willingness to help. He advised him not to press for a court of inquiry on the Shiloh matter and attempted to reassure him that neither Grant nor any other officer was hostile to him, though some "may have been envious of your early and brilliant career." Sherman cautioned that he should avoid controversy, remain quiet, be prepared to get into current events as quickly as possible, and hold his horses for the homestretch. "The war is not over. . . . For all real, hard working, and self sacrificing soldiers there is still a large future," he wrote. Impressed, Wallace withdrew his request for the court of inquiry and informed Stanton that he was "ready and anxious to go to any duty."[58]

True to his word, Sherman attempted to intercede with Grant concerning Wallace and wrote a confidential letter to Brig. Gen. John Rawlins, still serving as assistant adjutant general of Grant's department. "At Shiloh [Wallace] was laggard," Sherman bluntly stated, "but has he no good qualities which, with proper cultivation, might save his honor and be of use to the service?" Sherman's honest attempt at mediation failed, and in October he informed Wallace of the result, who then asked, "What next?"[59]

Some of Wallace's ordeal was of his own making. By not keeping his mouth shut, he had angered his superiors. Halleck, as general in chief, possessed the power to keep him on the shelf and away from the actual seat of war. He always felt that it was Halleck who had unofficially relieved him of command; he was probably right. Wallace also managed to anger the secretary of war with his persistent chafing over inactivity and the Shiloh affair. Stanton was not concerned with the plight of a troublesome Hoosier general. From the start of the ordeal, Wallace's old friend, the extremely influential Governor Morton, had refrained from speaking on his behalf. For a political general, Wallace appears to have had little clout.[60]

As commander of the Army and Department of the Tennessee, Ulysses S. Grant at any time could have made the request that Lew Wallace be reassigned to his command, but he did not. Wallace's seniority over other general officers in the department was a major obstruction to Grant's organizational desires. It is only reasonable to assume that as senior officer in the department Grant would desire to work with officers who, in his professional estimation, held the proper military capacity to command. To acknowledge that Grant wanted professionals—"Grant Men"—soldiers he trusted in the top commands, is only logical.

It is also reasonable to conclude that Grant may very well have held an experienced opinion that Lew Wallace had simply been promoted beyond his military capabilities. Even when one considers the brief time each was in the physical presence of the other, distinct differences in personality may have helped define the professional relationship between the commander and his lieutenant. It is notable, however, that Grant never officially raised any issue with Wallace's capacity to hold military command. He most certainly raised the issue of incompetence and inferior military capacity in the case of John McClernand—the correspondence with Halleck (December 14, 1862) being just one example of Grant's maturing professional impression on the subject of McClernand's generalship. As commander of the Western Department, Grant possessed the authority and responsibility to air similar informed impressions and concerns about Wallace's capabilities and competence. However, he did not. Thus, if the issues cited in his correspondence with Halleck shed any light on the professional impressions that Grant had of various lieutenants, it is reasonable to conclude that citizen-soldier Lewis Wallace simply held too much brass to suit him.[61]

In his attempt to secure the assistance of Grant's most trusted lieutenant, Lew Wallace "had cast [his] last throw" to get back his command. There was little that he could do other than remain quiet and patient, as Sherman had advised. Nearly two years had elapsed since Wallace had conducted his reportedly "laggard" march to the field of Shiloh, and the painful wound to his delicate sense of honor still festered. Only one person in the United States possessed supreme authority to pull him off the shelf, but Abraham Lincoln remained skillfully silent on the capabilities of General Lewis Wallace.

The Forging of Joint Army–Navy Operations

Andrew Hull Foote and Grant

Benjamin Franklin Cooling

Sometime late in the day on February 5, 1862, Brig. Gen. Ulysses S. Grant and Commodore Andrew Hull Foote stood watching sailors hoist a mine or torpedo aboard the river gunboat *Cincinnati,* downstream from the Confederate Fort Henry on the Tennessee River. As a naval armorer unscrewed a powder cap at one end of the polar bear–shaped device, the weapon emitted a loud sizzling noise. The army officers present dropped to the deck. Grant and Foote raced for the ladder leading back to the gun deck. Seeing the Jack Tars laughing uproariously at the brasses' discomfort, Foote turned to Grant and asked, "General, why this haste?" His typically unflappable colleague replied, "that the navy may not get ahead of us." Everyone got the point, for it had been Foote who earlier had boasted to his land comrades, "I shall take [Fort Henry] before you will get there with your forces."[1]

This good-natured banter revealed much about the partnership that Grant and Foote had personally forged over the past six months on the western rivers. It seemed to fly in the face of traditional service rivalries, and given the two men's apparently disparate personalities, it was surprising. But in reality, the competitive good humor reflected the pair's dedication to vision, mission, and cooperation in pursuit of a goal. The general and the commodore represented what the modern American military dogma calls "jointness"—service cooperation and operational cohesion without which combat objectives cannot be attained. In the words of one academic, lecturing over a century later to a class of military students, the Grant-Foote team represented the element "perhaps most important to any combined effort," that is, "the quality of 'selflessness.' "[2]

Foote, who lived from September 12, 1806, to June 26, 1863, was sixteen years Grant's senior when fate and the Civil War brought them together in 1861. Foote was the son of a well-to-do New Haven, Connecticut, family; his father was a merchant shipper, U.S. senator, and governor of the state. The son was raised in a strict moral and religious environment, with a private education and a brief matriculation at West Point in 1822. Later that year, he left the Military Academy and went to sea as an acting midshipman, eventually rising to the rank of rear admiral before his death. It was aboard the USS *Natchez* with the West India Squadron in the 1820s that he first expressed that powerful ethical and moral faith that subsequently attended his entire career. He became a strong temperance advocate during his service, both ashore (at the Philadelphia Naval Asylum and the Boston and Brooklyn Navy Yards) and afloat. He published *Africa and the American Flag* (1854), preaching opening darkest Africa to science, legal commerce, and Christian civilization. In fact, as John D. Milligan has succinctly put it, Foote could be seen as an "innerdirected" man for whom meaning in life came from "support for Protestant missionary activity, support for temperance, and suppression of the African slave trade."[3]

This deeply religious naval officer nonetheless also had a fighting side to his nature. Commanding the sloop of war *Portsmouth* on the East India Station when the second Anglo-Chinese war erupted in October 1856, Foote landed a force of marines in Canton to demonstrate the American presence. Two weeks later, in response to Chinese barrier forts' firing on his warships between Canton and Whampoa, he moved swiftly to capture and destroy those positions. Bravely upholding the honor of the United States against the belligerent Chinese, Foote's action paved the way for subsequent "gunboat diplomacy" in support of American policy and aims in the Far East. Moreover, his aggressiveness set a precedent for his own performance during the Civil War. Again, whether or not he was inner-driven because of passion in pursuit of a cause (response to a perceived insult to the American flag), Foote could be seen as (and may well have considered himself to be) an avenging agent of the Almighty. This dimension certainly surfaced during the period of his association with Grant.[4]

The opening shots of the Civil War found Foote employed as executive officer at the Brooklyn Navy Yard. In this capacity he helped outfit the expeditions for Forts Sumter and Pickens. Moreover, he enjoyed the patronage of Secretary of the Navy Gideon Welles, who never forgot or tired of telling people that he and the naval officer had been schoolboys together at the Cheshire Academy in Connecticut, where Foote had truly been his best friend. Little wonder then that Welles tapped Foote to go west in September 1861 to take charge of a gunboat squadron building for service on the Mississippi River and its tributaries.

Foote's predecessor, the respected commander John Rodgers, had, by dint of hard work, forged the beginnings of that squadron. But he had also incurred the enmity of his army superior, Maj. Gen. John C. Frémont, commanding the region. Frémont telegraphed Washington that he wished Rodgers to be replaced. Pres. Abraham Lincoln was not prepared to overlook such demands from the popular Pathfinder, sometime presidential candidate, and political general. Besides, Foote had that reputation as an aggressive, ever-driven fighter. So it was at St. Louis on September 6, 1861, that Foote took charge "of the naval operations upon Western waters, now organizing under the direction of the War Department."[5]

Indeed, in the words of the perceptive Richard S. West Jr., Foote was "tossed like his predecessor into the uncertainties of a new freshwater command in which ships of novel type had yet to be built with army money and manned by field and forest hands who had yet to be recruited and trained." And the initial period on the rivers was stressful for Foote. Like other naval officers, he would have preferred the smell of saltwater and sea air with the blockading squadrons. Instead, he had the challenges of contractor negotiation and oversight and constant interference, not only from army headquarters but also by having to dispatch a gunboat every time a regimental commander sensed some enemy presence. The crusty New Englander was adept at shaping his burgeoning flotilla of ironclads, converted riverboats, and mortarboat rafts, but it was in the unsung work of crew recruitment, effecting dilatory payments to contractors from Washington, and keeping close contact with army general Frémont and his successor, department commander Henry W. Halleck, that Foote made his mark. And he did it despite his belief that his naval rank of captain was equal to the much lower army grade of that title. Foote's dedication to God and country provided the persistence necessary to accomplish the administrative challenge of building a riverine navy.[6]

Of equal if not greater importance in the long run, Foote and Grant established relations at this time. The occasion for the beginning of the pair's cooperation stemmed from Grant's September 6 expedition to occupy secessionist-held Paducah, Kentucky, where the Tennessee River emptied into the Ohio. Foote had barely signed in at army headquarters and then gone on to the naval base at Cairo, Illinois, when he heard of Grant's expedition. Arriving in Cairo about midnight, he learned that Rodgers, with the gunboats *Tyler* and *Conestoga,* "in company with General Grant of the Army" and some two thousand troops had gone upriver to seize Paducah. Foote quickly commandeered a steamer and pursued them, overtaking Rodgers in the *Tyler* and witnessing what proved to be a virtually easy and bloodless takeover of that Kentucky river town. Whether or not Foote and Grant did anything more than exchange salutations is unclear. Nevertheless, the two men and the hour had met.[7]

Most certainly, Foote was impressed with Grant's action when he learned of the details. Until three days before, the Bluegrass state had been neutral in the unfolding civil conflict. Both sides had shadow-boxed while respecting that neutrality from their positions across the Tennessee border and north of the Ohio. Then, Confederate generals Leonidas Polk and Gideon Pillow had violated that neutrality by advancing and taking the Columbus bluffs on the Mississippi River, then spreading out into the western part of Kentucky, called the Purchase. Spies and rumors brought word to Grant in Cairo that they were poised to seize Paducah—key to any inland campaign using western waterways and crucial to freedom for river traffic of the Ohio Valley generally. Grant wired Frémont in St. Louis for permission to seize the town; none was forthcoming at his planned time of departure, but Grant had gone on with the operation. This was Foote's own kind of soldier—a man of action and daring, a fellow spirit.[8]

Much of autumn of 1861 brought the pair into steady but still somewhat distant contact. Grant was busy monitoring the troop buildup, studying maps and spy reports and restlessly awaiting an opportunity to strike the enemy. Foote, meanwhile, was likewise mired down, not only in monitoring the naval buildup but also in the ever-present call from land forces for support in minor reconnaissance, clandestine trade interdiction, and political control operations in western Kentucky, Northeast Missouri, and along the southern tier counties of Illinois, Indiana, and Ohio.

As a fretful Foote told Secretary of the Navy Welles, "every brigadier could interfere with [him]" as he chafed at the War Department's lack of centralized responsibility, which "made it all but impossible to obtain Army help in joint operations."[9] Historian Richard West is mainly alluding to the highest echelon's lack of command unity here, but the situation made it difficult to accomplish much on the western rivers. Arrangements improved in early October, when the entire naval force was transferred from War to Navy Department control; but before this, even Grant always seemed to be one step ahead of Foote in ordering gunboats hither and yon, much in the pattern of the Paducah expedition. Numerous communiqués passed between them concerning the navy's needs for storage facilities available at Cairo that conflicted with the need for similar space by Grant's logisticians. Perhaps it was mainly Foote's shuttle diplomacy between St. Louis and such river bases as Cairo, Mound City, and the like that minimized any schisms and difficulties. One also has the impression that Grant intended no slight toward or lack of respect for the navy. He was merely pressing on with his agenda, frustrated by Frémont's apparent lack of moral courage to support him promptly and completely with the task of getting on with the war in the West.[10]

Still, Frémont's October 11 order to Foote further exacerbated the situation. Frémont stated categorically that the navy captain "will officer, man, and equip" as well as "take charge of and prepare for immediate active service" not only the twelve gunboats proper but also "the mortar boats, propellers, transports, etc." belonging "to the entire floated expedition down the Mississippi River," and to "consider yourself in charge of, and commanding, this expedition." It was little wonder then that the older man took some umbrage when Grant rather peremptorily directed the gunboats to proceed with his small expeditionary land force on a movement against the Confederate fortress at Columbus, resulting in the battle of Belmont, Missouri, on November 7. Of course, Grant probably deduced correctly that Foote would have demurred in the first place, claiming his boats unready for such service.[11]

Foote thought that he had worked out a modus operandi with Grant, as he informed Welles two days later. "When last in Cairo," he had asked Grant "to inform me by telegram, at St. Louis, whenever an attack upon the enemy was made requiring the cooperation of the gunboats, that I might be here to take them into action." Grant had assented, "but no telegram was sent me, nor any information was given by General Grant when the movement upon Belmont was made." In fact, the army officer had not even informed the captains of the gunboats *Lexington* and *Tyler* of his intention until he directed them to proceed with his force on the armed reconnaissance. Foote considered it not only regrettable personally, "but it was a want of consideration toward the navy, a cooperating force with the army on such expeditions."[12]

Foote was in St. Louis when the battle of Belmont was fought. True, he told Welles, Grant had made subsequent amends, admitting that he had simply forgotten their agreement "in the haste in which the expedition was prepared, until it was too late for [Foote] to arrive in time to take command." Grant also profusely praised Foote's gunboat captains in his after action report. But because of similar affronts by Brig. Gen. Samuel Curtis, commanding at St. Louis, and Quartermaster General Montgomery Meigs in Washington, concerning naval parity with the land force, Foote remained peeved. He attributed the treatment to the fact that the army lacked experience, any appreciation of navy needs, and the general military "claiming rank over naval captains of under five years date of Commission," he told Welles. He had said the same thing, basically, a week earlier to Assistant Secretary of the Navy Gustavus V. Fox and even repeated it a third time, to Welles, on November 13. In today's terms, Foote was saying that he simply could get no respect as he requested the rank of flag officer from the Department of the Navy. Three more months and a more successful operation transpired before he won this rank.[13]

In the meantime, the drubbing that the amateurish Grant and his little force took in the battle of Belmont held other ramifications. "Belmont was not only a school for the troops but a classroom for their commander," Grant's biographer Geoffrey Perret has observed. Waging a fighting retreat and emerging "with a down payment on the renown that he secretly craved," suggests Perret, allowed the brigadier to paint Belmont as a success (despite major errors in tactics and in handling more than a squad of troops). Foote's subsequent reproach may have caused Grant to reflect more assiduously upon the changing nature of command relations and operational cooperation as core elements, in addition to impetuosity, in succeeding against a determined foe.[14]

In any event, it was during the months following Belmont that the soldier and sailor grew close. Frémont was gone, replaced by a crabby but intellectually brilliant departmental commander, Henry Halleck, and even in Washington there was a new general in chief of the army, George B. McClellan. Moreover, in the view of William B. Feis, the brownwater navy regularly provided invaluable assistance in the form of amphibious landing support, protected reconnaissance missions, and so-called "reconnaissance-by-fire" missions, throwing heavy naval shells into unsuspecting Confederate camps and positions. In addition to such psychological warfare contributions, Feis suggests that Foote's flotilla, in support of army commanders like Grant, Smith, and others, provided an intelligence-gathering dimension that proved decisive in the months ahead.[15]

At this time, Confederate defense in the West stagnated for want of men and supplies, frustrating senior Gen. Albert Sidney Johnston, who anxiously wanted to move the frontier of the Confederacy to the Ohio River from southern Kentucky. On November 8, Brig. Gen. Charles Ferguson Smith (another of Grant's promising subordinates and with whom Foote's gunboats had similarly cooperated during the autumn) wrote a report to the adjutant general in Washington. He spoke of both river and land threats to his position at Paducah as well as of Confederate positions strengthening just across the Tennessee line at Forts Henry and Donelson. During this period, too, Foote's individual gunboat captains, such as S. L. Phelps, supporting Smith, were busy running up the Cumberland and Tennessee Rivers reconnoitering, testing Confederate control, and generally developing a sense that these streams offered promising possibilities for circumventing the Columbus roadblock to Yankee invasion by way of the Mississippi River. And by December, small Confederate land and naval force activity suggested potentially troubling offensive intentions against Union positions in Missouri, Kentucky, and southern Illinois. All of this prompted increased message traffic between Grant and Foote beyond calls for normal support tasks such as blocking smuggling and protecting a steamer that Grant sent down "to bring up produce for some loyal citizens of Ky." Although the use of storage space aboard the Cairo wharf boat remained a sticking point, Grant apparently now felt comfortable enough in his relations with Foote to ask whether a young law student friend of his from Galena, Illinois, George Hicks, might visit one of the gunboats.[16]

The pace quickened with the new year. President Lincoln especially looked for movement in the war, having the notion that a wellspring of Unionism awaited Northern armies when they moved South: a popular force would rise up to aid them against the rebel oligarchy. Despite customary campaign lulls in winter (due to climatic effects on travel arteries as well as discomfort to men in the field), the chief executive pressed Halleck (and his departmental counterpart Don Carlos Buell in Louisville) to advance into Kentucky and then to Tennessee. Johnston's static front from west of the Mississippi to its eastern anchor in the mountains of eastern Kentucky and Tennessee fairly invited attack and victory—for some man of action. Halleck and Buell were not such men, but Grant and his compatriot Foote were. Still, there were roadblocks, not the least of which was Grant's reputation. His old army image of drunkenness, lack of snap, and the rather questionable Belmont affair kept Halleck at arm's length from his Cairo brigadier. What emerged then in January was shadowboxing and more demonstrations by Grant and C. F. Smith from Cairo and Paducah.[17]

Union goals remained limited—they were simply to move toward a major Confederate concentration point at Camp Beauregard in extreme western Kentucky to keep the enemy off balance as to Halleck's eventual goal of general invasion. Grant and Smith (whom the former now commanded) were to prevent Confederate reinforcements from being shifted eastward to counter Buell's intended offensives in response to Washington's directives. Thus, Union soldiers, supported by two of Foote's gunboats, sloshed about in the cold, rain, and mud of western Kentucky for a couple of days before returning to winter quarters in disgust, having accomplished nothing more than bewildering the enemy as to what was going on. Grant too was depressed, despite an upbeat-sounding dispatch to his chief, declaring, "The expedition, if it had no other effect, served as a fine reconnaissance." He asked permission to visit headquarters, which Halleck granted. But it was Smith who achieved more with his end of the exercise. Scouting aboard the gunboat *Lexington,* he and the navy discovered the abject weakness of the Confederate position at Forts Henry and Heiman on the Tennessee River. Suddenly, by January 24, such intelligence and other circumstances affecting Halleck, Foote, and Grant converged.[18]

Frankly, there was nothing novel about the discovery. Anybody on either side looking at a map that fall and winter could see the proper avenues for advance. The ever-conservative Halleck, knowing full well that he would use the twin rivers to outflank the Columbus bastion, simply bided his time until Foote's navy had come up to strength and added those critical mortar boats to bombard any rebel position into submission with less cost in life and material.

When Grant arrived at St. Louis headquarters that day in late January, the cold and punctilious departmental chief brushed aside his suggestion that it was time to take the Confederate forts. Halleck wanted Grant to stick to matters concerning the good of his command; he would do the decision making concerning the strategy of the situation. "I returned to Cairo very much crestfallen," Grant recalled in his memoirs, years later.[19]

It was here that Foote came to the fore. "He and I consulted freely upon military matters and he agreed with me perfectly as to the feasibility of the campaign up the Tennessee," Grant recalled later. Given his characteristic persistence and determination, he renewed the bidding in a January 28 wire to Halleck: "With permission I will take Fort McHenry [sic] on the Tennessee and hold & establish a large camp there." But this time he had the request reinforced with a separate telegram sent to Halleck that same day by Foote. "Grant and myself are of opinion that Fort Henry on the Tennessee can be carried with four Ironclad Gun-boats and troops to be permanent-occupied. Have we your authority to move for that purpose?" wrote the salty sea dog. At the bottom, he added, "I made the proposition to move on Fort Henry first to General Grant." Grant followed up with another wire the next day, noting that the window of opportunity was fast closing but then concluding, "The advantages of this move are as perceptible to the general commanding as to myself, therefore further statements are unnecessary."[20]

Halleck again tried to stall, telling Foote that he wanted a final report from Smith concerning road conditions between the latter's base at Smithland on the Ohio River and the rebel fort on the Tennessee. Still, the naval officer was to "have everything ready." The door half open, Foote replied the next day in greater detail as to his preparations and that "in consultation with Genl. Grant we have come to the conclusion that the Tennessee will soon fall as the Ohio is falling above and therefore it is desirable to make the contemplated movement the latter part of this week." He added that "it is said" that the road from Paducah to Fort Henry or opposite was good, "even at this season." Foote's and Grant's communiqués placed Halleck in a quandary. He flatly distrusted Grant's abilities and desperately wanted to await Foote's mortar boats before advancing. Yet just in from Washington was another wire from McClellan to both him and Buell stating that Confederate general P. G. T. Beauregard was coming west with fifteen reinforcing regiments from Virginia. Halleck's forces had to strike hard and strike fast.[21]

Little wonder then that on January 30, Halleck fired off the pivotal wire to Grant: "Make your preparations to take and hold Fort Henry," with written instructions to follow. The Grant-Foote team had been forged. But Halleck's longer instructions that same day hardly did justice to appreciating either that new team or the possibilities for joint operations on the rivers. It was to be a land operation, pure and simple. Foote's gunboats would protect the troop transports (that is, any not left for the defense of Cairo). And the real rush for the advance was the rumor of Beauregard and his reinforcements. Central to cutting the Confederate line between Columbus and Bowling Green was getting Grant's cavalry to break up the railroad that linked those points by rendering bridges and track impassable. That this could be accomplished by Foote and his gunboats, once past Fort Henry, never seems to have occurred to the St. Louis–bound departmental commander.[22]

At least the expedition would be fairly launched. Events moved quickly as Grant and Foote concentrated their force before Fort Henry by February 5. Halleck's dispatch mentioned "investing" the fort, so Grant personally hustled forward the land contingents on the limited number of available steamboats. Finally, determining it "imperatively necessary" that the enemy position be reduced on February 6, Grant had his men slogging forward on both sides of the flooding river. Foote, meanwhile, would plunge ahead with his gunboats to attack the fort directly. Grant delegated a company of Smith's infantry to go aboard the gunboats as sharpshooters. Nobody anticipated the rapidity of what transpired. In fact, writes James Milligan, "Caution had no place in Foote's plan." The favorable results of his experience in China uppermost in his mind, and faith in God's will against the heathen (whether Chinese or Southern), drove the flag officer toward the enemy's jugular. He intended proving his earlier prediction—his boats would take the fort before Grant's soldiers ever got into position.[23]

Indeed, it happened just that way. Jointness in principle gave way to service singularity in practice. Yet there was no reason to think Grant disapproved of letting the navy win a bloodless victory for him. Both men had great faith in the new weapon—the ironclad river gunboat. Still, the all-navy show had ramifications for the future. About an hour and a half of battering by the heavy bow guns in Foote's four ironclads convinced Fort Henry's commander, Kentuckian Brig. Gen. Lloyd Tilghman, to surrender. Working the heavy ordnance of the fort was his forlorn hope, a last-ditch contingent of seventy artillerists. The rest of the garrison had been sent overland to Fort Donelson on the Cumberland—suggesting how much confidence Tilghman had in the low-lying position of Henry. The navy advanced to point-blank range and quickly suppressed the fort's counterfire (the Confederates helped by accidentally spiking one of their own pieces). Inside the fort, the carnage shattered the rebels' will to fight. The demanded surrender was "unconditional" (thus coining the phrase for Grant's later use) and was taken by a naval party simply rowing through the sally port and onto the flooded parade ground. There was nothing army about the battle. In fact, the soldiers spent the day sloshing into position around the fort's outworks, although Smith's people managed to occupy an incomplete and abandoned position styled Fort Heiman on high ground opposite Fort Henry, across the river.[24]

Still, there were some wrinkles. For one thing, Confederate gunners were better than the Chinese. Although unable to penetrate the iron-plated casemate sides of the gunboats, they found unsheathed portions and gunports. One particular shot exploded the *Essex*'s boiler. Tilghman even told Foote afterward that had his best guns not burst or been otherwise rendered inoperable, he would have cut the flotilla to pieces. In his official report, the Confederate general further iterated that the gunboats' weakness was their hurricane deck or roof, susceptible to plunging fire (unattainable by Fort Henry's gunners). But Grant and Foote probably missed the point in the euphoria of the Union's first major victory. "Fort Henry is Ours," read Grant's wire to Halleck at the end of the day. The gunboats silenced the batteries before the investment was complete, he added. Displaying the victor's joy, Grant concluded in words entirely oblivious of Halleck's original instructions: "I shall take and destroy Fort Donelson on the 8th and return to Fort Henry." It all seemed that simple.[25]

Grant's and Foote's longer dispatches to headquarters noted the damage to the flotilla but dismissed its seriousness. The pair were intent not only on consolidating their foothold on the Tennessee and exploiting that avenue to the Confederate heartland but also on promptly moving the remaining twelve miles to capture Fort Donelson on the Cumberland River. Foote had his wooden gunboats moving upriver to take and disable the railroad bridge above Fort Henry the day after the fort's fall. Later, they continued for a 150-mile sweep all the way to north Alabama, discovering latent Unionism and destroying vast quantities of Confederate war materiel on the riverbanks and several enemy gunboats under construction. They spread fear among the secessionist populace as to the invulnerability of the Union naval force on western waters. But meanwhile, Foote needed to return to base with the battered gunboats *Essex* and *Cincinnati*.[26]

A week passed before he and Grant could resume cooperation. Halleck sent Foote congratulations for the Fort Henry victory. Suddenly, Grant's impatience (not to mention Halleck's fears about the column's exposed position, inviting Confederate counterattack) intruded on the comity of the partnership. Halleck wanted Grant to cut the railroad bridge at Clarksville, above Fort Donelson; and by February 10, both generals were pressing to get Foote's full flotilla back into service on the Cumberland. Grant somewhat petulantly wrote his partner that he had been "waiting patiently" for the return of the gunboats from their raid up the Tennessee and passage around to the Cumberland so that he could strike overland. "I feel that there should be no delay in this matter, and yet I do not feel justified in going without some of your gunboats to cooperate," he told him. "Please let me know your determination in this matter, and start as soon as you like," he continued. "I will be ready to co-operate at any moment."[27]

Finally, by February 12, Foote had resolved repair and manning problems with his boats, Halleck and others had begun rushing reinforcements to strengthen Grant's land force, and it was a question of a footrace with time. Although he mistakenly missed the greatest opportunity of his career to go in person and take charge of throwing the Union invaders back from their lodgment on the twin rivers, Albert Sidney Johnston did muster Confederate reinforcements to move against Grant and Foote. Still, the Federals held the initiative as they encircled Fort Donelson and began to peck away at the defenses the next day. They discovered a more resolute enemy and better prepared fortifications than at Fort Henry. Anticipating a long and possibly bloody siege, Grant once more looked for the navy to bring quick resolution. But Foote's gunboats and accompanying army transports made slow progress against the Cumberland's floodwaters, and they did not arrive until the evening of February 13. Grant had the land side well covered; it was up to Foote to deal with the naval batteries attached to the rebel fort.[28]

Early on Valentine's Day morning, Grant and Foote conferred aboard his command boat. The naval officer still wanted to await arrival of the much-vaunted mortar boats, which might reduce the fort by high-angle fire. He was adamant in feeling unprepared for battle. Grant, however, thought they could not wait—winter weather, moves by their opponents, pressure from headquarters all spoke against an investment. He suggested that while his troops held their position, the four iron-clads might run past the batteries and station themselves in the Confederate rear. "That position attained by the gunboats, it would have been but a question of time—and a very short time, too—that the garrison would have been compelled to surrender," Grant wrote years later in his memoirs. Foote acquiesced, and Grant left the conference in a jaunty mood of anticipated victory. Foote gloomily told his boat captains that orders were orders and cooperation with the army imperative. They spent the next four or five hours preparing to steam into battle.[29]

The St. Valentine's Day massacre at Fort Donelson was not a repeat of Fort Henry. True, Foote confidently advanced with his four ironclads in midafternoon. Once more, the Confederates quickly lost one of their best rifled cannon when a priming wire jammed in its vent. But Foote chose to repeat Fort Henry by closing rapidly. This time the enemy's superior position, which allowed directing a severe plunging fire into the boats, Foote's own constant overshooting of targets, and the grim determination and prebattle practice by the Confederate gunners gave victory to the defenders. Foote himself was injured, two of his gunboats were reduced to almost floating wrecks, and by nightfall he was back at his mooring, a wiser, defeated warrior nursing not only a physical but also a psychic wound. It was in such a condition that Grant found him the next morning when the general rode over to confer with the flag officer aboard his command boat.[30]

Grant had left his own headquarters behind the lines, thinking that the confined rebels would take no overt action in the wintry dawn of mid-February. He "had no idea that there would be any engagement on land unless I brought it on myself," he jotted in his memoirs after the war. Thus he rode to see Foote; the pair compared notes on the previous day's setback and agreed that Foote would squire the damaged craft to Cairo for repairs, retrieve the mortar boats, and then return to Fort Donelson. Meanwhile, Grant and the army would hang on and try to wear down the Confederates, partially aided by the remaining two ironclad and three timberclad gunboats that had survived the fight with the water batteries. A disappointed Grant left his naval partner to ride back to headquarters, and Foote steamed downriver later that morning by transport, the two wounded gunboats to follow. Neither man heard the sharp sounds of gunfire, cut off from the landing by intervening woods.[31]

The sounds were there, however, as Grant soon learned from an aide. The unpredictable Confederates had staged an elaborate and successful breakout attempt. What transpired was a close call with disaster, requiring all the help the army could muster from the rump navy left to it before Fort Donelson. Fortunately, the goodwill built up by Foote and Grant served the Union well at this point, for Grant's scribbled note to the navy asking for a supporting appearance before the fort brought just that (and nothing more). It was enough, however, apparently providing inspiration for ground force counterattacks that finally wrested the fort and its outer defenses from the Confederates in the famous surrender by Brig. Gen. Simon B. Buckner the next morning. By this time, Foote was well downriver; his subordinates, however, had known what to do. In the words of Kenneth P. Williams, although the impact of the moral effect of the navy can never be clear, at this point in the battle, "It is certain that there was smooth and harmonious coordination of Army and Navy on the Cumberland on that turbulent February day." Grant could thank his naval friend for that.[32]

Grant had written his wife on Valentine's Day that the taking of Fort Donelson "bids fair to be a long job" and suggested that she go home rather than await his return in Cairo. Then luck had swept victory once more into Grant's lap. Whether or not it was due to his personal partnership with Foote, the cooperativeness the two had developed had accomplished the task. Foote subsequently rejoined Grant on the Cumberland within the week, and the pair once more badgered Halleck for new action. They wanted to be allowed to ascend the river and capture Nashville. But their ever-cautious, somewhat devious departmental superior demurred. The gunboats could go no farther than Clarksville—another railroad crossing point on the Confederates' lateral line of communications. And just as after Fort Henry's fall, he wanted to make absolutely certain that his opponents could not get in the exposed rear of any precipitous dash upriver. Moreover, Nashville lay in Buell's line of advance. Further, Halleck was angling for power over the consolidation of the whole Western Theater and thus awaiting sanction from Washington for his every move.[33]

Grant continued to consolidate his gains at Fort Donelson, spending time counting prisoners and trophies. Foote had to content himself with boat repairs and supervising random reconnaissance on the rivers.

The naval officer was much more under Halleck's direct management rather than Grant's by this point. At least, he kept a barrage of missives going back to headquarters, reiterating that "General Grant and myself consider this a good time to move on Nashville." Water levels were perfect in the rivers, and the pair thought the capital city could be taken with little trouble. "Please ask General Halleck if we shall do it," he plaintively requested the departmental chief of staff on February 21.[34]

Halleck's approval was slow in coming; Foote meanwhile moved ahead to secure a brilliant diplomatic ploy, peacefully occupying Clarksville on February 20. He assured town fathers that lives and personal property would be protected in the community. The river city never overcame its secessionist roots, but Foote at least helped calm fears about the treatment that might be expected from Union invaders. In fact, up and down the rivers, Grant and Foote established a rule of law that promised justice for loyal and disloyal alike while promising destruction or confiscation only of identified Confederate war materiel. The expeditionary force conscientiously went after only iron works, fortifications, and supply dumps, leaving slaves, food, and the civilian sector largely undisturbed. By this point, dedicated Confederate citizens, like their comrades in the army, had long since departed southward for the deeper heartland, away from the joint army–navy force of the enemy.[35]

Indeed, Johnston set in motion a general retirement of his army that eventually ended only in northern Alabama and Mississippi. Nashville and all the region drained by the Tennessee and Cumberland Rivers were effectively given over to the Yankees. This movement enabled Foote and Grant to make an unsanctioned visit to Nashville, but it also meant that the gunboat flotilla was now needed elsewhere. There were no more heavy Confederate positions left on the twin rivers to deter further Union army advance into the heartland. Such was not the case on the Mississippi, however. Confederate positions continued to command that river southward from the Tennessee line to Memphis. Foote was soon called to that new axis of advance while Grant (with gunboat accompaniment) moved his army farther up the Tennessee River by steamboat as a means of outflanking those rebel positions.[36]

That Grant and Foote had grown close was reflected in the random personal correspondence between the two. On George Washington's birthday, Foote had sent congratulations to his land comrade "for your well-earned major-generalship." In turn, the soldier responded on

March 3, decorously enclosing a letter from his young sister "from which you will see how you are appreciated, deservedly, by the people of Covington [Kentucky] as well as the remainder of this broad country." Foote replied a week later, sending "the love of an old man to your accomplished sister who I know will take it from the friend of her distinguished brother." Here then was something more than just a professional bond between warriors. Their shared experience of the past six months had spawned a true friendship, which, unfortunately, fate did not permit to ripen further.[37]

Foote saluted his own new mission unenthusiastically, it seemed. More army cooperation with a new land force under Brig. Gen. John Pope should have been amenable to him. The design was to capture Island No. 10, impeding Union progress down the Mississippi. Certainly everyone expected Foote and his gunboats simply to add to their Henry-Donelson laurels. But Foote himself was a changed man after the latter campaign. Now more cautious, he sought to await completion of the mortar fleet and other improvements to his force. He admitted to his wife that he was disheartened by the petty jealousies of the army's top command that had prevented him and Grant from rapidly taking Nashville. "I am now determined to wait till I get the gun and mortar boats ready, and will not obey any orders except the Secretary's and the President's." He could well afford to be independent now, he observed, but chiefly he was "used up with fighting and working for the last ten days." The injured foot troubled him, too.[38]

"I tell you the last was a bad fight," Foote informed his wife about Fort Donelson. "I was touching the pilot with my clothes when he was killed, but I won't run into the fire so again, as a burnt child dreads it." Truth be told, Fort Donelson had spooked this aging sea fighter. Thus in his cooperation with Pope he did not enjoy the close affinity he had had with Grant. Eventually, Island No. 10 fell to the very subterfuge that Grant had suggested at that early February morning meeting aboard Foote's command boat. Only now it was Pope's suggestion that Foote simply run two of his gunboats past the island's bristling guns and force a surrounded enemy to yield. Reluctantly, he did so on two successive stormy nights, and bloodshed was minimal. Still, the glory was not the navy's, for Foote had dallied and sidestepped the straight-forward mission. He simply feared to risk gunboats and crews in another bloodbath like the massacre on the Cumberland.[39]

Beyond this point, Grant's and Foote's careers diverged sharply.

The army commander kept his appointment with destiny at Shiloh and weathered the troublesome relations with Halleck. The momentum of Henry-Donelson returned, albeit without Foote nearby. The old man never recovered health or spirits, despite months of recuperation after the Island No. 10 campaign. Welles secured a desk job for him in Washington as chief of the new Bureau of Equipment and Recruiting. Then Foote was slated to take over the South Atlantic Blockading Squadron. But he never did so, taking ill and dying of Bright's disease in the Astor House in New York City on June 26, 1863, en route to his new assignment. Grant, of course, went on to top army command and eventually the postwar White House. Yet he carried with him Foote's legacy—the truth of mutual early victories, shared with a comrade and the navy.[40]

Assistant Secretary of the Navy Gustavus Fox wrote Grant on October 20, 1865, that one Capt. Augustus Russell Street Foote, U.S. Volunteers, had applied for an extension of his commission. Apparently, young Foote had received a midshipman's appointment in the navy as of October 1, 1863, but resigned to enter army service on February 15, 1865, gaining his army rank and an adjutant position on March 22. The son of Grant's old comrade, the admiral, noted Fox, "is a waif" without parents or near relation and asked simply to remain in the Federal service as long as possible. Fox did not know that this course was the best for him, "as he is young enough to start on some secure path," but he still felt compelled to bring the matter to Grant's attention. Grant may have been sympathetic but possibly could do little, given the precipitous postwar demobilization. Foote was retained only until the end of October and was honorably mustered-out on January 12, 1866.[41]

Through the postwar years, Grant garnered the honors for the twin victories at Henry and Donelson. In the naval service, however, Foote was not forgotten, and both men reflected well John Keegan's declaration about Grant, an exemplar of "unheroic leadership." In fact, both Grant and Foote were unheroic types, individuals who would have readily accorded others all honors and glory due to success. Perhaps that was what made their partnership workable in the first place. Grant never denigrated the "jointness," born of partnership between himself and sailors such as Foote, Henry Walke, David D. Porter, and others, as a component of Union victory.[42]

Years later, in a possibly apocryphal instance, a professor lectured to a class of modern young officers about the Grant-Foote partnership. He declared that proper army–navy coordination demanded not only a variety of professional techniques but also some strong character traits. He enumerated courage, tact, judgment under pressure—all qualities found in Grant and Foote at this early stage of the Civil War. But he concluded that "perhaps most important to any combined effort is the quality of 'selflessness.' " Certainly this early pair of war professionals working together on the western rivers made a high art of that personal quality. And they spread that spirit of jointness among their subordinates, helping to make possible the final victory three years later.[43]

The Failed Relationship of William S. Rosecrans and Grant

℮ Lesley J. Gordon

In 1882 famed Civil War general and former president Ulysses S. Grant was broke. He had squandered money in a number of unwise investments, and his loyal friends in Congress wanted to find a way to help him. A bill was proposed that would restore him to his rank as lieutenant general and backdate his pay to 1869. William S. Rosecrans, chairman of the House Military Affairs Committee, and former subordinate of Grant's during the war, defiantly blocked the bill. This was a "proposition to reward Grant for his distinguished military service," Rosecrans contended, but "when true history is written," he maintained, Grant's record would not look so stellar. Grant, Rosecrans said, had made public statements that "were false and which he knew to be false at the time he made them, and which I have shown in my official reports to be false." He went on to condemn the business Grant engaged in as activity "which has been done as to rob some people of millions, and which, if done on a smaller scale would have sent its managers to prison." The bill passed, but Rosecrans's bitter words showed that his hostility toward Grant, hostility that began in the Civil War, showed no sign of abating.[1]

William S. Rosecrans and Ulysses S. Grant had started out as friends. On the surface, they had a lot in common. Both were natives of Ohio, both attended West Point, and both opted to leave the prewar army to pursue business endeavors. Rosecrans, like Grant, struggled financially as a civilian, but when war began he immediately offered his services to the Union. By summer 1862, Rosecrans had performed admirably, especially in western Virginia, where he won significant victories while serving under George McClellan. Transferred to the west, and under Grant's command, Rosecrans seemed destined for more impressive deeds on the battlefield. Grant himself told Henry Halleck on August 9, 1862, "I regret that Genl Rosecrans has not got rank equal to his merit."[2] Nearly two months later any respect between Rosecrans and Grant was quickly dissipating. Two years later all friendly feelings had vanished, replaced by intense dislike and resentment. On December 2, 1864, Grant wrote Edwin Stanton: "Rosecrans will do less harm doing nothing than on duty. I know of no department or any commander deserving such punishment as the infection of Rosecrans."[3] Rosecrans was removed from command and spent the final four months of the war sitting idle in Ohio with no assignment. He had his share of enemies, but he remained convinced that Ulysses S. Grant was the man who engineered his military demise.

How did this happen? How did these two Ohioans, who began the war mutually respecting each other, end up so bitterly hating one another? In examining the relationship between Grant and Rosecrans, I shall focus on their falling out in autumn 1862. Both men played a role in creating this breach, but circumstances also came into play. The Civil War careers of Rosecrans and Grant seemed to collide at the wrong time and place.

The story of William Starke Rosecrans begins in central Ohio. The eldest of four sons born to Crandell and Jemima Rosecrans, William was born on September 6, 1819, in Delaware County. His ancestral roots were Dutch, and his parents were devout Methodists. Crandell Rosecrans was a veteran of the War of 1812 who ran a tavern and store in addition to a family farm. William's mother, Jemima, and grandmother, Thanksgiving, were important women in his life, pious and strong. Young William grew up an avid reader, working in the family store and helping to keep his father's books. Perhaps it was in his genes or even learned on the rugged Ohio frontier, but something or someone instilled in him a tireless work ethic and a stubborn strong will.[4]

William was clearly a bright young man, but his parents could not afford to send him to college. Instead, they opted for an appointment to the U.S. Military Academy, and Rosecrans entered as part of the class of 1842. His classmates included James Longstreet, Don Carlos Buell, Earl Van Dorn, and John Pope. Other fellow cadets included William T. Sherman, George Thomas, Josiah Gorgas, and Ulysses S. Grant. One evening, Rosecrans first encountered Grant standing outside barracks intently guarding a pump. Rosecrans told him that he no longer had to stand guard: "You go to bed at tattoo, and douse your lights at taps." The naive plebe hesitated: "But how do I know that you're not playing a trick on me too?" Rosecrans pointed to his chevrons and proclaimed, "I'm officer of the day." It was perhaps the first time Rosecrans could pull rank on Grant, who no doubt was happy to obey.[5]

Rosecrans graduated from West Point fifth in his class, earning a commission in the prestigious engineering branch. He soon gained a professorship at the Academy, teaching for three years until 1847, when he began a series of stints overseeing various engineering projects in Rhode Island, Massachusetts Bay, and Washington, DC. He did not serve in Mexico, and by 1853 he had had only one promotion in eleven years. Pay was notoriously low in the prewar army, and he began to worry about supporting his growing family. He had married Anna Elizabeth Hegeman on August 24, 1843, and within ten years the couple had four children. William, like so many of his fellow West Point classmates, decided to leave the army to try his hand in business; in March 1853 he resigned. He spent the next eight years throwing his tireless energies into business and various inventions. In June 1855, he obtained employment as engineer and superintendent of the Canal River Coal Company and for a short period served as elected president of the New Coal River–Slack Water Navigation Company. With two other partners, he built an oil refinery in Cincinnati, but business faltered. Rosecrans, seeking a more marketable kerosene, was one day working on a "safety lamp" when an explosion occurred, burning him so severely that it took him over a year to recover. His face was scarred for life, leaving what seemed to some a permanent smirk on his face. He continued experimenting with inventions, creating an odorless oil from petroleum, producing an improved kerosene lamp, and making less expensive chlorine soap. By early 1861, his refinery business was finally beginning to show a profit. But then the war came, and seven days after Fort Sumter he offered his services to his native state of Ohio.[6]

Rosecrans began the Civil War as a civilian aide to George McClellan, in charge of Ohio volunteers. In April and May he laid out Camp Dennison for Ohio troops and traveled to Philadelphia and Washington, DC to obtain guns and uniforms. By the end of May he had gained commission as a brigadier general in the U.S. Regular Army and was given command of four Ohio regiments. He wrote his wife Annie: "I am appointed a Brig. General in the Regular Army. So, my dear your old ambition must now feel gratified."[7]

Soon after receiving his commission, Rosecrans joined McClellan in western Virginia and participated in the battle of Rich Mountain on July 11, 1861. He designed the battle plan that called for McClellan to press forward at the sound of guns from Rosecrans's advance. McClellan displayed his patented hesitation, and Rosecrans attacked alone but masterfully won the battle, giving the Union its first victory. McClellan claimed that he had expected to hear from Rosecrans "every hour," and when he heard nothing, he did nothing. In his official report McClellan praised Rosecrans: "I cannot, however, let the present occasion pass without making mention of the services of Brigadier-General Rosecrans in conducting his command up the very precipitous sides of the mountains and overcoming the formidable obstacles which impeded his progress; also for the very handsome manner in which he planned and directed his attack upon the rebels at Hart's farm, carrying them after a stout and determined resistance."[8]

Rich Mountain was a small battle compared to the size and human cost of future engagements, but it highlighted many of Rosecrans's talents as a strategist and determined fighter. In the midst of the battle, men spotted the general astride his horse, oblivious of danger, nervously relaying messages to his staff, and watching the battle unfold through a spyglass. The plan was a good one and caught Confederates entirely off guard, despite McClellan's failure to attack. But Rich Mountain also revealed Rosecrans's weaknesses. He resented the attention McClellan got for the win, and as fellow Ohioan and journalist Whitelaw Reid noted, Rosecrans "already exhibited symptoms of the personal impudence which was to form so signal a feature of his character, by casual hints as to his dissatisfaction with the conduct of his superior officers, dissatisfaction which he afterwards expressed officially, by complaining that 'General McClellan, contrary to agreement and military prudence, did not attack' the enemy in front."[9]

Rosecrans was a man of obvious emotion and unable to conceal his sentiments, whether good or bad. Gen. Jacob Cox recalled, "His impulsiveness was plain to all who approached him; his irritation quickly flashed out in words when he was crossed and his social geniality would show itself in smiles and in almost caressing gestures when he was pleased."[10] He kept his staff officers awake all night discussing his favorite subject, Catholicism. If he felt wronged, his hot anger flashed and his fury was unleashed. Col. John Beatty recounted an episode with Rosecrans when a confusion over names led to a mix-up with orders. When Beatty realized what had happened he quickly informed Rosecrans of the mistake. Rosecrans was furious, yelling and swearing at Beatty, as several other officers looked on. Beatty recalled, "His face was inflamed with anger, his rage uncontrollable, his language most ungentlemanly, abusive and insulting." Beatty was mortified. He later wrote Rosecrans a letter demanding an apology for such treatment, but he refused to comply. A private talk with Rosecrans eventually calmed Beatty, and their relations apparently returned to normal. But Rosecrans's sharp temper became well known to most people who had any dealings with him.[11]

Rosecrans's high emotion also showed itself in the field. He apparently needed little sleep and worked nonstop. One soldier described him early in the war: "Our General is an incessant worker. He is in his saddle almost constantly. He has not had a full night's sleep since he has been in Virginia, and he takes his meals as often on horseback as at his table."[12] In the midst of battle he nervously rode from place to place, and many observers attested that he frequently became so excited that he began stuttering. William Shanks, a reporter for the *New York Herald*, asserted that Rosecrans's nervousness interfered with his ability to command: "I have known him when merely directing an orderly to carry a dispatch from one point to another, grow so excited, vehement and incoherent as to utterly confound the messenger. In great danger as in small things, this nervousness incapacitated him from the intelligible direction of his officers of effective execution of his plans."[13]

Victory in West Virginia catapulted McClellan to national attention, and when he left to take command of the Army of the Potomac, Rosecrans assumed command of the Department of the Ohio. For several months, he worked at training green troops and at keeping peace in the loyal communities of western Virginia. He continued fighting and beating Confederates in the region, including Robert E. Lee. On September 21, 1861, the *Charleston (SC) Courier* praised Rosecrans as "probably the best general in the Northern armies."[14] Henry Adams wrote his father Charles Frances Adams, "Rosecrans seems to be a good deal of a man if I understand his double victory over John B. Floyd and Robert E. Lee."[15] The legislatures of both Ohio and West Virginia offered Rosecrans an official thanks for his achievements in the campaign. Indeed, the forty-two-year-old's Civil War career seemed off to an exceptional start.[16]

But as he gained accolades for his performance in West Virginia, Rosecrans was also making political enemies in Washington, DC. Edwin M. Stanton, made Secretary of War in January 1862, became one of his worst critics. When Rosecrans offered his own plan to unite forces in western Virginia, Stanton allegedly lashed out at him: "You mind your business and I'll mind mine."[17] Secretary Stanton was not a man who welcomed advice, especially from generals in the field. His increasingly radical Republican politics also worked against Rosecrans.

In early spring 1862, political pressure from the Radical Republicans caused Pres. Abraham Lincoln to convert the Department of the Ohio to the Mountain Department and to replace Rosecrans with John C. Frémont. Rosecrans was without command. After spending some time in Washington, DC, orders came in May for him to head to the Western Theater to join Henry Halleck near Corinth. He initially was given two divisions in John Pope's Army of the Mississippi, an obvious demotion from his independent command in the East. But Rosecrans was opening a new chapter in his military career: he was about to reunite with his West Point classmate and old army comrade, Ulysses S. Grant.[18]

By May 1862, a series of Union victories in the West had brought Ulysses S. Grant to national attention. But they also brought him headaches and controversy and worsened his relationship with Halleck, his immediate superior. Halleck, a jealous, petty man, resented any positive attention Grant received in the press and credited others with the success. Just before the battle of Shiloh, Halleck blasted Grant for leaving his command without orders to visit Don Carlos Buell in Nashville, where he was out of contact with Washington for more than a week. McClellan urged Halleck to arrest Grant for leaving his command without permission, but Halleck instead fumed from far away. Shiloh did not silence Grant's critics, even though it was a Union win, with the Confederates in retreat. The battle was terribly bloody (it was the bloodiest battle to date, April 1862), and Grant, not anticipating a Confederate attack, was not even on the field at the onset of battle. Rumors swirled that he was drinking excessively, and Halleck himself rushed from St. Louis to take personal command of the army. These were dark days for U. S. Grant.[19]

In July 1862, when Henry Halleck became general in chief of the

Union armies, Grant assumed responsibility of the District of Western Tennessee, which consisted of two armies: the Army of the Tennessee and the Army of the Mississippi. Grant personally led the Army of the Tennessee, and after John Pope went east, William Rosecrans headed the Army of the Mississippi. Neither army was in good fighting condition—both suffered from weeks of inactivity, hot weather, and bad drinking water.[20]

During these hot summer months Rosecrans and Grant appeared to enjoy pleasant relations. They dined together regularly at Grant's headquarters, and the two men conferred over improving the state of affairs in the district and strengthening Corinth's defenses. Rosecrans was a welcome addition to Grant's command: he was an experienced officer who had proven himself in battle. He quickly become popular with the men and significantly improved discipline, camp conditions, and morale in his army. It was in early August 1862 that Grant had written Halleck of his regret that Rosecrans was not promoted to a rank "equal to his merit."[21] But just a few days before Grant penned these lines to Halleck he confided to his father that he preferred to serve in the field rather than in departmental command. "I do not expect to be overslaughed by a junior," he wrote, "and should feel exceedingly mortified should such a thing occur, but would keep quiet as I have ever done before."[22]

Although his relationship with Grant seemed fine, Rosecrans was increasingly troubled by his situation. His relations with Stanton were worsening, and McClellan was openly critical. His wife Annie was having a difficult pregnancy, and he waited anxiously for letters from home to inform him of her condition. And he was impatient with his new command. In West Virginia, Rosecrans had had a good deal of autonomy, planning his own campaigns and controlling his own department. He was a perfectionist, a man who demanded the best in himself and everyone around him. There seems little question that he was a man of talents—he was confident, courageous, knowledgeable, and a skilled strategist. But his impatience, excitability, and quick temper could quickly overshadow these abilities. He chafed at any criticism from anyone, but especially from men whom he deemed less able than himself.[23]

In September 1862 the Confederacy was on the move in three key locations: Robert E. Lee invaded Maryland, Braxton Bragg advanced into Kentucky, and Sterling Price marched toward Iuka, Mississippi. It was unclear where Price was ultimately headed, whether it was toward Braxton Bragg in Tennessee or to join forces with Earl Van Dorn farther south. Grant considered gathering his scattered troops and attacking Price hard before there was any chance of his uniting with Van Dorn. Rosecrans, however, suggested Grant divide his command into two parts and use one part to block Price's movement to Tennessee and the other to prevent his escape south. The two parts would strike Price simultaneously, hitting him from two directions. This strategy was a complicated one that required cooperation, careful timing, and coordination; and it was paramount that the Union troops defeat Price before Earl Van Dorn had a chance to arrive and reinforce him. Grant accepted it, believing that Rosecrans's familiarity with Iuka merited such a plan, and he put Rosecrans in command of 9,000 men to block Price's retreat routes to the south; Edward O. Ord with about 6,500 men was to attack Iuka from the direction of Memphis, west of Iuka. Price had 12,000 men and could easily defeat either portion of Grant's army if the attack was not coordinated.[24]

On September 18, 1862, Rosecrans's plan was put into motion. He marched his men forward but initially took the wrong road. It was raining and he was behind schedule, but he repeatedly sent word to Grant that he still expected to arrive on the field by the agreed-upon time. Rosecrans told Grant that when Ord heard the sound of firing, he should move forward with his men. But it was not until 4:00 P.M. on September 19 that Rosecrans finally attacked. Casualties were terrible, both sides withstanding high losses. However, neither Ord nor Grant ever heard the firing, and thus no second attack ever occurred. To Rosecrans it seemed like Rich Mountain all over again, where he waited in vain for McClellan to advance. Rosecrans had deemed it too risky to divide his force to try to prevent Price's escape route, and on the morning of September 20, Price slipped easily away. Rosecrans was livid. He confronted Ord, demanding to know why he had not come forward to fight. When Ord explained that Grant had told him to wait until he heard the sound of guns, Rosecrans turned his frustration on Grant.[25]

But Grant was equally displeased. His reasons for modifying the plan to attack from the west are unclear—some scholars have speculated that exaggerated news of a spectacular victory at Antietam in the East caused him to hesitate about causing further bloodshed if in fact the war was over. He did ask Ord to send a telegram to Price asking for his surrender, although Price refused. There is also a good deal of

controversy about whether men in Ord's command could hear firing—
this vacuum of sound that happened in other battles may have happened
at Iuka. Grant clearly did not know what was happening, and rather
than blindly commit more troops into combat, he opted to wait. But he
was astonished to learn that Rosecrans failed to cover both roads leading south. In his postwar memoirs he recalled, "I was disappointed at
the result of the battle of Iuka—but I had so high an opinion of General
Rosecrans that I found no fault at the time."[26] In fact, it seems that
Grant's high regard for Rosecrans's abilities had already begun to
wane.

Rosecrans's only biographer, William Lamers, has speculated that
Grant resented the tone and language Rosecrans used in a message he
sent late in the evening on September 19. In this missive he had urged
Grant, "You must attack in the morning and in force."[27] Lamers wrote,
"The positive tone of this order to his superior might have been regarded as insubordinate and used as a basis for misunderstandings to
come." But he defends Rosecrans by arguing that it might be seen as
"good advice from one leader in a joint movement to the other, with
whom he was on a friendly basis and who had failed to put in his appearance, how to get out of the mess."[28]

Grant and Rosecrans might have smoothed over any misunderstandings or disappointments had not the press and politics become involved. Both men made mistakes at Iuka, Grant for failing to support
Rosecrans's attack and Rosecrans for failing to stop Price's retreat.
Rosecrans's confident claim of familiarity with the area had also fallen
far short. Both men were dissatisfied with the battle's result. But when
newspaper reporters judged Iuka's winners and losers, these two individuals' frustrations and failures turned into personal antagonism. To
a Northern public clamoring for action, Rosecrans's performance was
heralded as exemplary, but Grant's seeming inaction was severely denounced. Newspapers praised Rosecrans while castigating Grant as
drunk and incompetent. In Washington, DC, politicians who wanted to
see Grant fail were too willing to believe the worst.[29]

These public attacks had stung Grant before. But he especially resented his subordinate's gaining recognition when in Grant's mind
Rosecrans had allowed Price to get away unmolested. At first, Grant
commended him: "I cannot speak too highly of the energy and skill
displayed by General Rosecrans in the attack, and of the endurance of
the troops under him."[30] He blamed the Confederates for preventing

Ord's advance and even offered praise to his unused troops. But as the weeks passed, and the attacks in the press grew more and more vicious, he began to feel differently toward Rosecrans. On October 22, 1862, a few weeks after the equally disappointing battle of Corinth, Grant submitted a report on the battle of Iuka that was entirely devoid of any compliments for him.[31]

Rosecrans meanwhile was not silent in expressing his displeasure. A few days after the battle he wrote his wife Annie, "The failure of proper co-operation unfortunately lost us the capture of Price and his entire army, which would have been inevitable had the attack from the west side been duly made."[32] Even in his official report he could not restrain himself. As Whitelaw Reid observed, "Of course, however, Rosecrans could not omit the opportunity to do himself an injury, so, even in his official report to General Grant, he curtly expressed his disappointment at Ord's failure, and elsewhere was even more explicit."[33]

September ended. Sterling Price and Earl Van Dorn were united and readying for another attack. Grant and Rosecrans were unsure of their destination but speculated that their target was Corinth, an important railroad town in northern Mississippi that had already changed hands once before from Southern to Northern control. Rosecrans directed the strengthening of the town's inner lines, confident that the enemy could not break the defenses.[34]

But he was soon proven wrong. On the morning of October 3, 1862, the Confederates began their advance on Corinth. Fighting raged for two days, and casualties were high. Rosecrans seemed at first confused and startled, unsure if in fact Corinth was the enemy's true target. At one point the Confederates pressed the Yankees in panicked retreat to the town's center. Rosecrans cursed and swore at his fleeing troops, but somehow he managed a counterattack that hurled the Southerners back. By 3:00 P.M. on October 4, Van Dorn led his bloodied and beaten army in a hasty retreat. Rosecrans, urged by Grant repeatedly to "push the enemy to the wall," waited several hours and then sent his men with five days' rations to follow.[35] One division took the wrong road, and the other started late and lost more time. But by then Grant believed the momentum was lost in the delay and soon ordered Rosecrans's men back.[36] He worried that Van Dorn would be reinforced and that Rosecrans was exposing his men, already low on food and water, to extreme danger. But Rosecrans, whose fighting blood was up, refused to obey. He pleaded with Grant, "I beseech you to bend everything and push them while they are broken, weary, hungry, and ill-supplied. Draw everything from Memphis to help move on Holly Springs."[37] Grant deferred to Halleck and asked for his advice. Halleck, displaying uncharacteristic aggressiveness, asked, "Why order a return of your troops? Why not reinforce Rosecrans and pursue the enemy into Mississippi, supporting your army on the country?"[38] Grant explained his concerns that his weary troops could not survive for long off the countryside and that the Confederates were being heavily reinforced. Then he sent Rosecrans his third request to halt.[39] Finally and reluctantly, Rosecrans obeyed. Meanwhile, Grant received a telegram from Stephen Hurlbut at Bolivar: "I have just heard from Holly Springs. There are no forces there; all left on Sunday." He concluded, "I am of the opinion that the rout of Van Dorn's army is complete, and that Pillow's force, late of Holly [Springs] has caught the panic."[40] Confederate correspondence shows that Vicksburg was essentially undefended. Rosecrans was right and Grant was wrong. But the point was moot; the battle of Corinth was over.[41]

If Iuka initiated a fissure in the relationship between Ulysses S. Grant and William S. Rosecrans, Corinth blew it entirely apart. In the weeks that followed the battle, correspondence between the two men grew increasingly strained and their ill will toward each other was unmistakable. Grant was irritated by Rosecrans's handling of prisoners and chastised him for seeming to communicate directly with Sherman for troops without going through Grant. He also accused several members of Rosecrans's staff for stirring bad feeling between his troops and those in the rest of the army. To the sensitive, wearied Grant, Rosecrans appeared to be demonstrating deliberate disregard for protocol and blatantly challenging his authority. Rosecrans responded that Grant was terribly mistaken and assured him that he had not meant in any way to challenge his authority. But Rosecrans was angry. Incensed that Grant did not support him and wholly convinced that he, not his superior, was right, Rosecrans brooded. And when he brooded he did not do so silently—he talked openly to his staff, his wife, to Halleck, and to friendly newspaper reporters.[42]

On October 9, 1862, the *Cincinnati Commercial* printed an account by Rosecrans's friend and biggest fan, W. D. Bickham, who unabashedly cheered Rosecrans: "And now to whom is due the honors of the battle of Corinth? The verdict of the whole army is in favor of General Rosecrans." Grant, however, deserved no accolades for the victory. "There is no doubt," Bickham declared, "that the public will give the credit to General Rosecrans where it belongs."[43]

Grant's official congratulations to the army in his General Orders no. 88 further added to the growing tensions between the two men. Grant mentioned the battle of Corinth only briefly, instead focusing on Stephen Hurlbut's brief encounter with the retreating Confederates after the battle. Grant added that he hoped there would be "the warmest bonds of brotherhood" between both divisions of the army. "Each was risking life in the same cause, and on this occasion risking it also to save and assist the other." Rosecrans took this order as a deliberate slight and resented the implication that there were poor relations between his men and those in Ord's command. He wrote Grant, "Under such circumstances the report is to be regretted, because our troops knowing that there was no foundation in it for them, will be led to think there is some elsewhere."[44]

There were a few days after Corinth when perhaps an honest personal conversation between the two men might have calmed tempers. Rosecrans in fact notified Grant on October 18 that he was going to try to come over to his headquarters and see him to discuss promotions and "other things."[45] But Rosecrans was sick, and his doctor advised that he not travel. A few more days passed, and rumors swirled and reports were issued. Both men believed the worst about the other, and without a personal meeting their negative thoughts only festered and grew. Rosecrans continued distracted and worried over his pregnant wife's condition, which had taken a turn for the worse. He was unable to consider Grant's point of view or admit his own mistakes in the campaigns. Instead, he lashed out at Grant, calling him a poor administrator, and said bluntly that he believed the victories at Iuka and Corinth were his alone. Grant, a man who himself was sensitive to criticism and rank, found Rosecrans irritating and arrogant and blamed his subordinate for failing to silence the gossip that cast him in a bad light.[46]

Correspondence between the two men became notably more strained, and on October 21 their hostility was clearly apparent in a series of telegrams they exchanged, ostensibly regarding the armament of some cavalry. Grant had asked Rosecrans if he had cavalry rifles for use of the troops at Corinth. Rosecrans, showing his vintage bad temper and brusque manner, rejoined that a shipment of rifles was en route but that it should go to his cavalry, who had done the most fighting at Corinth, rather than those troops closer to Grant. Grant was stunned: "Your remarkable telegram is just received. If the troops commanded by you are not part of my command what troops are?" He added, "General, I am afraid from many of your dispatches that you regard your command giving privileges held by others commanding geographical divisions.... This is a mistake." Rosecrans was insulted and demanded an apology for the tone of Grant's dispatch. "You have no truer friend no more loyal subordinate under your command than myself," he maintained. "Your dispatch does me the grossest injustice." Grant refused to apologize; instead he chastised him for improperly paroling prisoners and condemned the "leaky nature" of his staff. Rosecrans defended his staff, accused Grant's staff of harmful gossip, and threatened to resign.[47]

Despite this heated series of exchanges, Grant refused to reproach Rosecrans formally. On October 19, Col. Mortimer Leggett wrote John Rawlins that he was "exceedingly vexed and pained" to witness the vilification of Grant and the public acclamation of Rosecrans. "Major General Rosecrans, is undoubtedly an excellent officer—and I hope, for his honor, and the honor of his state, that he is not a party in this hellish attempt to ruin General Grant." But Leggett added, "I cannot rid my mind of the conviction that he must be at least, privy to the whole devilish scheme." Leggett feared that Rosecrans's ambition and jealousy "[lead] him to seek the downfall of Grant, hoping that thereby he may succeed to the command of the department." He asked Rawlins if something could not be done to stop the anti-Grant cancer from spreading.[48] Rawlins and two other officers even petitioned Julia Grant to try to persuade her husband to censure the outspoken Rosecrans, telling her, "In justice to General Grant—in fact, in justice to ourselves—General Rosecrans must be relieved." Grant listened to her pleas and admitted that Rosecrans's behavior "was all wrong"; but he told her, he is a "brave and loyal soldier with the best of military training, and of this kind we have none to spare at present." He assured his wife, "He is a bit excited now but he will soon come around alright."[49]

A few days later William Rosecrans received orders for a new assignment. The backbiting and incriminations had taken their toll, and Grant was none too displeased to be rid of his volatile subordinate, even though Rosecrans's transfer was unrelated to their quarrels. Rosecrans too was happy to leave an increasingly frustrating situation in Mississippi. Soon after he left, an aide on Grant's staff notified William T. Sherman: "Rosecrans has been ordered to Cincinnati to receive further orders. This is greatly to the relief of the General who was very much disappointed in him."[50]

Soon after arriving in Cincinnati, Rosecrans learned that he would be heading to Nashville to join Don Carlos Buell. But already he was annoyed. Just after Iuka he had received word of his promotion to major general, but when he realized that the date of it was September 17, 1862, rather than July 1861, the date of his success at Rich Mountain, he fumed. He demanded an explanation from Halleck:

> Why, I find myself promoted junior to men who have not rendered a tithe of the services nor had a tithe of the success. I find myself separated from the command of an army whose confidence I possess—a separate army in the field—to go and take a subordinate position—in a new & unformed one, where Buell, Gilbert, Schenck, Lew Wallace, Tom Crittenden and Bully Nelson are my seniors. Were it not a crisis for the country I would not trouble you to intercede, but would at once resign. As it is a crisis, I beg you to intercede for me, that some measure of justice may be done me.[51]

Rosecrans's promotion date was changed to March 1862, but he continued to cause problems in Washington, especially with Secretary of War Stanton. At one point, just before assuming command of the newly created Department of the Cumberland, he opted to bypass Stanton and appeal directly to Lincoln for authorization to promote an officer to inspector general. Lincoln forwarded the request to Stanton, who immediately lashed out at Rosecrans. He ordered Halleck to fire off a stern threat: "Your conduct in this matter is reprehensible and I am directed to say that unless you obey orders you will not receive the command."[52]

Rosecrans was still popular with the Northern public, and many newspapers welcomed the exit of Buell and the arrival of the "hero" of Iuka and Corinth. He also continued to have quite a reputation among the Confederates themselves. He boasted to his wife that the Confederates "have a wholesome regard for me, praise very highly the style of our troops and the tactics on the field of battle. They are more afraid of me than any other general in the service."[53] The men in Buell's former Army of the Ohio were pleased with the change, as Robert Stewart of the Fifteenth Ohio wrote: "There was silent rejoicing everywhere when Rosecrans took his [Buell's] place."[54] A few weeks after Rosecrans came to Nashville, Col. John Beatty described him as a "man from whom people are each day expecting some extraordinary action, some tremendous battle in which the enemy shall be annihilated." But Beatty doubted that his popularity would last: "I predict that in twelve months Rosecrans will be as unpopular as Buell."[55] Within twelve months his prediction came true.

But in fall 1862, neither Rosecrans nor Grant knew this. And although the two men did not have to deal directly with one another, Rosecrans's popularity continued to bother Grant. In November, he complained to his friend and political ally Elihu B. Washburne that newspapers failed to print his report of Iuka. Papers supportive of Rosecrans "have so much misrepresented the affair," Grant wrote, "I would like to see it in print." He felt troops under his command had been overlooked in the flurry to celebrate Rosecrans's men.[56]

Meanwhile, Rosecrans had a brand new army upon which to focus his boundless energy. He quickly concentrated on reorganizing and re-energizing his troops and made plans for a move on Braxton Bragg. After several weeks of preparation and repeated urgings from an impatient Henry Halleck, Rosecrans finally advanced on Bragg's position at Murfreesboro. The result was the Union victory at Stones River in late December 1862. This win, hard-fought and bloody, coming as it did just after the federal debacle at Fredericksburg and setbacks in Mississippi, gained him renewed recognition and gushing praise from President Lincoln: "God bless you and all with you. Please tender to all, and accept for yourself the nation's gratitude for your and their skill, endurance and dauntless courage."[57] Henry Halleck, too, who had threatened Rosecrans with removal if he did not do something, was ecstatic, and wrote, "The victory was well earned and one of the most brilliant of the war. You and your men have won the gratitude of your country and the admiration of the world."[58] Even Secretary of War Stanton was momentarily pleased with Rosecrans, informing him on January 7: "There is nothing you can ask within my power to grant to yourself or your heroic command that will not be cheerfully given."[59]

No congratulations came from U. S. Grant, though, who resented the continued positive attention paid to his former subordinate. A few months after Stones River, a reporter for the *Cincinnati Gazette* wrote Salmon Chase that Grant was "shamefully jealous of Rosecrans" and that his staff "would chuckle to see Rosecrans cut to pieces."[60]

Several months later, Grant's staff got their wish. In July 1863, Rosecrans had had brilliant success in maneuvering Braxton Bragg out of middle Tennessee in the Tullahoma campaign. But his victory was overshadowed by the Union triumphs at Vicksburg and Gettysburg. Then in September 1863, at the battle of Chickamauga, Rosecrans floundered and faltered and found himself and his army nearly surrounded at Chattanooga. He suffered an embarrassing defeat, his army saved from complete destruction only by the tenacity of George Thomas. It was U. S. Grant himself who came to relieve his former subordinate and rescue the Army of the Cumberland from Chattanooga. Grant's dispatch to Rosecrans and Thomas just before his arrival urged them not to give up the important railroad city. Rosecrans later complained to the Committee on the Conduct of War that he did not intend to abandon the city, and his biographer argues that had Rosecrans had more time and support from both Grant and Stanton, it would have been he who successfully defeated Bragg at Missionary Ridge and sent him hurrying back to Georgia. But by September 1863 Grant led nearly all Union forces in the West, and in consolidating his new command he got rid of a man who had remained a thorn in his side since Corinth. He replaced Rosecrans with George Thomas. On October 19, 1863, almost exactly one year after he left Grant's command in Mississippi, Rosecrans was again back in Cincinnati waiting further orders.[61]

This time the newspapers turned on Old Rosy. There were rumors of him suffering from epilepsy, using opium, and disobeying orders. He defended himself in a letter to the *New York Times* on November 2, 1863, calling them "infamous lies" and asserting that if the source of such duplicity was "our government I would despair of a nation headed by such a government."[62] Only in the South it seemed were Rosecrans's abilities still respected. The *Richmond Examiner* on October 26, 1863, announced, "Lincoln is helping us. He has removed from command the most dangerous man in his army. Rosecrans thus retired is unquestionably the greatest captain the Yankee nation has yet produced."[63]

A variety of people were responsible for Rosecrans's loss of command after Chickamauga. His critics included Edwin Stanton, Charles Dana, James Garfield, and even Abraham Lincoln himself, who lost faith in him. Although Sherman later assured Rosecrans that Grant had had nothing to do with his dismissal, in fact Grant played an active and direct role. Stanton offered Grant two sets of orders that placed him in overall command in the West: one option kept his former subordinate in command of the Army of the Cumberland and the other removed him. Grant opted for the latter, and Rosecrans was gone.[64]

Rosecrans did have enough political supporters in late 1863 to garner him one last assignment. He was given the Department of the Missouri—his third independent command of the war. For one year he headed a department with few troops and many headaches. He faced bushwhackers and guerrilla fighting and repeatedly complained that he lacked the resources to deal with either. His complaining did not earn him sympathy in Washington, and when Grant was made general in chief in March 1864, Rosecrans's continual complaining only added to Grant's dislike and distrust of him. In June, Assistant Secretary of War Charles Dana wrote Abraham Lincoln that Grant believed "the most useful way to employ Rosecrans would be to station him at some convenient point on the Northern frontier with the duty of detecting and exposing rebel conspiracies in Canada."[65] Halleck too had grown weary of the acerbic Ohioan. At one point in late September 1864, when Sterling Price threatened Missouri, Rosecrans anxiously ordered some of Sherman's troops to St. Louis. On September 29, Halleck informed Grant, "I have just learned that General Rosecrans has ordered to Saint Louis a veteran Illinois regiment belonging to General Sherman and also a Wisconsin [Minnesota] regiment en route to Nashville. He had no authority for this, but, on the contrary, I refused to permit him to stop troops belonging to General Sherman. I have telegraphed him to forward them on immediately, but I presume he will, as usual, disobey orders."[66] Grant replied, "If Rosecrans does not send forward the regiments belonging to Sherman as ordered arrest him by my order unless the President will authorize him relieved from command altogether."[67] Three weeks later Grant demanded to know if Rosecrans had yet taken on Price. "If he has not," Grant wrote Halleck, "he should be removed at once." He wanted John Logan to take over affairs in Missouri but added, "Anybody, however, will be better than Rosecrans."[68] Grant was convinced that Rosecrans had more than enough troops in Missouri to deal with Price, and in early November he sent his chief of staff, John Rawlins, to visit Rosecrans's headquarters personally to ensure that his orders were being obeyed. Rawlins reported that in fact, Rosecrans seemed "to appreciate fully the condition of affairs on the Mississippi and Tennessee Rivers, and will use every exertion, I have no doubt, to forward troops there."[69] Grant was unmoved by Rawlins's assurances. He wanted Rosecrans gone.

Finally, in December 1864 Grant got his wish. On December 2, Rosecrans received word that he was to turn over the Department of the Missouri to Grenville M. Dodge and return to Cincinnati to receive new orders. Edwin M. Stanton asked Grant what he should do with Rosecrans, and Grant's response was blunt: "Rosecrans will do less harm doing nothing on duty. I know of no department or any commander deserving such punishment as the infliction of Rosecrans upon them."[70]

Rosecrans returned home to Ohio to wait for new orders that never came. On December 30, he wrote a letter to James Garfield expressing his bitter dismay and frustration. "Greatly I am puzzled to know how it comes to pass that an officer who minds his own business, labors for the good of the country and the service, aiding merit and honesty to rise, and treating all with kindness and humanity, should be treated as I have been." He listed what he considered his many accomplishments, including "the first successful campaign against Lee" and winning "Iuka and Corinth against great odds." Why were younger, less experienced men with less rank "tainted with pecuniary speculation if not peculation" left in command while he, "an officer of sobriety, morality, industry [and] abstinence," sat out the war at home? He closed his letter with a postscript: "You know I consider my present situation an outrage on justice having few parallels in this or any other war. But I am a firm believer in the final downfall of iniquity."[71]

On April 14, 1865, Lincoln held a cabinet meeting, and Grant was in attendance. The president was remarking on the strange dream of a vessel he seemed to have before every Union victory. He listed the many times he had had this specific dream during the war, including having had it just before the battle of Stones River. Grant hastily interrupted Lincoln to say that in fact Stones River was "not victory—that a few such fights would have ruined us." Lincoln looked at Grant and remarked that he would have to disagree. Gideon Welles, who recorded the exchange in his diary, remarked that he took Grant's comments as evidence of his "jealous nature."[72] Just the hint of a compliment directed to Rosecrans set Grant on edge.

The feeling was mutual. Rosecrans too would cringe at hearing positive praise of Grant. Apparently, he hoped after the war to charge his former commander with conduct unbecoming an officer but never had the opportunity. He formally resigned from the army in December 1865 and began to direct his energies toward civilian pursuits. He worked in railroads and in 1868 gained appointment as the minister to Mexico from Pres. Andrew Johnson. However, when Pres. U. S. Grant came to office in 1869, Rosecrans lost the position.[73]

Both men lived well into old age, nursing their resentment. Grant's memoirs contain angry remarks about Rosecrans, and Rosecrans wrote several accounts of Iuka and Corinth, including one in *Battles and Leaders* that castigated Grant for failing to support him in his pursuit of Van Dorn. "If Grant had not stopped us," he insisted, "we could have gone to Vicksburg."[74] In 1885 Rosecrans's loyal friend and former chief of staff Arthur Ducat pronounced Grant's calling back of Rosecrans at Corinth "an unexplained military crime," and certainly Rosecrans believed it. That same year he tried to block the bill to award the impoverished former president more back pay.[75]

The relationship between William S. Rosecrans and Ulysses S. Grant was not doomed from the start. The two men actually began the war as respected comrades and friends. But a mixture of personality clashes, bad timing, bad press (for Grant), and poor communication destroyed their relationship. Rosecrans was arrogant and cocky; he chafed at being subordinate to anyone. Although not a man without talents, he fell short of the perfect general he claimed to be. He made mistakes, but he was unwilling ever to admit them, instead blaming others for his failings. Grant, too, had his foibles, including a heightened sensitivity to rank and authority, especially in summer and fall 1862, just when Rosecrans came to his command. Grant could not bear Rosecrans's arrogance, nor could he endure the press's continual favoring of his subordinate. In his memoirs he maintained that after Corinth he really was pleased that Rosecrans was given independent command: "I was delighted at the promotion of General Rosecrans to a separate command, because I still believed that when independent of an immediate superior, the qualities which I, at that time, credited him with possessing would show themselves. As a subordinate, I found that I could not make him do as I wished and had determined to relieve him from duty that very day."[76] In the end, neither man could make the other do as he wished.

Fighting Politician

John A. McClernand

℮⁓ Terrence J. Winschel

Embroiled in controversy throughout much of his military career, Maj. Gen. John A. McClernand remains a shadowy figure around whom controversy still swirls. He was a victim of his own actions as much as those of others, and history has all too easily come to accept and present the popular image of McClernand without questioning its validity or fairness. A troublesome subordinate, he has been characterized by his more famous contemporaries as inept, incompetent, and insubordinate. He continues to be maligned by his critics and writers of popular history and is nowadays all but ignored by even devout students of the Civil War. McClernand's biographer Richard Kiper concedes that the fighting politician "has become a footnote in the story of the American Civil War." Indeed, the politician-turned-soldier was a prominent figure in the Western Theater of operations, whose service was worthy of note; yet a clear and accurate portrait of the general remains to be painted by historians.[1]

McClernand's path to relative obscurity began in spring 1861 when he first met then-colonel Ulysses S. Grant. It culminated at Vicksburg, when by Special Orders no. 164 issued by Major General Grant on June 18, 1863, he was relieved of command of the Thirteenth Corps, stationed in the trenches before the Confederate Gibraltar. Less than two weeks later, McClernand requested that a court of inquiry be convened to examine the circumstances surrounding his removal from command. That court was never formed, and McClernand's reputation—hence his legacy—was never salvaged or refined.

The pretext for which McClernand was removed from command was the issuance of General Orders no. 72, a congratulatory order in which he praised the men of the Thirteenth Corps for their accomplishments in the opening stages of the Vicksburg campaign. Army regulations stipulated that any such orders be cleared by the War Department prior to publication. Either by design or error, the order was never submitted by the corps commander for such clearance.[2]

On the surface, it was a petty offense, hardly justifying McClernand's removal from command. But the incident reveals not only the deep animosity that existed between the army commander and his senior subordinate but also the jealous relationship between the professional soldiers and volunteer officers that was prevalent during the Civil War. How did their relationship, which began with such promise in 1861, erode to this extent? It was a complex relationship, deeper and more intimate than popular history leads us to believe and thus one that warrants further evaluation, particularly in the context of the Vicksburg campaign.

Frustration and death plagued the Union Army of the Tennessee throughout winter 1862–1863, as it maneuvered under the command of General Grant to seize the fortress city of Vicksburg. The Confederate citadel on the Mississippi River remained defiant, seemingly impervious to capture by Union land and naval forces. From Yazoo Pass and Holly Springs in north Mississippi, to Lake Providence in Louisiana, along the banks of Chickasaw Bayou north of the city, and the abortive canal across De Soto Point opposite Vicksburg, Grant's efforts had ended in failure. The only result of his operations thus far had been an ever-lengthening casualties list. The Northern press ridiculed him and clamored for his removal. Even members of the cabinet urged Pres. Abraham Lincoln to find a new commander for his western army. The president, however, answered Grant's critics by saying, "I can't spare this man, he fights. I'll try him a little longer."[3]

At forty-one, Sam Grant was at a crossroads in his military career. An 1843 graduate of the U.S. Military Academy at West Point and a veteran of the Mexican War, he was no stranger to adversity. Having battled his way to national prominence at Belmont, Fort Donelson, and Shiloh, he struggled with rumor and innuendo to establish a reputation of respectability. Cognizant of the criticism that swirled around him in both military and political circles, Grant appeared stoic but confided the torment he felt to his wife Julia. Determined to persevere, he ignored the critics and remained focused on his objective—Vicksburg. After months of frustration and failure, he examined his options.

Three possibilities were discussed at army headquarters. The first was to launch an amphibious assault across the Mississippi River and storm the Vicksburg stronghold. The second was to pull back to Memphis and to try once again the overland route, which had failed miserably the previous year. And the third option was to march the army down the west side of the river, search for a favorable crossing point, and transfer the field of operations to the area south and east of Vicksburg. In characteristic fashion and with grim determination, Grant boldly opted for the march south. On March 29, 1863, he directed General McClernand of the Thirteenth Corps to open a road from Milliken's Bend to New Carthage on the Mississippi River below Vicksburg. The movement started on March 31, and the Vicksburg campaign began in earnest.[4]

Energetic, aggressive, and ambitious, John Alexander McClernand was also bombastic, egotistical, and extremely irritating to those around him. Standing almost six feet tall, he was sparse of frame, heavily bearded, and had a rather large nose and scraggly hair, but he was of "tough and wiry fiber." He had piercing eyes, a hearty laugh, and an engaging smile yet at all times was calculating and deceitful. A lawyer by training and a politician by profession, McClernand looked to the field of battle to win victories and headlines in his quest for the White House.[5]

The man selected and entrusted by Grant for what was arguably to be the most important assignment of the campaign had been born near Hardinsburg, Kentucky, on May 30, 1812. He was the only child of John and Fatima McClernand, and his life prior to the Civil War mirrored that of Abraham Lincoln. (They were neighbors later, in Springfield, and perhaps that is why the two men got along so well.) McClernand's family moved to Shawneetown, Illinois, when he was quite young, and his father died not long after in 1816. Although he attended a village school in Shawneetown and benefited from some private tutoring, McClernand was largely self-educated. Throughout his youth, first as a boy, then as a young man, he worked at various jobs to support his mother. He went on to study law at a local attorney's office and was admitted to the bar in 1832.

As with most young men on the Illinois frontier that summer, he served as a private in the Black Hawk War. He was later involved in Mississippi River trading and came to appreciate the economic importance of the great river to America. McClernand also edited the *Gallatin Democrat and Illinois Advertiser,* but it was politics that attracted the young man and his many talents. A fiery orator, he proved to be a gifted politician. He served as an Illinois assemblyman for seven years, beginning in 1836, and was elected to the U.S. House of Representatives as a Jacksonian Democrat in 1843—the same year that he married Sarah Dunlap of Jacksonville.

In Congress, he joined the faction led by Stephen A. Douglas, whose doctrine of popular sovereignty was embraced by McClernand's constituents in southern Illinois, many of whom like himself were natives of slaveholding states. McClernand was reelected four times, serving until 1851. Harboring a strong dislike for abolitionists, he watched with mounting anxiety as the nation drifted to the brink of civil war. Entering the political arena once again, he won election to Congress in 1859 and quickly rose to the pinnacle of power in the House of Representatives, only to be narrowly defeated for the speakership by a coalition that opposed his moderate sentiments on slavery and disunion.

After the election of Abraham Lincoln and the dissolution of the Federal Union, McClernand threw his considerable influence behind the administration's war policy. Although a Democrat, he was considered by the president as an ally in the maintenance of midwestern support for the Union and was rewarded with appointment as a brigadier general of volunteers in August, to rank from May 17, 1861. Reluctant to yield the power he wielded as a member of Congress, the self-serving general did not resign his seat in the House until October 28.[6]

He first served in the District of Southeast Missouri in command of the First Brigade, then stationed around Cairo, Illinois. As part of Grant's force, McClernand moved down the Mississippi and led his brigade in the battle of Belmont on November 7, 1861. In this bizarre little action, in which untested Union troops drove equally green Confederate soldiers from their encampment, McClernand distinguished himself. "In this charge," wrote Col. John A. Logan (himself a political officer), "I saw General McClernand, with hat in hand, leading as gallant a charge as ever was made by any troops unskilled in the arts of war." Victory, however, was short-lived as the Confederates, reinforced from across the river by the garrison at Columbus, counterattacked. Soon the Federals were in retreat toward their transports and narrowly averted disaster.[7]

In a manner that became characteristic of McClernand, he placed the best possible light on events in his report and claimed great credit for his command, and thus for himself. Of his brigade's action he boasted in his report that "we beat them, fighting all the way into their camp immediately under the guns at Columbus; burned their encampment, took 200 prisoners, a large amount of property, spiked two or three guns, and brought away two." In this, his first test in combat, the politician-turned-soldier earned the praise of Grant, who wrote, "General McClernand was in the midst of danger throughout the engagement, and displayed both coolness and judgment. His horse was three times shot under him." The Federal commander further stated that McClernand "acted with great coolness and courage throughout, and proved that he is a soldier as well as statesman."[8]

On February 1, 1862, in a reorganization of Grant's force, he assumed command of the First Division, District of Cairo, in the Department of the Missouri. The feisty officer next fought at Fort Donelson, where on February 13 he launched a premature attack in an attempt to silence a Confederate battery that was playing upon his command. The attack was easily repulsed, and he was criticized by Grant for recklessness, who reported that McClernand attacked "without orders or authority." Two days later, the Confederates attempted to break through Grant's encircling lines and withdraw toward Charlotte, on the road to Nashville. The attack was directed against McClernand's sector of the line, on the Federal right, and the battle soon raged in fury. Although his troops fought with grim determination, they were not supported, and he complained bitterly in his report that "up to this and a still later hour a gun had not been fired either from the gunboats or from any portion of our line, except that formed by the forces under my command." Poor staff work at all levels throughout the inexperienced army further placed his men in a precarious situation and resulted in the troops of McClernand's division running out of ammunition—although tons of it were lying around in crates. His troops were outflanked and forced to fall back: the road to Nashville was temporarily open to the Confederates.[9]

Grant, who had been absent from the field throughout the morning, arrived on the scene and, in his words, witnessed "great confusion in the ranks." Although relieved to see the commanding general, McClernand expressed his displeasure with Grant, muttering, "The army needs a head." (This is the first indication of the rift that developed between the two generals.) Grant ignored this rebuke and simply replied, "It seems so." Along with McClernand, he brought order to the troops, saw to it that ammunition was distributed, and directed the men to seal the breach. The Federal commander later wrote that McClernand's advance, "notwithstanding the hours of exposure to a heavy fire in the forepart of the day, was gallantly made, and the enemy further repulsed." The following day Fort Donelson surrendered, resulting in the capture of thirteen thousand Confederate soldiers.[10]

In the wake of victory there was much glory to go around. McClernand, however, irritated Grant and his fellow division commanders by claiming the fruits of victory for his division in his lengthy report filed on February 28, 1862. Grant forwarded the report to his immediate superior, Maj. Gen. Henry W. Halleck, commander of the Department of the Missouri, with the observation that the account was "a little highly colored." McClernand's experience as a politician, coupled with a rather large ego and thirst for higher office, helps explain—though does not justify—this tendency for self-aggrandizement, a tendency that grew more irritating to his fellow officers as the war progressed and that finally proved to be his undoing. Regardless, his actions at Donelson helped seal for him the confidence of his men and gain the respect of his superiors. In his report, however, Grant informed the War Department, "I must do the justice to say" that General McClernand was with his command in the midst of danger and was always ready to execute all orders, no matter what the exposure to himself. A future critic, Charles A. Dana, noted that McClernand "behaved with the most conspicuous gallantry."[11]

The Union victory at Fort Donelson was hailed across the nation, and the political general basked in the public acclaim he received in the papers. In this bloody affair, McClernand had again demonstrated that he was an aggressive and courageous officer. More important, his tactical handling of troops evidenced his maturation into a capable and effective combat officer. In recognition of his service he was elevated to the rank of major general of volunteers on March 21, 1862. It was a promotion that Grant admitted was well deserved.

In the wake of victory, the Federal force moved downriver and less than two months later was again engaged at Pittsburg Landing. In the first day of fighting in the battle of Shiloh on April 6, 1862, McClernand's division moved quickly to the support of Maj. Gen. William T. Sherman's hard-pressed troops and established a formidable line of resistance. Throughout the day he and his men fought with both valor and skill but were forced to fall back from one position to another as the Federal army was driven toward the Tennessee River. Grant noted that the "hardest fighting was in front of these two divisions." Despite the confusion and casualties of the day, McClernand's exertions worked to ensure that his division retained a semblance of order and combat capability when the sun set. His performance in the bloody fray had been solid and again earned for him the praise of Grant, who stated in his report that McClernand maintained his place with credit to himself and the cause.[12]

Reinforced during the night by Maj. Gen. Don Carlos Buell and his Army of the Ohio, the combined Federal force counterattacked the next morning. In close cooperation with Sherman, McClernand's division advanced over much of the same ground yielded the previous day. Overcoming obstinate resistance, the Illinois politician exhorted his men forward and by late afternoon reoccupied the lost ground as Confederate troops fled toward Corinth.

Union victory at Shiloh polished his reputation as a fighting general. Yet despite the acclaim he received, it was a spring and summer of frustration for McClernand, who rankled under the harness imposed by subordination to Grant and others, who, he felt, treated him unfairly while showing favoritism to West Pointers. A series of incidents occurred in which McClernand believed that Grant was meddling in his authority and questioning his actions. There was considerable disagreement between the two generals, even signs of hostility that strained their relationship. McClernand yearned for an independent command and wrote letters to both Lincoln and his political ally Gov. Richard Yates of Illinois for assistance.

At the request of Governor Yates, he was sent home in mid-August to raise troops in Illinois, Indiana, and Iowa, a role in which he was highly successful. McClernand seized upon his popularity and traveled to Washington in search of greater opportunity for political gain, following the battle of Antietam. Accompanying the president to the battlefield near Sharpsburg, Maryland, he played a subversive role in the army, seeking to supplant Maj. Gen. George B. McClellan in the East and criticizing Grant's operations in the West for his failure to pursue the enemy after Shiloh. Such criticism only worked to widen the rift between McClernand and Grant.[13]

Although he failed to gain command in the East, McClernand did receive authorization from the president and Secretary of War Edwin M. Stanton to raise and command a force for operations on the Mississippi River aimed at Vicksburg. While this force assembled at Memphis, the general, who by this time was a widower, courted Minerva Dunlap, his sister-in-law, and was married on December 26, 1862. The honeymooners traveled south only to learn that McClernand's command had been taken over by Sherman and led to defeat on the banks of Chickasaw Bayou.[14]

Rushing to the vicinity of Vicksburg, McClernand assumed command on January 4, 1863, and christened his force the Army of the Mississippi. Anxious for action, he embraced Sherman's recommendation to seize Arkansas Post—a suggestion that concurred with his own estimation of the strategic situation. Located fifty miles up the Arkansas River from its confluence with the Mississippi, Arkansas Post was a point from which the Confederates could send gunboats into the Mississippi. Moving with remarkable speed, McClernand's force reached its objective on January 9 and two days later forced the surrender of Fort Hindman and almost five thousand enemy soldiers. Although the victory secured headlines for McClernand, it was downplayed by Grant, who said it was not the proper theater of operations and termed it "a wild goose chase"—that is, until he found out that his friend Billy Sherman had recommended the campaign. In all fairness to McClernand, it must be recognized that his actions eliminated a major threat to Union operations on the Mississippi River aimed at Vicksburg and a potential source of trouble for Grant's operations in Louisiana and Mississippi in the campaign soon to be initiated.[15]

Fearful lest McClernand launch an operation of greater consequence, Grant hastened from his headquarters in Memphis to the front. On January 30, 1863, he issued General Orders no. 13, announcing, "I hereby assume immediate command of the expedition against Vicksburg, and department headquarters will hereafter be with the expedition." By such action, McClernand's command was limited to that of the Thirteenth Corps, a reduction in authority that did not sit well with the fiery political general. McClernand, however, replied that he would "acquiesce in the order for the purpose of avoiding a conflict of authority in the presence of the enemy" and asked that his protest be forwarded to General Halleck and through him to the secretary of war and President Lincoln. Along with the protest, Grant sent a cover letter in which he expressed a lack of confidence in McClernand's "ability as a soldier to conduct an expedition," and by that he meant an independent expedition. Unfortunately for McClernand, Washington remained deathly quiet on the matter, and he had to content himself with corps command.[16]

In spite of his expressed lack of confidence in McClernand and an obvious personality clash that severely strained the relationship between the two generals, Grant selected the commander of the Thirteenth Corps to lead the army's vanguard through Louisiana in spring 1863. That choice is still a source of controversy today. As a political appointee in the military, McClernand was at times inept in the handling of troops. The former congressman had repeatedly demonstrated his disdain for administrative details and contempt for military protocol. He did not work well with superiors or subordinates, and his hatred for West Pointers did not endear him to his fellow corps commanders—Sherman and Maj. Gen. James B. McPherson. McClernand, however, had proven his willingness to fight at Fort Donelson and Shiloh and had developed into an able combat officer. Although Grant knew of the widespread distrust of the corps commander within the combined force operating against Vicksburg, and later wrote that he "doubted McClernand's fitness," in spring 1863 he was confident that the former congressman could and, if necessary, would fight.[17]

On March 29, 1863, Grant directed McClernand to open a road from Milliken's Bend to New Carthage on the Mississippi River below Vicksburg. The troops of the Thirteenth Corps were in high spirits as they pushed south from Milliken's Bend, followed by McPherson's Seventeenth Corps. Over the next month, McClernand's veterans marched through sixty miles of Louisiana swamp and bottomlands, corduroying roads and building bridges virtually each step of the way. He later wrote, "The 2,000 feet of bridging which was hastily improvised out of materials created on the spot . . . must long be remembered as a marvel." He justly boasted of his men with pride that their labors produced "the highest examples of military energy and perseverance."[18]

By the end of April, the Thirteenth Corps was concentrated at Hard Times Landing and boarded the transports of the invasion armada in preparation for a landing at Grand Gulf. The Union fleet, however, was unable to silence all the guns at Grand Gulf. Not wishing to send the transports, loaded to the gunwales with troops, to attempt a landing in the face of enemy fire, Grant had the troops disembark, march five miles farther down the levee, and rendezvous with the fleet at Disharoon's Plantation, below Grand Gulf. On April 30 Grant hurled his army across the mighty river and onto Mississippi soil at Bruinsburg. Soldiers and sailors gave a cheer when a band aboard the flagship *Benton* struck up "The Red, White, and Blue" as McClernand's men jumped ashore. By noon, much of the Thirteenth Corps—seventeen thousand–strong—was ashore and the inland campaign begun.

Over the next seventeen days, in what is often referred to as the blitzkrieg of the Vicksburg campaign, the Union army marched more than two hundred miles, fought and won five engagements, and drove the Confederates into the defenses of Vicksburg. The Thirteenth Corps played a stellar role in these operations, during which the Confederacy was struck a fatal blow.

Having landed at Bruinsburg, the Thirteenth Corps pushed inland through the night until Confederate resistance was encountered west of Port Gibson. In a furious battle that raged throughout the day on May 1, 1863, McClernand's troops fought determinedly to secure the Federal beachhead on Mississippi soil while Confederate soldiers fought with equal determination to drive the invaders into the river. McClernand worked his superiority of numbers to advantage by applying pressure all along the front and on the enemy's flanks. His force, later augmented with one division of the Seventeenth Corps, overwhelmed the Southern troops and drove them from the field. In the opening action of the campaign, McClernand reported the loss of 125 killed, 678 wounded, and 23 missing; the Seventeenth Corps lost a total of only 49 men. The Thirteenth Corps had carried the day, and McClernand boasted with justification that this was "the most valuable victory won since the capture of Fort Donelson."[19]

Rather than move north, directly on Vicksburg, Grant pushed his army deep into Mississippi. His objective was to strike the railroad between Vicksburg and Jackson, sever that vital line of communications and supply, and isolate the fortress city on the river. During this phase of the campaign, McClernand's corps was on the left—closest to the enemy at the point of danger. Throughout this critical period, he handled his troops with consummate skill and was prepared to meet the enemy, at all times confident of the results.

By May 12, elements of the Thirteenth Corps had crossed Fourteenmile Creek and moved to within four miles of Edwards, Mississippi, where Confederate Lt. Gen. John C. Pemberton was massing his army. In response to the sharp engagement at Raymond that day, a battle fought entirely by the soldiers of McPherson's corps, Grant decided to move on Jackson. McClernand's corps would be used as a shield to cover the movement. The crusty officer skillfully disengaged his command from the enemy near Edwards (always a potentially hazardous operation) and crossed Bakers Creek to the east, taking up a blocking position on a line running from Bolton to Raymond. Thus protected in the rear, the other corps of Grant's army marched on Jackson and seized the capital city of Mississippi on May 14. Not wishing to detach combat troops for occupation, Grant neutralized Jackson with the torch, then turned his army west toward Vicksburg—the Thirteenth Corps was again in the lead.

En route from Jackson to Vicksburg, Grant's army encountered Pemberton's force near Edwards on May 16. McClernand's divisions led the three Federal columns that converged on the small town. Cautioned not to bring on a general engagement until the army was well in hand, the commander of the Thirteenth Corps acted accordingly when the enemy was encountered, first along the Raymond-Edwards Road, then along the Middle Road farther to the north. The third Federal column, with which Grant traveled, advanced along the Jackson Road, on the Union right. Undetected at first by the Confederates, this column was in position to flank the Southerners. Grant seized the opportunity and ordered his columns to advance all along the front.

In the largest, bloodiest, most significant action of the Vicksburg campaign, Grant's men overcame stiff Confederate resistance at Champion Hill, inflicting devastating casualties on the enemy and driving Pemberton's army from the field. The Thirteenth Corps was engaged all along the front and in the bitter fight suffered the loss of 218 killed, 987 wounded, and 145 missing. McPherson's corps reported 300 fewer casualties than did McClernand's; elements of the Fifteenth Corps engaged that day suffered no reported loss. Yet credit for the victory was given by Grant, and by historians ever since, to McPherson, whose actions that day only revealed that his meteoric rise through the ranks from first lieutenant to major general had not prepared him for the level of command responsibilities he now faced.[20]

Pursuing the routed enemy the following morning, the Thirteenth Corps again formed a line of battle and overwhelmed Pemberton's rear guard at the Big Black River. In this brief affair fought by his corps alone from the Union army, McClernand's troops captured almost 1,800 prisoners, 18 cannon, 6 limbers, 4 caissons, 1,400 stands of arms, and 4 battleflags while suffering a combined loss in killed, wounded, and missing of less than 300 men. Bridging the stream on May 18, he then pushed his troops to the outskirts of Vicksburg.[21]

The campaign thus far had been a stunning success for the Union army, thanks largely to the hard-marching, hard-fighting soldiers of the Thirteenth Corps and their commander. Anxious for a quick victory, Grant ordered an attack against the city's defenses on May 19. His three corps, however, were unable to concentrate in time, and only Sherman's troops were in proper position to make the attack. Although his men fought with commendable valor and succeeded in planting several stands of colors on the exterior slope of Stockade Redan, Sherman's troops were repulsed. In this assault, his corps lost more than 700 men. McPherson reported 130 casualties; McClernand, whose troops were only lightly engaged, suffered the loss of 100 men.[22]

Realizing that he had been too hasty, Grant decided to make a more thorough reconnaissance and gathered his forces in hand for a second strike. Three days later, on May 22, he moved his army over a broad three-mile front against the Vicksburg fortifications. Sherman and McPherson were stopped cold by the deadly fire, which poured from Confederate rifle-muskets. But McClernand's troops withstood the galling fire and, advancing with sheer determination, reached the ditches that fronted the Confederate fortifications. Although his troops penetrated Railroad Redoubt and threatened to enter at Second Texas Lunette, he had few reserves with which to exploit the situations. (McClernand was a puncher who always threw in everything he had. His failure to hold a ready reserve was perhaps his most significant tactical weakness.) He knew they could not consolidate their gains without reinforcements or a diversion in their favor. He quickly wrote a note to Grant: "We are hotly engaged with the enemy. We have part possession of two forts, and the Stars and Stripes are floating over them. A vigorous push ought to be made all along the line."[23]

Grant was skeptical about accepting the note at face value. Although he doubted the veracity of it, based on the information provided him by his subordinate on the scene of action, Grant had no option but to order the attacks renewed all along the front. Beneath a blistering sun, Federal soldiers surged forward with a mighty cheer only to be checked and driven back with heavy loss. McClernand was also forced to relinquish the ground gained, and the bodies of his dead and wounded littered the field in abundance. Death had reaped a bountiful harvest. In the assault on May 22, the Thirteenth Corps suffered the heaviest casualties in Grant's army. The returns on this bloody day tallied McClernand's loss at 1,275 men killed, wounded, or missing. Yet he could boast that his was the only corps to gain a lodgment in the enemy works.[24]

Failing to carry Vicksburg by storm, the Union army settled into the routine of siege life. As the army completed its dispositions around the beleaguered city and perfected its alignment, Lt. Col. James Harrison Wilson delivered an order from Grant to the commander of the Thirteenth Corps, who viewed it as yet another incident of meddling in his command prerogatives. Wilson, another West Pointer, class of 1860, was astonished when McClernand exclaimed, "I'll be God damned if I'll do it—I am tired of being dictated to—I won't stand it any longer, and you can go back and tell General Grant." The corps commander then issued a stream of oaths against Grant and West Pointers in particular to which Wilson took umbrage. The young officer remarked angrily, "In addition to your highly insubordinate language, it seems to me that you are cursing me as much as you are cursing General Grant." He then added, "If this is so, although you are a major general, while I am only a lieutenant colonel, I will pull you off that horse and beat the boots off of you." McClernand attempted to placate Wilson, saying, "I am not cursing you. I could not do that. Your father was my friend, and I am yours. I was simply expressing my intense vehemence on the subject matter, sir, and I beg your pardon." From that time on, whenever anyone around army headquarters raised his voice, it was referred to as "simply expressing intense vehemence on the subject matter." The incident was indicative of the rising storm clouds that were gathering over the Thirteenth Corps commander.[25]

On May 30, 1863, McClernand issued General Orders no. 72, in which he congratulated his troops on their achievements and, in typical fashion, claimed credit for the victories thus far achieved in the campaign.

General Orders, no. 72
HDQRS. Thirteenth Army Corps Battlefield,
in rear of Vicksburg, May 30, 1863

COMRADES: As your commander, I am proud to congratulate you upon your constancy, valor, and successes. History affords no more brilliant example of soldierly qualities. Your victories have followed in such rapid succession that their echoes have not yet reached the country. They will challenge its grateful and enthusiastic applause. Yourselves striking out a new path, your comrades of the Army of the Tennessee followed, and a way was thus opened for them to redeem previous disappointments. Your march through Louisiana, from Milliken's Bend to New Carthage and Perkins' plantation, on the Mississippi, is one of the most remarkable on record. Bayous and miry roads, threatened with momentary inundation, obstructed your progress. All these were overcome by unceasing labor and unflagging energy. The two thousand feet of bridging which was hastily improvised out of materials created on the spot, and over which you passed, must long be remembered as a marvel. Descending the Mississippi still lower, you were the first to cross the river at Bruin's Landing [Bruinsburg] and to plant our colors in the State of Mississippi below Warrenton. Resuming the advance the same day, you pushed on until you came up to the enemy near Port Gibson. Only restrained by the darkness of night, you hastened to attack him on the morning of May 1, and by vigorously pressing him at all points drove him from his position, taking a large number of prisoners and small-arms and five cannon. General [John A.] Logan's division came up in time to gallantly share in consummating the most valuable victory won since the capture of Fort Donelson.

Taking the lead on the morning of the 2d, you were the first to enter Port Gibson and to hasten the retreat of the enemy from the vicinity of that place. During the ensuing night, as a consequence of the victory at Port Gibson, the enemy spiked his guns at Grand Gulf and evacuated that place, retiring upon Vicksburg and Edwards Station. The fall of Grand Gulf was solely the result of the victory achieved by the land forces at Port Gibson. The armament and public stores captured there are but the just trophies of that victory. Hastening to bridge the South Branch of Bayou Pierre, at Port Gibson, you crossed on the morning of the 3d, and pushed on to Willow Springs, Big Sandy, and the main crossing of Fourteen-Mile Creek, four miles from Edwards Station. A detachment of the enemy was immediately driven away from the crossing, and you advanced, passed over, and rested during the night of the 12th within three miles of the enemy, in large force at the station.

On the morning of the 13th, the objective point of the army's movements having been changed from Edwards Station to Jackson, in pursuance of an order from the commander of the department, you moved on the north side of Fourteen-Mile Creek toward Raymond. This delicate and hazardous movement was executed by a portion of your number under cover of [Brig. Gen. Alvin P.] Hovey's division, which made a feint of attack in line of battle upon Edwards Station. Too late to harm you, the enemy attacked the rear of that division, but was promptly and decisively repulsed.

Resting near Raymond that night, on the morning of the 14th you entered that place, one division moving on to Mississippi Springs, near Jackson, in support of General Sherman; another to Clinton, in support of General McPherson; a third remaining at Raymond, and a fourth at Old Auburn, to bring up the army trains.

On the 15th, you again led the advance toward Edwards Station, which once more became the objective point. Expelling the enemy's pickets from Bolton the same day, you secured and held that important position.

On the 16th, you led the advance, in three columns upon three roads, against Edwards Station. Meeting the enemy on the way in strong force, you heavily engaged him near Champion's Hill, and after a sanguinary and obstinate battle, with the assistance of General McPherson's corps, beat and routed him, taking many prisoners and small-arms and several pieces of cannon. Continuing to lead the advance, you rapidly pursued the enemy to Edwards Station, capturing that place, a large quantity of public stores, and many prisoners. Night only stopped you.

At day-dawn on the 17th, you resumed the advance, and early coming upon the enemy strongly intrenched in elaborate works, both before and behind Big Black River, immediately opened with artillery upon him, followed by a daring and heroic charge at the point of the bayonet, which put him to rout, leaving eighteen pieces of cannon and more than 1,000 prisoners in your hands.

By an early hour on the 18th, you had constructed a bridge across the Big Black, and had commenced the advance upon Vicksburg.

On the 19th, 20th, and 21st you continued to reconnoiter and skirmish until you had gained a near approach to the enemy's work.

On the 22d, in pursuance of the order from the commander of the department, you assaulted the enemy's defenses in front at 10 A.M., and within thirty minutes had made a lodgment and planted your colors upon two of his bastions. This partial success called into exercise the highest heroism, and was only gained by a bloody and protracted struggle; yet it was gained, and was the first and largest success achieved anywhere along the whole line of our army. For nearly eight hours, under a scorching sun and destructive fire, you firmly held your footing, and only withdrew when the enemy had largely massed their forces and concentrated their attack upon you. How and why the general assault failed, it would be useless now to explain. The Thirteenth Army Corps, acknowledging the good intentions of all, would scorn indulgence in weak regrets and idle criminations. According justice to all, it would only defend itself. If, while the enemy was massing to crush it, assistance was asked for by a diversion at other points, or by re-enforcement, it only asked what in one case Major-General Grant had specifically and peremptorily ordered, namely simultaneous and persistent attack all along our lines until the

enemy's outer works should be carried, and what, in the other, by massing a strong force in time upon a weakened point, would have probably
insured success.

Comrades, you have done much, yet something more remains to be
done. The enemy's odious defenses still block your access to Vicksburg.
Treason still rules that rebellious city, and closes the Mississippi River
against rightful use by the millions who inhabit its sources and the great
Northwest. Shall not our flag float over Vicksburg? Shall not the great
Father of Waters be opened to lawful commerce? Methinks the emphatic
response of one and all of you is, "It shall be so." Then let us rise to the
level of a crowning trial. Let our common sufferings and glories, while
uniting as a band of brothers, rouse us to new and surpassing efforts. Let
us resolve upon success, God helping us.

I join with you, comrades, in your sympathy for the wounded and sorrow for the dead. May we not trust, nay, is it not so, that history will
associate the martyrs of this sacred struggle for law and order, liberty
and justice, with the honored martyrs of Monmouth and Bunker Hill?

John A. McClernand
Major-General Commanding

Within days, the order appeared in the pages of the *Memphis Evening
Bulletin,* the *Missouri Democrat,* and other influential newspapers in
the Midwest, copies of which circulated throughout the Union camps
around Vicksburg.[26]

On the evening of June 16, following an inspection tour of the
works at Snyder's Bluff, north of Vicksburg, Sherman was handed one
such paper by Maj. Gen. Frank Blair with the advice, "I should notice
it, lest the statements of fact and inference contained therein might receive credence from an excited public." Sherman was incensed at what
he read, and the following day wrote at length to Grant, "It certainly
gives me no pleasure or satisfaction to notice such a catalogue of non-
sense—such an effusion of vain-glory and hypocrisy; nor can I believe
General McClernand ever published such an order officially to his
corps. I know too well that the brave and intelligent soldiers and officers who compose that corps will not be humbugged by such stuff."
The note reveals the level of contempt Sherman harbored against Mc-
Clernand. Seeing the order for what it was, he lashed out, "If the order
be a genuine production and not a forgery, it is manifestly addressed
not to an army, but to the constituency in Illinois, so far distant from
the scene of the events attempted to be described, who might inno-

cently be induced to think General McClernand the sagacious leader and bold hero he so complacently paints himself." In a rare display of vindictiveness, he continued:

> I beg to call [your] attention to the requirements of General Orders, No. 151, of 1862, which actually forbids the publication of all official letters and reports, and requires the name of the writer to be laid before the President of the United States for dismissal. The document under question is not technically a letter or report, and though styled an order, is not an order. It orders nothing, but is in the nature of an address to soldiers, manifestly designed for publication for ulterior political purposes. It perverts the truth to the ends of flattery and self-glorification, and contains many untruths, among which is one of monstrous falsehood. It accuses General McPherson and myself with disobeying orders of General Grant in not assaulting on May 19 and 22, and allowing on the latter day the enemy to mass his forces against the Thirteenth Army Corps alone.

To justify this he explained, "I would never have revealed so unwelcome a truth had General McClernand, in his process of self-flattery, confined himself to facts in the reach of his own observation, and not gone out of the way to charge others for results which he seems not to comprehend." He then patronized Grant: "With these remarks I leave the matter where it properly belongs, in the hands of the commanding general, who knows his plans and orders, sees with an eye single to success and his country's honor, and not from the narrow and contracted circle of a subordinate commander, who exaggerates the importance of the events that fall under his immediate notice, and is filled with an itching desire for 'fame not earned.'"[27]

On June 18, McPherson also read a copy of the congratulatory address in a newspaper and fired a note of complaint to Grant: "The whole tenor of the order is so ungenerous, and the insinuations and criminations against the other corps of your army are so manifestly at variance with the facts, that a sense of duty to my command, as well as the verbal protest of every one of my division and brigade commanders against allowing such an order to go forth to the public unanswered, require that I should call your attention to it." The junior corps commander continued:

> After a careful perusal of the order, I cannot help arriving at the conclusion that it was written more to influence public sentiment at the North and impress the public mind with the magnificent strategy, superior tac-

tics, and brilliant deeds of the major-general commanding the Thirteenth Army Corps than to congratulate his troops upon their well-merited successes. There is a vain-gloriousness about the order, an ingenious attempt to write himself down the hero, the master-mind, giving life and direction to military operations in this quarter, inconsistent with the high-toned principles of the soldier.[28]

Grant, however, had already taken measures to deal with McClernand and quiet the uproar among his subordinates. On June 17 he demanded of McClernand: "Inclosed I send you what purports to be your congratulatory address to the Thirteenth Army Corps. I would respectfully ask if it is a true copy. If it is not a correct copy, furnish me one by bearer, as required both by regulations and existing orders of the Department." That evening McClernand responded, "The newspaper slip is a correct copy of my congratulatory order, No. 72. I am prepared to maintain its statements."[29]

After receiving McClernand's admission, Grant issued General Orders no. 164, by which the unrepentant subordinate was relieved of command and replaced by Maj. Gen. Edward O. C. Ord. The order was delivered with great delight by Lt. Col. James H. Wilson. McClernand scanned the note and said, "Well, sir! I am relieved," to which Wilson remarked gleefully, "By God, sir, we are both relieved!"[30]

Outraged by Grant's action, McClernand immediately protested his removal in characteristic tenor. In writing to Grant, the dismissed officer was quick to point out, "Having been appointed by the President to the command of that [Thirteenth] corps, under a definite act of Congress, I might justly challenge your authority in the premises, but forbear to do so at present." Confident that his actions would be vindicated by a court of inquiry, he stated, "I am quite willing that any statement of fact in my congratulatory [order] to the Thirteenth Army Corps, to which you think just exception may be taken, should be made the subject of investigation, not doubting the result."[31]

His protest notwithstanding, McClernand returned quietly to Illinois, where he waged a battle to regain his command. On June 27 he wrote to General in Chief Halleck a long letter in which he identified a major component of the enmity against him and perhaps the reasons he was removed—jealousy and resentment. "The real motive for so unwarranted an act," he wrote, "was hostility—personal hostility—growing out of the early connection of my name with the Mississippi

River expedition and your assignment of me to the command of it."
Embellishing this claim, he continued, "This feeling subsequently became intensified by the contrast made by my personal success at Arkansas Post with General Grant's retreat from Oxford and his repulse
at Chickasaw Bayou, and still, more intensified by the leadership and
success of my corps during the advance from Milliken's Bend to Port
Gibson, to Champion's Hill, and to Big Black." Seeking to shift the
focus of attention, he requested an investigation into Grant's conduct
as an officer and demanded "that I be restored to my command, at least
until the fall of Vicksburg."[32]

While the noose around Vicksburg tightened, Illinois's governor
Richard Yates came to the support of his political ally and friend. On
June 30 the governor wrote Lincoln, "Major General McClernand arrived here on the 26th instant. He has been received by the people here
with the greatest demonstrations of respect, all regretting that he is not
now in the field. I desire to suggest that if General McClernand, with
some Western troops, was put in command in Pennsylvania, it would
inspire great hope and confidence in the Northwest, and perhaps
throughout the country." Fortunately, the president did not act on this
suggestion, and he remained quiet on the subject of McClernand until
he received Grant's report of the campaign.[33]

On July 19 Grant forwarded a copy of McClernand's report to
Washington with the following endorsement: "This report contains so
many inaccuracies that to correct it, to make it a fair report to be
handed down as historical, would require the rewriting of most of it. It
is pretentious and egotistical, as is sufficiently shown by my own and
all other reports" (which in the case of many of his subordinates were
also "pretentious and egotistical").[34]

In light of Grant's victory at Vicksburg, Lincoln wanted to put the
matter to rest. On August 29 McClernand was notified by Halleck that
the president had declined to order a court of inquiry. The general in
chief informed McClernand that "the President, . . . directs me to say
that a court of inquiry . . . would necessarily withdraw from the field
many officers whose presence with their commands is absolutely indis-
pensable to the service, and whose absence might cause irreparable injury to the success of operations now in active progress."[35]

And so the court was never convened. Although McClernand sent
a lengthy defense to Halleck on September 28, it was ignored by officials in the War Department, and the matter was closed.

In evaluating the case of John McClernand, one must ask: Did Grant have the authority to relieve McClernand? McClernand would certainly argue the point, as have many historians and military professionals since. In reference to Lincoln's appointment of him to command the Vicksburg expedition, historian Edwin C. Bearss asserts, "The President's decision thus constituted an independent command in Grant's department." Those who support McClernand argue that as the president appointed him, only the president could relieve him of his command responsibilities. But as Grant's actions were sustained by the administration, it is a moot point. Was such a petty offense as the issuance of General Orders no. 72 sufficient grounds to relieve McClernand of command of the Thirteenth Corps? If not, were the statements made in General Orders no. 72 untrue or misleading? Regardless, such statements were certainly in keeping with McClernand's previous actions to which Sherman, McPherson, Grant, and the entire army should have been accustomed.[36]

We have yet to get to the underlying reason of why McClernand was relieved of command, for which the issuance of General Orders no. 72 was simply the pretext. Why then did Grant relieve him? Was it due to lack of confidence? Although Grant frequently expressed a lack of confidence in McClernand and later wrote that he "doubted" his fitness to command, his actions do not support those claims. Among the factors to consider is that McClernand commanded the largest corps in the army. It led the march down the west side of the river in the opening stage of the Vicksburg campaign. His troops were the first to cross the river and land on Mississippi soil, potentially requiring them to fight an engagement independent of the other corps still in Louisiana. Moreover, his corps was positioned on the left flank at the point of danger as the army pushed deep into Mississippi. It maintained the longest section of the siege lines. And, Grant was on the verge of strengthening McClernand's command responsibilities by increasing the number of men under him and lengthening the sector of siege lines for which he was responsible, prior to removing him. A general does not entrust such vital assignments and levels of command responsibilities to someone in whom he has no confidence.

Was it due to the professional jealousy that West Pointers harbored for volunteer officers? Perhaps, in part. It certainly appears that Sherman and McPherson, at least, were somewhat envious of McClernand's success during the Vicksburg campaign. Grant himself clearly preferred that his subordinates be West Pointers rather than volunteer officers.

In spite of his many shortcomings as an officer, declaring him to be "unmanageable and incompetent," Grant could and did tolerate McClernand's irascible nature and often insubordinate actions. He even tolerated McClernand's repeated efforts to secure political advantages in his "highly colored" after action reports. But when that tendency to embellish his success appeared in communications on the field of battle and resulted in the useless effusion of blood, McClernand's integrity as a combat officer was compromised and Grant's trust and confidence in him shattered.[37]

Recall the note on May 22 in which McClernand stated he was in "part possession of two forts and the Stars and Stripes are floating over them" and asked that the assaults be renewed as a diversion in his favor. When Grant discovered the true extent of the Federal penetration at Railroad Redoubt and grasped the number of lives lost as a result of the afternoon assaults, he determined that someone would pay for those losses and that someone would be John McClernand. Grant had no recourse but to relieve McClernand of command, his integrity compromised and no longer trustworthy. Unfortunately, rather than make public the true reason, Grant used the issuance of General Orders no. 72 as the pretext for his removal, and the issue boiled in controversy for months.[38]

Although McClernand returned to command of the Thirteenth Corps briefly in 1864, his military career was over. Following service in the field, he returned to the arena of politics but never again exercised the powerful influence he once held in Congress. However, he did serve as chairman of the 1876 Democratic National Convention that nominated Samuel J. Tilden for president. McClernand led a long and active life and finally succumbed to the effects of dysentery on September 20, 1900. He was survived by his wife and by four children from his first marriage.

An objective evaluation of McClernand's military performance reveals that he demonstrated many fine qualities of leadership. He had unshakable confidence in himself and always acted from his strengths, he knew his men and their abilities, and he did not care about what the enemy did; rather, he focused on what he could do to the enemy. Most important, he was not afraid to fight, a fact that earned him the respect of his soldiers. "A personality that responded to the challenges and difficulties in the political arena was apt to accept those of the battlefield and respond similarly," writes his biographer Richard Kiper. "Ambition, oratory, determination, confidence, and courage were the heart and soul of John McClernand's composition. Properly harnessed, those qualities could make a great politician or a great general. Unharnessed by self-control, they could lead to insubordination, inflexibility, and want of introspection."[39]

Unfortunately for both the Illinois general and the nation he served, the qualities of leadership that he lacked, he never developed—chief among which was selflessness. Ezra Warner sums it up best: "McClernand's chief failing as a troop commander, aside from inexperience, was his fatal proclivity to display the fruits of victory, no matter how garnered, upon his own standards." And that failing ushered him into obscurity, where he remains to this day.[40]

The tarnished image of the fighting politician is worthy of polishing to a luster more deserving of his service. Perhaps historians will someday reevaluate John Alexander McClernand and the significant role that he played in the Civil War. Only through objective evaluation will the shroud that continues to veil him be lifted, enabling the portraiture of this historical figure to be completed.

A Matter of Trust

Grant and James B. McPherson

℮~ Tamara A. Smith

Maj. Gen. Ulysses S. Grant must have known that he was being evaluated in January 1862 when his senior commander, Maj. Gen. Henry W. Halleck, sent an old friend, his young assistant chief engineer, to act as Grant's chief engineer in the attack on Forts Henry and Donelson. What he did not know, at least directly, was that this officer, one Lt. Col. James B. McPherson, was also specifically charged to observe and report on the rumors of Grant's drinking.[1] As Maj. Gen. William T. Sherman later remarked, "Whenever I had occasion to learn any thing that I wished to know, I invariably went to McPherson, who, while he attended to his own business, was very observing of every thing that interested the whole army."[2]

Although no written record of their meeting or of his report to Halleck, at least on the drinking matters, exists, McPherson apparently later told him that Grant was indeed sober and that the rumors were unfounded.[3] Grant, in turn, found McPherson to be remarkably unstodgy for a brainy West Pointer who had graduated first in his class. A tall, gentle, gregarious man with a sparkling personality, McPherson was also most accommodating; he easily stepped aside, allowing Grant's chief of staff, Joseph D. Webster, to continue as unofficial chief engineer at Henry and Donelson, despite his official orders to the position. Uncertain about McPherson's reliability, Grant sent both men into the field to collect information on the roads around the two forts. Apparently acting under verbal orders from Grant, McPherson did reconnaissance, built bridges, and destroyed the railroad bridges over the Tennessee River between the battles; and during the Donelson fight, he reinforced Grant's artillery on his own initiative.

Throughout the campaign, McPherson acted more as a staff officer than as an engineer and demonstrated his desire to fit in with Grant's staff. Impressed both by his actions as well as by his deference to volunteer staff, unexpected from a regular army engineer, Grant cautiously requested that Halleck assign McPherson to him in "any future movement" both "as a personal favor" and for the good of the service.[4] McPherson, impressed by witnessing Grant's first capture of an entire army, never wanted to go anywhere else. After Donelson, McPherson could always be found in the thick of any action, particularly that surrounding Grant.

Their friendship was really joined under fire at Shiloh, literally and figuratively. Both Webster and McPherson had agreed that the Union army's position at Pittsburg Landing was indefensible due to the terrain; thus no entrenchments were dug, as they had planned on attacking the Confederates instead at Corinth. When the Confederates attacked first at Shiloh Church, McPherson worked again under verbal orders from Grant, placing divisions on the field and looking for Lew Wallace's lost reinforcements. Racing under fire with Grant on the second day, McPherson had his horse shot out from under him by snipers. He and Grant remained close enough on the field for the former to witness the latter's remarkable reversal of his army's fortunes, which he promptly reported to Halleck in person. Later criticism for Grant's failure to entrench at Shiloh followed them both. Grant's refusal to retreat after the terrible losses of the first day impressed McPherson, who grew closer to both him and Sherman amid the carnage. After Shiloh, McPherson adopted Grant as his mentor, seeking Sherman's friendship but Grant's approval.[5]

Two years later, when he died in the battle of Atlanta, McPherson was commanding Grant's Army of the Tennessee. News of McPherson's death reached Sherman just moments after his body was recovered. Sherman cried as McPherson's body lay in headquarters, then wrote dolefully to his wife, "I lost my Right *bower* in McPherson."[6] To a staff member, he declared, "The army and the country have sustained a great loss by the death of McPherson. I had expected him to finish the war. Grant and I are likely to be killed or set aside after failure to meet popular expectation, and McPherson would have come into chief command at the right time to end the war. He had no enemies."[7]

Grant uncharacteristically wept also when he heard of McPherson's death, over one year after they had last seen action together. "The Country has lost one of its best soldiers and I have lost my best friend," he said.[8] "The nation had more to expect from him than from almost any one living," he declared, rare praise from Grant.[9] He openly mourned the loss, believing that the "brave, accomplished, and noble-hearted McPherson" remained one of the Union army's "ablest, purest and best generals . . . the most promising officer of his age in the army."[10] To McPherson's family Grant expressed the depths of his personal sorrow. "Your bereavement is great," he wrote, "but cannot exceed mine."[11] No wonder McPherson's army's survivors lobbied to place his striking equestrian statue at a crucial juncture of roads in Washington, DC, allowing President Grant to observe McPherson seemingly riding directly toward him into the White House.

Many Civil War scholars have long held the belief that the striking and natural friendship among Grant, Sherman, and McPherson was so strong, and McPherson so knowing, that if only the scattered fragments of his remaining letters could be collected it would reveal much of their characters and their relationship. Unfortunately, this has proved not to be the case. McPherson's cautious nature and Victorian rectitude did not permit him to commit much to paper, and many of his letters were dispersed by his family to his admirers and friends. Any intimate revelations to his fiancée were most likely destroyed by her loyal Confederate family. As a result, one must largely turn to the remaining evidence of McPherson's life, to Grant's own letters and memoirs, and to their own staffs' and friends' reminiscences to reconstruct the relationship that Grant himself deemed of the highest significance.

James B. McPherson was born at an Ohio crossroads later named Clyde. His farmer father dabbled in trade and blacksmithing and worked as a postmaster, but he lost everything in speculation in the panic of 1837, which physically and mentally destroyed him. At the age of twelve, McPherson left home to support his family. For seven years, he worked as a clerk in a general store in a nearby town, earning the affection of his employer, who kept him from enlisting during the Mexican War by promising him a modest education to meet the entrance standards for West Point.[12]

McPherson blossomed at West Point. He studied endlessly yet made friends easily, with Southerners as well as Northerners. With a magnetic personality and a constant willingness to lend a hand, he befriended his successive roommates, John Bell Hood and John M. Schofield, as well as classmates Oliver O. Howard, Philip H. Sheridan, Joshua W. Sill, and J. E. B. Stuart and underclassmen like G. W. Custis Lee, whose father, Robert E. Lee, was superintendent. Ranking second in his class his plebe year, he ranked first the following three years, earning every possible promotion in the Corps of Cadets and a total of only fifty-seven demerits in four years. He obtained his first choice of duty in the elite Corps of Engineers easily. Dennis Hart Mahan, the Academy's famous professor of engineering and military theory, claimed that McPherson was "among the ablest men sent forth from the institution; . . . his brilliant after-career in the field surprised no one who had known him intimately."[13]

Like Halleck, McPherson did not leave West Point after graduating but was kept on the faculty as an assistant instructor of practical engineering for a year, before being assigned to engineering duty at headquarters in New York City. For two years he boarded at a rooming house, where he made friends of fellow boarders John G. Barnard and William T. Sherman, and, through army connections, as a friend of a friend, assisted in the successful courtship of Halleck and his eventual wife, a small favor Halleck never forgot. McPherson was the kind of friend many fellow officers trusted with investments and secrets and who stood by them at their weddings and as godfather to their children. Promoted early in his career to temporary superintending engineer at Fort Delaware, he so impressed Chief Engineer Joseph G. Totten that he was named superintending engineer to complete the construction of the defenses at Alcatraz Island in San Francisco Bay in 1857 while still a second lieutenant, passing over senior officers with more than a decade at higher rank.[14]

In his first two years in San Francisco, McPherson lived primarily on Alcatraz and completed building most of the defenses. In 1860 he moved to his shore-based office on the city side of the bay and became active enough in San Francisco society to be listed in the city's social manual. It was there that he finally met Halleck, reacquainted himself with the now-banker Sherman, and became engaged to Miss Emily Hoffman, from a socially prominent and strongly pro-Confederate Baltimore shipping family. The advent of war sealed her family's opposition to their marriage. After months of petitioning for a transfer east, McPherson was finally ordered to recruiting duty in Boston in August 1861.[15]

After two months in Boston, McPherson began actively seeking an engineering command in the field by applying to his old friend, John G. Barnard, chief engineer of the Army of the Potomac. Commanding Gen. George B. McClellan approved his transfer, though the Corps of Engineers did not, but friends did pass McPherson's plea for "*active duty somewhere*" to the attention of Halleck, then forming the Department of the Missouri at St. Louis. Halleck quickly appointed him assistant engineer, brought him west as a lieutenant colonel, and sent him to Grant.

McPherson's reward for loyal service under Grant at Henry and Donelson and at Shiloh was a brigadier generalcy of volunteer troops. In the homey atmosphere of Grant's headquarters in the lull after Shiloh, Julia Dent Grant sewed McPherson's first general's stars on his uniform. Halleck also appointed him as military superintendent of railroads in the District of West Tennessee in June 1862.[16]

In less than one month, McPherson had reorganized the captured railroads, reopened 367 miles of track, and had linked all the major portions of Halleck's command. Within two months he had fully staffed the railroad with efficient personnel, including counterespionage agents, and had very little to do. As soon as Halleck was appointed general in chief of the Union army and Grant gained command in the West, McPherson asked Grant to find him a more active command. When Confederates attacked William S. Rosecrans at Corinth, Grant gave McPherson an improvised division and, once again, verbal orders, and hurried him down in support.[17]

Organizing en route, McPherson's force moved swiftly to Corinth and arrived just after the battled ended, followed fifty-two miles in pursuit, then returned to shore up Corinth. Pleased at his attempt, Grant requested McPherson be regularly assigned to command of troops. "I would feel more strengthened to-day," Grant wrote, "if I could place McPherson in command of a Division than I would to receive a whole brigade of new levies."[18] Rosecrans concurred, claiming McPherson "adds twenty per cent to any troops he commands."[19] A few days later Grant gave McPherson a division and requested that Halleck appoint him as major general of volunteers. Within twenty-four hours, both Halleck and Secretary of War Edwin M. Stanton had approved the appointment. "General McPherson," Halleck loftily declared, "has distinguished himself in nearly every battle fought in the west."[20] Whether the swiftness of McPherson's promotion was due mainly to his minor battlefield actions or to his growing friendships with Grant and Halleck is unclear. When told of his major generalcy, McPherson honestly replied, "I don't know what for."[21]

McPherson's promotion reflected faith in his potential as well as any of his actual battlefield achievements. Both Grant and Halleck recognized that his adaptability made him an able subordinate officer. Visitors to the army noted how he seemed "the antithesis of Sherman in temperament" while resembling Grant in manner, and noted his reliance on Grant's "judgment and executive ability."[22] As for McPherson, what he really wanted, from his first taste of battle at Donelson, was to get back into the fight.

On reaching his new command in late 1862, he found that he had been assigned a division of unruly midwesterners whose habit was to pillage everywhere they stopped. While McPherson worked to reorder and discipline his force, Grant ordered him to command a wing of his army advancing down the Mississippi Central Railroad toward Vicksburg. During his first independent field command on a reconnaissance in force toward Holly Springs, Mississippi, McPherson intelligently deployed his forces and so confused the Confederates at Lamar that they believed they were surrounded by Grant's entire force and fled.[23] Grant then named McPherson his second in command and gave him the lead in the advance on Oxford, Mississippi. When the supply depot at Holly Springs was destroyed by Confederate cavalry, Grant trusted McPherson to cover the rear of the army in their retreat. Despite reduced rations and a hard march, few grumbled in his wing. Observers noted that he was "always with his men, toiling with them." While doing so, he noted that his men's destructiveness and fighting spirit were among their strongest talents, requiring strict control.[24]

Politics intervened to further solidify the relationship among Grant, Sherman, and McPherson. John A. McClernand, an Illinois politician and a friend of Abraham Lincoln, who had shown some military promise at Donelson, had convinced the president to give him a major generalcy and an independent command to take Vicksburg by water. McClernand quickly alienated both the army and the navy with his arrogance, and soon Sherman and McPherson urged Grant, who outranked McClernand, to take over on the river. Grant reorganized his command, the Army of the Tennessee, into three invasion corps, headed equally by McClernand, Sherman, and McPherson. With the Mississippi River soon at flood stage for the long winter, Grant sought water routes among the river's many tributaries to bypass the strong Vicksburg batteries. McPherson's assignment, to dig a canal from Lake Providence through the flooded swampland to the Mississippi River, was an engineering nightmare, but it kept the corps busy over the long, fruitless winter. Of all Grant's canal attempts, only McPherson's succeeded, but Grant lacked sufficient shallow-draft boats to use it. When spring came and the swamps dried up, Grant decided to march his army on the Louisiana side of the river and to cross below Vicksburg, invading from the south.[25]

On April 16, 1863, Rear Adm. David Dixon Porter, under cover of darkness, ran part of his fleet past the Vicksburg batteries. While Sherman feinted north to Haynes's Bluff, the navy bombarded Grand Gulf, covering McPherson's and McClernand's crossing of the river at Bruinsburg. Grant's cleverly planned cavalry raid, led by Benjamin Grierson, drew Maj. Gen. Joseph E. Johnston's support troops away from assisting the garrison at Vicksburg. After crossing the river, Grant directed McPherson's and McClernand's corps in repulsing a sturdy defense of Port Gibson by Confederate brigadier John S. Bowen. McPherson personally directed the fight on the far left, which drove Bowen off the field, and took the lead in the following days, pressing the Confederates hard while quickly rebuilding bridges along the way.

On May 3 McPherson encountered a Confederate force and personally led five regiments in an attack, which captured a portion of the main road to the capital in Jackson, Mississippi. Pressing on, he outflanked the Confederates, capturing the crucial bridge at Hankinson's Ferry before it could be burnt. Acting on information that McPherson uncovered through reconnaissance and his own spy network, Grant sent him on to Rocky Springs and Utica, then to Raymond for supplies. The destruction of Grant's supplies at Holly Springs five months earlier was still devastating to the army, and Grant ordered McPherson to capture what they needed at Raymond, little expecting opposition.[26]

McPherson gave his own protégé, John A. Logan, the lead, unwittingly exacerbating a running feud between his officers and offending his other division commander, Marcellus M. Crocker. On approaching Raymond and meeting unexpected resistance in his front, McPherson ordered Logan forward but he hesitated, forcing McPherson to order him in again. Crocker, in a huff, decided not to support Logan as ordered, and the cavalry, for similar reasons, acted no better. Correctly convinced that he faced a smaller foe, McPherson quickly sent in a skirmish line, which was repulsed by the tenacious Brig. Gen. John Gregg.

Gregg held all the advantages, including terrain, position, and the determination to avenge his surrender at Donelson. For two hours the two generals directed a determined contest to outflank the other, their vision strained by unusually thick dust and smoke on the humid field. McPherson slowly advanced under withering fire across a deep creek and eventually ended the contest with a charge on the left when Crocker finally deigned to appear, sweeping Gregg from the field in great disorder. Refusing to stop to tend the wounded, McPherson pressed Gregg on through Raymond, slowed by the difficult terrain. On gaining Raymond, McPherson stopped his exhausted men, sending the cavalry in pursuit. That evening when Grant ordered McPherson to advance on Clinton, he immediately began the march, his men finishing their dinners on the road.

Skirmishing quickly to Clinton, McPherson's men captured several dispatches from Confederate general John C. Pemberton inside Vicksburg to Gen. Joseph E. Johnston, coordinating opposition to Grant's movement outside. McPherson met the Confederates outside Jackson and fought during a torrential thunderstorm, pushing the Confederates through the capital. His spies captured further dispatches between Johnston and Pemberton indicating immediate action, and Grant hurried McPherson back the way he had come to oppose Pemberton. When McClernand reached the field and ordered McPherson to assist him in fighting Pemberton much further south than McPherson's more reliable intelligence reports indicated, McPherson hurriedly sent for Grant, who commanded the battle fought at Champion's Hill. Returned to his preferred subordinate role, McPherson flanked Pemberton, forcing his retreat into fortified Vicksburg.[27]

McPherson's troops held the center of the siege works at Vicksburg, with Sherman in the north and McClernand in the south. Two attempts to storm the entrenchment failed, and when McClernand claimed victory too early in the last attempt, urging Sherman and McPherson to fight harder, all three corps were bloodily repulsed. Almost everyone had had enough of McClernand, whose politicking had delayed the campaign and who had brought his new bride and all her luggage to the seat of the war with him. When McClernand officially congratulated his troops for their splendid victories in the campaign, hinting that they had won thus far on their own, Sherman and McPherson protested, and Grant replaced McClernand with a far more amenable commander.

As the siege progressed, McPherson experimented with mined explosives in an attempt to blow a hole in the Vicksburg lines. Two times he successfully shattered portions of the lines, slowly whittling away the bastion in his front. The surrender of the Vicksburg garrison canceled the third attempt. Grant gave McPherson's Seventeenth Army Corps the honor of occupying the city as the unit most responsible for the victory. After McPherson helped negotiate the terms of surrender, urging Grant to parole the captured soldiers and send them home rather than further crowd Northern prison camps, Grant gave McPherson command of the city and the "District of Vicksburg."[28]

While the nation applauded Grant's army for its success, its commanders hoped for more lucrative attention. "In the events resulting thus," Sherman complained, "the guiding minds and hands were Grants, Shermans & McPherson's all native of Ohio, and we have yet to see the first honest impulses of thanks or appreciation of our native state."[29] Grant, due to receive a promotion for the victory, recommended McPherson and Sherman equally for brigadier generalcies in the regular army, which meant job security in the postwar world. He cited them equally for their "great fitness for any command." In recommending them for promotion, he clearly stated that he trusted these men above all others and wanted them by him in future campaigns. No more would political appointments interfere with his command. Determined to keep effective leadership in the West, he urged their promotions with full faith in their abilities to succeed him.[30]

"Gen. McPherson," Grant stated, "has been with me in every battle since the commencement of the rebellion except Belmont." Concerning Vicksburg, he stressed McPherson's immediate direction of events, conspicuousness, and abilities in command. Grant portrayed him as a man of action, always riding at the forefront of his corps, skillfully managing troops on the field, always pressing forward. "He is one of our ablest Engineers," Grant wrote, "and most skillful Generals."[31] Sherman agreed with Grant's assessment of McPherson, reportedly declaring that "he is as good an officer as I am—is younger, and has a better temper."[32] Both Sherman and McPherson received their promotions that summer, and Sherman wrote Grant that "I value the commission far less than the fact that this will associate my name with yours and McPherson's in opening the Mississippi, an achievement the importance of which cannot be overestimated."[33]

In a war where command personalities had become significant, affecting actual military operations, McPherson must have become even more valuable to Grant than even he realized. Grant, the taciturn, unmilitary general, felt at ease with McPherson, who looked like a general and acted like a regular soldier. They enjoyed relaxing together of an evening and socializing when possible. When the assignment required brashness and risk, Grant could turn to Sherman and his good friend Admiral Porter, two unrelentingly energetic officers, who loved nothing better than stirring up a good fight, no matter what the consequences. But when consequences did matter, he sent in McPherson, who approached everything in Grant's more methodical, practical style.

Left to command Vicksburg for the foreseeable future, McPherson spent the next full year dealing with the problems of holding and reconstructing the city and district. Most of the citizens liked him, and Southern newspapers pointed to his administration as a model for the rest of the Union. This did not sit well with Radicals in Congress, who questioned his appointment and delayed his confirmation. Ultimately, Grant stepped in and, as McPherson had no political friends in Congress, applied to his own congressional friends to secure McPherson's confirmation.[34]

Twice again during McPherson's administration of Vicksburg, he received verbal or undefined orders to field duty. In October 1863, Grant sent him on a reconnaissance toward Canton, Mississippi. In February 1864, he accompanied Sherman on a similar expedition to Meridian, Mississippi. Both adventures were less military maneuvers than destruction missions, at which McPherson's rowdy veteran troops excelled. In the Canton expedition, McPherson never even reached the railroads Grant hoped he would destroy, hampered by poor cavalry, Confederate concentration, and threats to the security of Vicksburg, which hastened his return. He did, however, according to Grant, achieve his express mission by diverting the Confederates from Sherman's reinforcement of Chattanooga. On the march to Meridian, McPherson commanded the right wing, which did the major share of the damage to Confederate communications and whatever else got in their way. In fact, he so thoroughly destroyed the town of Chunky Station that one man followed the army, seeking to obtain an insurance affidavit that the town had indeed once existed. Returning victorious from the expedition, McPherson secured the reenlistment of his entire Seventeenth Army Corps, offering thirty-day furloughs and using revival-meeting tactics.[35]

Awaiting orders, McPherson finally embarked on his own furlough in spring 1864 and headed upriver to go to Baltimore to marry

Emily Hoffman, sending his fiancée telegrams from every stop. At Cairo, Illinois, he was halted and given new orders: to return to the field immediately and take command of the Army of the Tennessee at Huntsville, Alabama, for Sherman's campaign toward Atlanta, Georgia. McPherson did go to Huntsville, but he made Sherman telegraph the news to Emily. He took over Grant's and Sherman's army with both pride and uneasiness. To his mother he confessed, "I have a much greater responsibility than I desire."[36]

With fully one-third of his effective troops and all his veteran Seventeenth Army Corps and intelligence officers on expedition and on furlough, McPherson reorganized his depleted army and joined Sherman on the field. Thus far in major campaigns, McPherson had always acted under Grant's orders, often verbal ones. Grant knew him well. A shrewd reader of army men, Grant rarely, if ever, mistook their military skills. Sherman, however, was a different story. His first orders to McPherson proved how little he really knew the man whom he also later claimed as a "brother."

Sherman planned to force Johnston and his army into fighting a pitched battle in Georgia, even if it meant pushing them all the way back to the crucial rail center of Atlanta. To dislodge Johnston from his mountain fortification at Dalton, he ordered McPherson to swing his army south to the railroad at Resaca, cutting the railroad with cooperating cavalry and forcing Johnston's retreat. But Sherman's written orders prescribed McPherson's movements in minute detail and attempted to cover every contingency. If he found Resaca too strongly held, Sherman ordered, he was "to draw back four or five miles, to Snake Creek Gap, make it secure, and wait for orders." Over the next several days, Sherman oversaw McPherson's advance with a number of messages limiting his actions, ordering him to move to exactly marked spots on the map, and reassuring him of the reliability of the forthcoming cavalry, whose job it was actually to cut the railroad.

McPherson pushed a portion of his army quickly through the narrow Snake Creek Gap, secured it, and left some forces behind to widen it enough to get the rest of the army through while he advanced on Resaca. The promised cavalry never arrived. Past the gap, the road to Resaca went straight uphill for several miles, a fact not noted on the army's maps. By the time they arrived at the steep hillside overlooking Resaca, it was nearly dark, and the cavalry was nowhere in sight. McPherson attempted to hold the hillside while part of his infantry swung north to cut the railroad. The center of his line, led by a drunken Ohio colonel, faltered and threatened to give way under unexpectedly spirited Confederate resistance, and McPherson recalled the advance. As darkness fell, with reinforcements under John Bell Hood rumored approaching, McPherson withdrew his force to the safer position near Snake Creek Gap, little suspecting that only four thousand Confederates actually opposed his six thousand effective troops.[37]

Sherman was so enraged by McPherson's failure to cut the railroad that McPherson never told him fully what had actually happened. Denying him the chance to make a planned second attempt the following morning, Sherman modified his language in official reports, claiming he was "somewhat disappointed at the result, still appreciative of the advantage gained."[38] After the war, Sherman admitted that McPherson had acted strictly according to his written orders, but he altered his assessment eleven years later in his *Memoirs,* calling him "timid" at Resaca. After vociferous protest by McPherson's former field officers, Sherman again reevaluated him in the second edition, changing the word "timid" to "nervous." "Still," Sherman continued, "he was perfectly justified by his orders."[39]

McPherson's advance on Resaca was also his first independent operation under his friend, Sherman, rather than his mentor, Grant, whose methods were quite different. Grant always made sure that his trusted subordinates, like Sherman and McPherson, understood his goals, then allowed them to plan and execute the tactical details. For McPherson, Grant almost always wrote open-ended orders when he did write them, setting limits on his initiative only when necessary. Grant would never have written McPherson's orders for Resaca with the diffusion of mission and plethora of contingency clauses that Sherman used.[40]

In retrospect, McPherson's old roommate and fellow army commander under Sherman, John M. Schofield, claimed that "the error was Sherman's, not McPherson's; that McPherson was correct in his judgment, which certainly was mine (after passing over the same ground and fighting the battle of Resaca), that his force was entirely too small for the work assigned it." Schofield characterized McPherson's actions as "wise prudence" for not sacrificing his force in a bloody assault on Resaca and castigated Sherman for a "faulty system of organization and command" throughout the campaign. Of McPherson himself, Schofield judged that "his was the most completely balanced mind and character with which I have ever been intimately acquainted, although

he did not possess in very high degree the power of invention or origi-
nality of thought," and defined his failure at Resaca most accurately.
"McPherson," he said, "was a subordinate in spirit as well as in fact,
and cannot fairly be charged with timidity for not attempting what he
was not ordered to do, and what, in fact, was no part of the plans of his
superior so far as they were indicated in his orders."[41]

McPherson's failure to take Resaca, and Sherman's reaction,
greatly affected him. Grant and Sherman had both made mistakes in
battle, but McPherson had never failed at anything he had ever tried.
His inherent cautiousness was a part of his makeup. Grant had recognized this and had used it to advantage, giving him the lead or having
him cover the retreat in dangerous territory, but Sherman simply denied
it. In this case, it made a difference. Determined to please Sherman,
and to make up for this blot on his otherwise ideal career, McPherson
threw his army into the campaign with vigor. At the battles of Resaca,
Dallas, and Kenesaw Mountain, he acted decisively, employing inven-
tive tactics and repulsing, at Dallas, the attack of nearly all of Johnston's army. Over and over, Sherman flanked Johnston with McPherson's army, the "whip-lash" of Sherman's force. As Sherman steadily
pressed Johnston back toward Atlanta, he left the safety of his most
endangered flanks entirely in McPherson's hands, seemingly oblivious
of the need for adequate cavalry protection, while McPherson showed
a more restrained exercise of the caution that Sherman lacked.

At last, before Atlanta, they faced a different foe. Jefferson Davis,
angered by Johnston's strategic retreat, put McPherson's old roommate
Hood in command of Johnston's army. On the night of July 21, 1864,
Sherman, who had already sent McPherson's cavalry away to break up
railroads in the rear, and who sincerely believed that Atlanta was being
evacuated overnight, ordered his armies forward. He also ordered a
substantial portion of McPherson's infantry away to Decatur for further
railroad destruction. McPherson pressed forward and found Hood still
in Atlanta. Refusing to obey Sherman's orders, McPherson sent
Grenville M. Dodge to reinforce his left and rear and rode off to see
Sherman.

McPherson convinced Sherman that his old friend Hood, an in-
ventive and aggressive man, would never abandon Atlanta without a
fight and that he would most likely attack on the left, which Sherman
had once again weakened. He was right. Hood had sent Gen. William
J. Hardee's corps to get in McPherson's rear, but his early morning

deployments had placed most of Dodge's Sixteenth Corps in their path. When Hood attacked, portions of McPherson's army fought both front and rear, saved from immediate destruction only by his earlier concern for his flank. Corps Commander Francis P. Blair later claimed that "the Lord placed Dodge in the right place on 22 July," but the author of that act was really McPherson, who had set Dodge's course at 8:00 A.M.[42]

McPherson died in the second wave of attacks at noon that day, when shifting battle lines brought Confederate skirmishers onto a previously safe road. Still recovering from the anger meted out by Sherman after his failure to retake Resaca, McPherson apparently could not face the ultimate humiliation of surrender, parole, and exchange. Politely, he removed his hat, bowed to the approaching soldiers, wheeled his horse off to the right, and was shot in the back. If captured, he would have lived to become, at the very least, general of the army after Sherman.

Men in the ranks felt McPherson's loss keenly. After hearing the news, his army charged off into its bloodiest battle of the war, shouting, "McPherson! McPherson!" Their victory over John Bell Hood's desperate troops on that day did not appease them for his loss. Again on August 28 and 31 they repelled the Confederates in his name, but even the capture of Atlanta did not reconcile them. John A. Logan noted that often in the weeks after his death, his men would sit around their campfires and exchange reminiscences of him. Soldiers in every theater of war noted his death in their diaries and letters, even those who never knew him, and recalled instantly the moment they heard of McPherson's death. Southerners to whom he had shown a kindness even decorated his death site long after the war, and his former professors joined the swelling numbers of those who gave him credit for planning Grant's Vicksburg campaign, which he actually led only under his mentor's direction. Indeed, he was so universally admired in life and venerated in death that little gossip ever spread about him in army circles, no small distinction in a profession where gossip was widespread, pernicious, and often motivated by rivalry. When Sherman announced his death he created an ideal of McPherson more saintly than he could ever have been, the true ideal soldier of the Old Army. "General McPherson," he declared, "fell in Battle, booted and spurred as the Gallant Knight and Gentleman should wish."[43]

In light of the paucity of documentation chronicling their friendship forged in war, Grant's similar, highly emotional reaction to the news of McPherson's death seems somewhat odd. It is only when we look at the surviving evidence in light of their friendship that we can see why he felt so devastated. Although conventional wisdom has determined throughout the years that Grant never gave verbal orders after the debacle of the first day at Shiloh, his own words attest to the many instances in which he continued to give only McPherson verbal or open-ended orders and the complete latitude to carry them out. He trusted McPherson in a way that he was rarely ever able to trust any other man, in complete confidence that he would do whatever could be done while not foolishly risking the mission. That he never found anyone else to trust similarly during the remainder of the war only emphasized, for him, the personal magnitude of McPherson's death.

Ultimately, McPherson succeeded in being remembered only for his death. That he was a trusted protégé, confidant, and an able lieutenant to Grant, a close friend to Sherman, and an able member of the Union high command in the West was soon largely forgotten. His actions on the field before Vicksburg and Atlanta are only vaguely remembered.

But the army with which Sherman reshaped Georgia and South Carolina did not forget him. The right wing of Sherman's march, composed solely of McPherson's reshaped Fifteenth and Seventeenth Army Corps, was the most destructive and "flexible" of the invading force. It was McPherson's men who captured Fort McAllister and occupied Charleston, Bentonville, and Raleigh. Whatever caused the burning of Columbia, it was the men of McPherson's Fifteenth Corps who commanded it. His men raged through the South with a fury that astonished their new commander, who found that he could not control his troops' wanton tendencies as McPherson had before Atlanta. In honor of their signal achievements on this march Sherman allowed men from each of McPherson's old corps to receive Johnston's surrendered arms.[44]

After the war the officers of McPherson's old army formed a social organization, the Society of the Army of the Tennessee. Its first meeting was held in Ohio on what would have been McPherson's thirty-seventh birthday, and its first goal was to erect a suitable memorial statue to him.[45] The society met yearly in midwestern cities, ate and drank impressively, and relived the war years ferociously. Their campaign to memorialize McPherson was enormously successful. As contributions flowed in, a fight began over where the memorial should be placed and, ultimately, over control of McPherson's body. Despite the army's desire to have the statue placed at West Point and his body reinterred there, most people generally agreed that the best spot would be over his original grave site at Clyde, Ohio. The citizens of Clyde, outraged by suggestions of removing his body and putting the monument elsewhere, formed a competing monument association. Ten years of negotiations over the statue's placement ended after Congress passed an act in 1875 creating McPherson Square in Washington, DC, especially for the society's statue. McPherson's family agreed to the Washington location and exhumed his body for reburial in the base of the statue, but the Clyde association obtained an injunction when he was already partially disinterred and quickly and permanently encased him in the concrete pedestal for the Clyde monument, leaving the society no alternative but to agree to erect a second McPherson memorial over his grave at Clyde.[46]

Five years later, in 1881, more than twenty thousand people went to northern Ohio to dedicate the second statue. Pres. James Garfield, who had promised to attend the unveiling "if nothing especial or unlooked for occurred," was prevented from doing so by an assassin's bullet.[47] Thousands of people traveled hundreds of miles to attend ceremonies for a man they had barely, if ever, known, and who had been dead for over seventeen years. They hailed him, as they had in Washington, as their army's martyr and an irreplaceable comrade. Ultimately three statues, one monument, several forts, and at least one ship were dedicated to McPherson, but such honorific attempts to remember him failed to commemorate anything but his death.

Whatever else he was, McPherson was all army, much more so than Grant or Sherman ever were. He had gone to West Point like so many, a young idealistic midwestern boy, but had emerged a soldier, totally shaped by the ideals and education of the Old Army. While success in war rarely correlated to the army's ideals, McPherson's attempt to meet them advanced him within the army system, earning him promotion after promotion in rank long before he gained leadership of any troops. Without the experience of early failures in command, like Grant and Sherman, or the boldness of Lee, he was only just learning at the very end of his life how to take chances and to survive great loss. An excellent subordinate officer, when given flexibility in command and told to use his own judgment, he proved to be quick thinking and capable; when told exactly what to do, he did that and no more. Grant used this aspect of McPherson's personality to advantage, and Sherman did not. While McPherson was not a gambler or an instinctive tactician, under an incisive superior he demonstrated a high degree of leadership. What he did do, he did well, and he also never lost a battle.

His death at age thirty-five reduced him to a Civil War statistic: the highest-ranking Union officer killed in the war. McPherson's reputation never transcended either his "heroic" death or Sherman's *Memoirs*. Those writers who accepted Sherman's later version of events at Resaca over his contemporary correspondence or more reliable testimony portrayed McPherson as always ineffective and overly cautious. Sherman's critics blamed him for neglecting to coordinate and control his command, regarding McPherson's real weaknesses too lightly. Aside from one published popular, eulogistic biography, McPherson remains a shadowy figure, alternatively considered bright, heroic, or competent but largely unexamined.

Even McPherson's most jealous acquaintances noted that he was "justly regarded as an ideal soldier." The ideals of the Old Army did make good soldiers, but experience and natural ability made great generals. Both Grant and Sherman believed McPherson had that ability but needed command experience to develop it. At McPherson's death, Sherman called him "the best hope for a great soldier that I had in my mind's eye."[48] When McPherson finally overcame his own spirit of subordination long enough to disobey Sherman's direct orders on the morning of July 22, 1864, and began to trust his own instincts, he showed the true promise of which Sherman spoke and in which Grant always trusted.

"We Had Lively Times up the Yazoo"

Admiral David Dixon Porter

ᴄ⁓ *R. Blake Dunnavent*

Acting Rear Adm. David Dixon Porter watched as his flagship, the gunboat *Benton,* slowly churned the dark water as it steamed closer to the ominous cliffs. As he peered out of his gunboat, he noticed that his flotilla was no longer shrouded in darkness, for the graycoats had lit fires to illuminate the oncoming Union fleet. When it came within range of the Confederate gunners, who had been carefully scanning the darkness for Federal movement, the rebel batteries belched fire and shot at the closing ironclad goliaths. The deafening sound of musket-fire, ship's broadsides, and the fire of the shore batteries engulfed the surrounding area. Like hail bouncing off a roof, the musket balls ricocheted off the iron hulls. When the Confederate gunners obtained their range, a number of cannon balls struck the *Benton,* with one passing through the casemate, injuring several men and spraying blood inside the gunboat. Yet the *Benton* and six other craft made it intact below Vicksburg's batteries.[1]

David Dixon Porter was born on June 8, 1813, to Commodore David Porter, veteran of the engagement between the *Constellation* and the *L'Insurgente,* the Barbary Wars, and the War of 1812. Porter's desire for life in the navy emerged at an early age, inspired by his father's sea stories and those of other colorful naval figures such as Oliver Hazard Perry, John Rodgers, and Stephen Decatur, who recounted their yarns at the Porter family estate on Meridian Hill in Washington, DC. While his father was stationed at the Washington Navy Yard following the War of 1812, young Porter would scamper across the entire facility, examining every inch, and further exciting his curiosity about the sea. Above all, his father's expectations that his sons become sailors destined Porter for a life in the navy.[2]

In 1824 Porter's father sent him to Columbia College to gain the mathematical knowledge necessary for navigation. While he was at school, his father became embroiled in a diplomatic incident. Cruising the Caribbean in search of depredating pirates, Commodore Porter learned that an American naval officer, Lt. Charles T. Platt, had petitioned the alcalde at Fajardo, Puerto Rico, to assist in the recovery of stolen American goods in the town. Instead of finding a conciliatory town official, the "authorities horse-collared Platt, accused him of piracy, and threw him in the local guardhouse." After Platt returned to his ship and reported the incident, the commodore, having learned about Platt's treatment, departed for Fajardo, anchored off the town, and with an armed landing party forced the alcalde to apologize. When his father reported the event to the Navy Department he was recalled to Washington, court-martialed, and given a six-month suspension. Infuriated, despite being exonerated "from the charge of misconduct at Fajardo and praised . . . for upholding the honor of the nation and her navy," the commodore resigned his commission and became the general of marines for the Republic of Mexico. Because of these events, the young Porter began his days at sea in a foreign navy.[3]

From 1826 to 1828, Porter served in the Mexican navy as a midshipman, receiving instruction in the ways of leadership, weaponry, and navigation. In 1828 he assumed duties aboard his cousin's ship, *Guerrero.* On a foray against Spanish shipping around Cuba, the *Guerrero* engaged the *Lealtad.* Following several hours of combat, resulting in the death of Porter's cousin, Henry Porter, and a large number of the crew, the Spanish captain took the remainder of the survivors, including Porter, to a prison ship off Havana. Although the authorities offered him better quarters until his famous father could arrange parole, Porter chose to endure prison hardships with his fellow crewmen. When General Porter bargained his son's release six months later and sent him home, Cong. William Anderson, Porter's grandfather, acquired the sixteen-year-old an appointment as a midshipman in the U.S. Navy.[4]

Over the next seventeen years, Porter served in the Mediterranean Squadron and the Coast Survey and attended school to study mathematics. Rising to the rank of lieutenant and fearful of remaining there, he knew that only war would permit advancement. Hostilities with Mexico provided him with the opportunity to demonstrate his talents.[5]

Transferred to the home squadron aboard the *Spitfire,* on March 10, 1847, Porter took part in the Vera Cruz landings. Initially, the *Spitfire* provided direct fire support for Gen. Winfield Scott's amphibious landings; then, on March 22, it shelled the southernmost bastion protecting Vera Cruz, Fort Santiago. Before dawn the next morning, Porter, using experience gained from coastal survey duties, made soundings of the channel. Later the same morning, the *Spitfire* steamed up the waterway and attacked Fort Santiago and San Juan de Ulloa before returning to the fleet. On April 18, Porter participated in his first riverine operation when Commodore Matthew Calbraith Perry led a flotilla against Tuxpan. Porter remained on board the *Spitfire* and directed cannonfire against enemy positions while the landing force disembarked and stormed the two forts guarding the river city. The small fleet proceeded toward Tuxpan and landed the troops while the vessels provided fire support for the ground forces. On May 24, he served on another riverine expedition when Perry deemed Tabasco, which had already been attacked in 1846, significant enough to merit an additional assault. The riverine armada entered the Tabasco River and returned fire at enemy ambush sites along the river bank. Several miles away from the city, the Mexicans placed obstructions in the middle of the river. Perry disembarked and commanded the ground forces, which marched toward Tabasco. The waterborne commander, using underwater explosives, dislodged the log barricades. In temporary command of the *Spitfire,* Porter pulled the obstacles clear, and the flotilla churned upriver. When the craft reached Fort Iturbide, protecting the approach to the town, he led a landing party that routed the defenders. Hours later, the naval element steamed upriver and forced the town's surrender. It was not until later that Perry's ground force wearily walked into the captured city. For his performance, he gave Porter command of the *Spitfire.* All his experiences during the Mexican War provided him with valuable knowledge, which he applied fourteen years later on the Mississippi River.[6]

Following the war with Mexico, Porter held several duties until the outbreak of the Civil War. He served in the Coastal Survey, took a leave of absence from the navy and captained mail steamers, returned to the navy to transport camels for the army, and contemplated a civilian career, until South Carolina seceded from the Union.

Porter's first involvement in the Civil War nearly led to events mirroring the severity of his father's Fajardo debacle. In early spring 1861, before open hostilities surfaced between the North and South, Pres. Abraham Lincoln listened to future assistant secretary of the navy Gustavus Fox, who set forth a plan to relieve Fort Sumter. According to its commander, Maj. Robert Anderson, the fort could hold out only until mid-April. Lincoln readily embraced Fox's scheme to resupply the Union stronghold in Charleston Harbor.

Meanwhile, in addition to Sumter, the only other remaining Union outpost in the would-be seceding states was Fort Pickens, near Pensacola, Florida. Located across from Pensacola Navy Yard (which had already been seized by the Florida militia), Fort Pickens was also considered valuable to the United States, and therefore it warranted reinforcement. Porter and army captain Montgomery C. Meigs devised plans for this contingency. With growing concern about the loyalty of certain officers and the possibility of departmental leaks, Lieutenant Porter went to Secretary of State William H. Seward instead of to the secretary of the navy. The three men presented the plan to the president, who, assured by Seward that Secretary of the Navy Gideon Welles would be informed, requested that Porter and Meigs write the orders and then he would sign them. Lincoln's missives provided for the outfitting of the *Powhatan* for Porter's Fort Pickens expedition. That vessel, however, was earmarked for the chief role in Fox's Fort Sumter relief operation. Unaware of this, Lincoln then ordered Porter to "proceed to Pensacola Harbor, and at any cost or risk prevent any expedition from the mainland reaching Fort Pickens."[7]

While Porter prepared the *Powhatan* to put to sea, Welles met with Lincoln and Seward, and the latter changed his mind. Early on April 6, Welles forwarded a message to Porter ordering him to hand over command of the vessel to another captain. By the time the telegram reached the navy yard, Porter was steaming to Florida. Although a ship was dispatched with the new orders, Porter refused to accept them, reasoning that his orders were from the president. On April 17, Meigs and his transports reached Fort Pickens, first discovering that Confederates had positioned guns opposite the fort and all around the harbor entrance. Meigs, observing the *Powhatan* approaching, sent a tug out to Porter with a request from the fort's commander, Col. Harvey Brown, and himself to remain outside the harbor. Meigs's correspondence to Porter alluded to executive authority, stating, "My knowledge of the views and intentions of the President justify me in making this request with almost the force of an order from the President." Despite his desire to run the harbor's gauntlet, the brash lieutenant acquiesced and informed Brown that his request for "me not to go in and draw the fire on you before you had time to prepare is quite sufficient to satisfy me that such a course on my part would be very indiscreet." Because Lincoln assumed responsibility for the episode, Porter received little rebuke from Washington and was transferred to blockade duty off the mouth of the Mississippi River. While there he was promoted to the rank of commander.[8]

As captain of the *Powhatan* off the Mississippi, Porter gained extensive knowledge of the passes and waterways providing routes to New Orleans. This, coupled with his awareness of the importance of the Crescent City, enabled him to formulate a plan for its capture. When he brought his vessel north for repairs, he immediately went to the Navy Department to voice his ideas. With the department already examining and contemplating New Orleans's capture, Welles listened, without prejudice, to Porter's plans. He proposed that a fleet of ships, combined with a mortar flotilla and two thousand ground troops, attack the forts guarding the advance up the river from the Gulf. Although he stressed the capitulation of the forts first by mortar bombardment, he emphasized, "If the ships can get by the forts, and there are no obstructions above, then the plan should be to push on to New Orleans." Secretary of the Navy Welles selected Adm. David Glasgow Farragut, Porter's adopted brother, to lead the assault. On April 18, Porter's mortar boats began a six-day bombardment of the two Confederate river forts. With mortar ammunition running low, the admiral decided to pass the guns of the forts and take New Orleans. In the early morning hours of April 24, Farragut's armada, although under continuous fire from enemy cannon, slipped past the forts, successfully engaged a small rebel naval force, and captured New Orleans. Days later the fort's defenders surrendered to Porter.[9]

Following the success of New Orleans, Porter assisted Farragut in the first naval operations against Vicksburg. He then steamed to Mobile, laid buoys for Farragut's fleet, which he believed was making preparations for an imminent attack on that port, and then departed for home. Shortly after Porter's arrival, Welles ordered the commander to assist Commodore J. B. Hull in overseeing the construction of gunboats in Cincinnati. Recognizing that his new command relegated him to a noncombatant post, Porter went to the president, and the resulting meeting may have decided his fate. On September 22, while Porter was convalescing from an intermittent fever, Welles forwarded to him a message: "You will be assigned to duty West, and on your way report in person to this Department for further orders." On October 1, Welles handed orders to Porter to assume command of the Mississippi Squadron from Acting Rear Adm. Charles H. Davis, "who will transfer the command of that squadron to yourself, when you will immediately hoist your flag as acting rear-admiral." The following day the gunboat flotilla was transferred from the War to the Navy Department.[10]

Acting Rear Admiral Porter realized that his primary responsibility with his new command was the seizure of Vicksburg. Yet he grimaced at the thought of working with army officers. The admiral's feelings existed as a result of Maj. Gen. Benjamin F. Butler's claims, during the New Orleans campaign, that the army had forced the surrender of Forts Jackson and St. Phillip. This incident not only soured Porter's attitudes toward Butler but also toward the concept of working with other political generals. Nonetheless, when Secretary Welles ordered him to work jointly with Major Gen. John A. McClernand against the Confederate river stronghold, he cooperated.[11]

When Porter arrived at his new command and began building a fleet, McClernand was recruiting troops in Illinois. For weeks, Porter awaited news from him. Once the admiral's riverine armada was mobilized, he became anxious for action and frustrated with McClernand's absence and lack of communication. Maj. Gen. Ulysses S. Grant was also concerned about McClernand, but for other reasons. He became suspicious that his appointment created an independent command that might supersede his own. Astute and ambitious, Grant raced to initiate operations against Vicksburg before McClernand's arrival. Through various channels, Porter learned of Grant's actions and feared the exclusion of the navy, until an impromptu meeting occurred between him and Grant in early December. Porter was enjoying dinner with the army quartermaster of Cairo when Grant entered, Porter was introduced, and the two officers took a private table to discuss Grant's plan for assailing the Confederate bastion. This brief rendezvous demonstrated to both men that each was willing to work jointly to accomplish a common goal, and it was the origin of a mutually respectful relationship. In Grant, Porter had found an army general who shared his own aggressiveness and tenacity.[12]

In accordance with the plans he had outlined to Porter, Grant ordered Sherman to Memphis to "assume command of all the troops there . . . [and] as soon as possible move with them down the river to the vicinity of Vicksburg and with the cooperation of the Gunboat fleet under command of Flag Officer Porter proceed to the reduction of that place." While Porter and Sherman moved along the river, Grant would march from Holly Springs to Granada in hopes of drawing out a number of Vicksburg's defenders. The well-prepared plan dissolved when Confederate forces attacked Grant's supply line, forcing him to withdraw. Unaware of this, Sherman and Porter pressed forward.[13]

Sherman selected the Chickasaw Bluffs on the Yazoo River just north of Vicksburg as the location from which his troops would attack and then move on to Vicksburg. Although Porter had previously ordered the clearing of torpedoes from the Yazoo, which resulted in the sinking of a gunboat, steadfastly he ordered another "expedition up the Yazoo for the purpose of securing a good landing place for [the] troops." For days, under constant harassing fire from Confederate sharpshooters, Union naval forces attempted to clear the river of torpedoes, bombarded possible landing sites, engaged enemy batteries, and prepared to support Sherman's assault. The day after Christmas, Sherman's troops, soaked from rain that had begun to fall, disembarked and slowly plodded through the muck and mire to their assigned positions. The following morning and throughout the day, Porter's gunboats unleashed a withering fire on the enemy gun emplacements at Drumgould's Bluff. Despite Porter's attempts to cover Sherman's troops, topography prevented direct fire support from the gunboats. On December 29, Sherman's men attacked the cliffs but were forced to withdraw because of a murderous Confederate crossfire. After the failure to storm the bluffs, the two commanders conferred and decided on a new plan the next day for a subsequent assault on the enemy positions. Their concepts never came to fruition, as a thick fog enveloped the area, forcing a mutual decision to cancel the operation. The failure at Chickasaw Bluffs forced Grant to devise new means for capturing Vicksburg.[14]

To the chagrin of Porter and Sherman, McClernand arrived on the Yazoo days after the Union attack at Chickasaw Bluffs and assumed command of the army. Sherman recommended to McClernand that a combined army–navy force should move up the Arkansas River and eliminate a Confederate strong point called Fort Hindman, at a bend of the river traditionally known as Arkansas Post. Behind this suggestion was an annoying incident. During the Chickasaw Bluff operation a Confederate craft "had seized a Government transport, the *Blue Wing*, laden with valuable munitions on their way to General Sherman." McClernand listened to Sherman's proposal and pondered its outcome.

When McClernand approached the admiral with the plan, Porter, skeptical of McClernand's abilities, assured the new army commander that his forces would assist in the operation but only if the general's subordinate, Sherman, led the assault. McClernand acquiesced and the armada of gunboats and transports transited the Arkansas on January 9, 1863. The next day navy gunboats shelled the rebel fort with astounding accuracy, demoralizing its defenders. On January 11, as bluecoats disembarked and struggled into position in the swampy terrain, Porter conferred with McClernand, who informed him "that the army was waiting for the navy to attack, when they would assault the works." With orders to close and engage the fortress, the gunboats' cannon aimed belching fire, smoke, and death at the rebel emplacements. According to Porter, the navy's barrage knocked "everything to pieces," whereupon "the enemy held out a white flag, and I ordered the firing to cease." The occupants surrendered to Porter before the bluecoats could occupy the fort. Reports of the victory released by the press greatly exaggerated McClernand's role and incensed Porter, who conveyed his thoughts to Welles that "army officers are not willing to give the Navy credit." Porter's disgust dissipated when Grant met the returning forces and assumed command of operations against Vicksburg. Porter had confidence that Grant was a capable warrior; he had no such confidence in McClernand.[15]

With the hard lessons learned about a direct assault on the bluffs north of Vicksburg, Grant next proposed to enhance Williams's Canal, "which would enable gunboats and army transports to cross the peninsula at Young's Point and reenter the river below Vicksburg's batteries." On January 10, Grant queried Porter as to the feasibility of this action. Although this effort, as well as other attempts at gouging canals at Duckport and Lake Providence, appeared to some observers as foolhardy, Porter supported Grant's ideas, as always.[16]

Meanwhile, Grant, in a continued attempt to get above Haynes's Bluff, came up with a plan to surprise the rebel forces at Vicksburg by using waterways east of the Mississippi. He proposed to Porter that a combined army–navy force should proceed through the Yazoo Pass "into Coldwater river thence down the stream into the Tallahatchie which with its junction with the Yalobusha forms the Yazoo which it is the great object of the enterprise to enter." On February 6, Porter ordered the naval commander of the expedition to begin the operation. Carrying infantry aboard the naval craft, the joint forces churned up the muddy waters. From February 6 to April 12 the army–navy riverine forces engaged rebel troops, cleared clogged waterways, and doggedly but unsuccessfully attacked a Confederate earthwork, Fort Pemberton, that blocked their further progress. Yet despite their efforts, the fort proved impregnable, and the operation was scrapped.[17]

As the Yazoo Pass expedition stalled, Porter informed Grant that he had another route selected to secure the Yazoo. Still wishing to avoid attacking the bluffs, Grant listened to the plan. The admiral asserted that by penetrating Steele's Bayou and then proceeding through Black Bayou, Deer Creek, Rolling Fork, and the Big Sunflower River, Union forces could hack their way through the heavy vegetation and into the Yazoo River "and thus get into the rear of Vicksburg without loss of life or vessels." Grant adopted the plan. Demonstrating his faith in the proposal, Porter chose to lead the thrust into Steele's Bayou. On March 14, the navy, with its infantry support, moved into the bayou, with Sherman's ground forces slated to follow shortly thereafter. The relative ease of movement of the initial leg of the journey kept Porter's hopes high for the success of the operation. When the force reached Black Bayou, which permitted entrance into Deer Creek, Porter's men manned the upper decks with saws and ropes and began the tedious duty of clearing the bayou for the flotilla's passage. After plying the four miles to Deer Creek, gunboats and transports turned north toward Rolling Fork. The flotilla never made it. Underwater growth, overhanging branches, and thick trees prevented Porter's force from proceeding faster than one mile an hour. By March 20, Confederate units discovered the oncoming Federals and began sniping at men on the vessels' decks and felling trees to impede Union movement. Still, Porter pushed forward until several of his gunboats became entangled in underwater vegetation. Attempting to dislodge the craft proved difficult, and by the evening of March 21 he knew that the rebels had cut timber to his front and rear. He was trapped. He prepared his gunboats for the long night. Sherman, learning of the expedition's peril, pushed his men relentlessly to rescue the stranded boats. While Porter prepared for a Confederate attack, "Sherman undertook a night march, daring and eerie, through swamp waters, the troops' only light provided by candles stuck in their rifle barrels." Around noon the next day, he and his men reached the beleaguered Union flotilla. Grant wrote to Porter, requesting his opinion about the continuance of the operation and stating, "I will heartily cooperate with you in the present enterprise so long as you deem it advisable to push it." But Porter knew to continue was inappropriate, so he ordered the flotilla to return to Steele's Bayou.[18]

Following the failure of the Steele's Bayou operation, Grant pondered again the idea of attacking Haynes's Bluff. Then messages from Farragut and Banks south of Vicksburg triggered an idea in his mind. With the rainy season ebbing, he could move his men to the west bank of the Mississippi, maneuver them through the bayous and swamps, transport them across the river, and attack Vicksburg from the south. On March 29, Grant asked Porter to consider "occupying New Carthage with troops, and opening the bayous from here to that place sufficiently for the passage of flats." The general further contended that with "this passage I can run the blockade with steamers sufficient to land troops . . . either at Grand Gulf or Warrenton." Grant stressed the need of fire support from Porter's gunboats. Porter responded the same day, promising him his support but emphasizing that once the gunboats transited below Vicksburg, any assistance from the navy to attack Haynes's Bluff would be impossible. On April 1, Porter, Grant, and Sherman, weighing their options, observed the positions from which naval fire support would be rendered and where bluecoats would assail the bluffs, if the attack were made there. Following this investigation, Grant informed Porter that "an attack on Haynes Bluff, would be attended with immense sacrifice of life, if not with defeat," and he requested that the admiral run past the guns as soon as possible. Porter, ready to assist Grant, prepared seven of his gunboats and additional craft for the sortie under the Confederate guns at Vicksburg. On the evening of April 16, the gunboats, with coal barges lashed to their sides, quietly began their journey downriver to run the gauntlet of the Vicksburg batteries. About two hours into the mission, the Confederate batteries opened fire on Porter's boats. Despite a heavy fusillade from rebel gunners, his little fleet slipped past Vicksburg's guns relatively unscathed.[19]

After this harrowing experience, Porter's gunboats gave fire support for Grant's abortive attack on Grand Gulf. With the navy unable to reduce the Confederate batteries, Grant had to disembark his men farther south. Soon thereafter, the Federal siege of Vicksburg began in earnest. Throughout the siege, Porter's forces provided fire support, transport, cannon, and anything that Grant's command requested to ensure a successful outcome. When the end came on July 4, 1863, Grant praised Porter by expressing his "thankfulness at being placed in cooperation with an officer of the Navy who never throws obstacles or objections in the way of any move, but gives it whatever it may be an efficient and active support." Moreover, he extolled "Admiral Porter, and the officers under him, [for they] have ever shown the greatest readiness in their cooperation no matter what was to be done or what risk to be taken, either by their men or vessels." He continued by contending that without Porter's assistance, Vicksburg's collapse would not have occurred.[20]

Following the victory at Vicksburg, the promoted Admiral Porter had minimal contact with Grant for about a year. During that time he adopted patrolling districts for his riverine forces operating on the Mississippi River and provided assistance to army units. In spring 1864 he participated in the ill-fated Red River campaign with Maj. Gen. Nathaniel P. Banks. Then the tides of war carried him from brownwater warfare back to the bluewater navy and General Grant.

Secretary of the Navy Welles had wanted to seal off the port of Wilmington, North Carolina, for some time to prevent Confederate blockade runners from taking cotton to foreign shores and returning with material for rebel forces. He had urged Secretary of War Edwin M. Stanton to furnish troops for "joint operation against the defenses of Cape Fear River." When Stanton deferred the decision to Grant, the general "though not explicitly refusing cooperation, saw no strategic purpose in it at that time." Lieutenant General Grant's ambivalent attitude was later interpreted by the Navy Department as passive acceptance. On September 6, 1864, two plans were drawn for operations against Wilmington and presented to Grant. Naval leaders adopted the second plan, proposing a direct attack on Fort Fisher with ten thousand infantry. The navy men pushed forward with their preparations and assumed the army would provide support. The Navy Department's first choice as commander of the expedition was the hero of the battle of Mobile Bay, Admiral Farragut. Surprisingly, he turned down the secretary, claiming his health would prevent him from successfully carrying out the mission. Historian Rowena Reed notes that "Fox got the message at once. Wilmington was considered a nasty job, likely to end in defeat and humiliation for the Navy." Yet Fox knew another commander remained who, regardless of the outcome, would interpret the facts in favor of the navy's performance. When offered the position, Porter did not hesitate, and on October 12 he assumed his duties as commander of the North Atlantic Blockading Squadron. The navy's assumptions that Grant would furnish troops for the expedition proved a problem. On October 15, Porter visited Grant, requesting troops for the attack against Fort Fisher. When Grant, who was preoccupied with more than an assault on Wilmington, apprised Porter of his limited manpower due to ongoing operations in Virginia, Secretary Welles, about two weeks later, pleaded with President Lincoln for men. On December 6, Grant acquiesced and ordered Maj. Gen. Godfrey Weitzel, with 6,500 men, to cooperate with the navy in a joint venture against Fort Fisher. Grant had not anticipated that General Butler, whose district Wilmington fell under, would actively participate in the assault. When Butler surprised Grant with his decision not to take merely an administrative role, Porter feared the worst and told Grant so. Despite their differences, which had existed since New Orleans in 1862, Porter found Butler ready to attack the North Carolinian fort.[21]

Following an unsuccessful attempt to blow up the fort using a ship loaded with gunpowder, the joint force prepared for action. On December 24, the guns of Porter's fleet commenced a bombardment of the fort to soften up the Confederate defenses. The next morning, Christmas Day, Porter's fleet unleashed another bombardment onto the rebel bastion. That afternoon a portion of Weitzel's men climbed down from the navy ships into their landing boats and pulled for shore. While the bluecoats clambered onto the beach, Porter's ships provided fire support. Through the smoke and haze, Weitzel surveyed the gun emplacements. Observing that the navy's shelling had not eliminated all the enemy cannon, he reported to Butler the situation at the fort. Believing the bluecoats were now exposed to overwhelming firepower, Weitzel and Butler ordered a withdrawal of the ground troops. But the reembarkation was so expeditious that a detachment of soldiers remained isolated on the beach. Infuriated with army carelessness, Porter dispatched his sailors to retrieve the stranded men. Meanwhile, Butler, with his entire force, departed the area and left Porter without infantry.[22]

Tempers flared following the failed attempt to storm Fort Fisher, and Porter's and Butler's correspondence assigned blame to each other for the operation's outcome. Afterward, Porter wrote his old friend, Lieutenant General Grant, asking for army assistance to launch a second assault on the garrison. On December 30, Grant stressed to Porter to "hold on where you are for a few days and I will endeavor to be back again with an increased force and without the former commander." The admiral responded to Grant's missive on January 1,

1865, writing, "I shall be all ready, and thank God we are not to leave here with so easy a victory at hand. Thank you for so promptly trying to rectify the blunder so lately committed. I knew you would do it." As promised, Grant chose Maj. Gen. Alfred H. Terry to lead the ground forces in the second attack on Fort Fisher. On January 13, Porter and Terry's huge amphibious armada deployed surfboats from which army infantry, sailors, and marines jumped onto the beach and entrenched. By January 15, the Federal ground elements had moved forward. Having fought a pitched battle resulting in close-quarters fighting, the combined army–navy forces secured Fort Fisher. The Porter/Grant relationship had produced another victory for the Union.[23]

The good relationship forged between Porter and Grant was necessary for the Vicksburg and Fort Fisher campaigns to have successful outcomes. Although Porter disliked army generals because of his experience with Butler during the New Orleans operation, the admiral overcame his prejudices and kept an open mind when he met Grant. The initial meeting left an indelible positive impression on Porter about the determination of the unpretentious general from Illinois. Throughout the many pitfalls of the Vicksburg campaign, Porter never faltered in his support of Grant. Usually, Grant solicited Porter's perspective on a given operation or an idea to end the siege. In 1865, this respect for Porter's capabilities still remained, as indicated in Grant's orders to Terry: "I have served with Admiral Porter, and know that you can rely on his judgment and his nerve to undertake what he proposes. I would defer to him as much as is consistent with your own responsibilities." Because of his faith in Porter's judgment, Grant supplied a new commander and troops for the second assault on Fort Fisher. Porter also shared mutual regard for Grant, revealed when he wrote Secretary Welles: "So confident was I of the ability of General Grant to carry out his plans when he explained them to me, that I never hesitated to change my position from above to below Vicksburg." The combined army–navy operations at Vicksburg and Fort Fisher resulted in Union triumphs because Porter and Grant possessed the martial qualities that inspired mutual respect between these two warriors.[24]

Grant and Grenville M. Dodge in the West, 1862–1864

e~ William B. Feis

Anxious and nearly out of breath, Brig. Gen. Grenville M. Dodge rushed to catch the train for Jackson, Tennessee. Earlier that October afternoon he had been supervising crews repairing the Mobile and Ohio Railroad, a vital supply line for Union forces in West Tennessee and northern Mississippi. He then received orders to report immediately to Jackson for a conference with the commanding general. A railroad engineer in civilian life and now in late 1862 a brigadier general of volunteers, Dodge had never met his superior and wanted to make a good impression, despite the fact that he still wore his dirty work clothes. As the train neared the Jackson depot, Dodge only hoped that his appearance would not overshadow his solid war record. A staff officer boarded and informed him that the commanding general waited on the platform. As they left the train, Dodge apologized for his attire. Without blinking, the staff officer replied, "Oh, we know all about you; don't mind that." When he finally stood before his commander, all discomfort vanished. As was his nature, Ulysses S. Grant had also dressed down for the occasion. During their brief meeting, Grant assigned Dodge to command a division in the Army of the Tennessee stationed at Corinth, Mississippi.[1] In the months ahead, Dodge rarely set foot on a major battlefield or participated directly in important campaigns, but that awkward moment on a railroad platform in Tennessee marked the beginning of an important partnership that bore fruit in the areas of army logistics and military intelligence, two essential yet less glamorous facets of warfare. This relationship between an Illinois store clerk and an Iowa railroad builder contributed significantly to Union victory in the West.

Born in Danvers, Massachusetts, on April 12, 1831, "Gren"

Dodge developed an early interest in military matters. He attended Norwich University, which was founded by a former commandant of the U.S. Military Academy at West Point, and graduated in 1851 with a degree in civil and military engineering. Choosing railroad building over soldiering, Dodge ventured to Illinois, Iowa, and Nebraska Territory as an engineer and surveyor with the Mississippi and Missouri Railroad. After battling Indians and constructing hundreds of miles of track, he settled in Council Bluffs, Iowa, became captain of the local militia, and wholeheartedly supported Republican efforts to build a transcontinental railroad, a project for which he stood to profit handsomely. When the Civil War erupted in 1861, his military-oriented education, militia experience, and prominent status in the community made him a candidate for command of one of Iowa's volunteer regiments. When he became colonel of the Fourth Iowa Infantry, a position procured mostly through political connections, Dodge thought little of railroading and only of leading men into battle, an activity better suited to winning the acclaim and glory he longed to attain.[2] Little did he know that rebuilding, repairing, and protecting railroad supply lines and gathering military intelligence—not his prowess as a combat commander would constitute his major contributions to the Union war effort.

At first, however, it appeared as if Colonel Dodge was destined to rise through the ranks as a fine combat officer. After brief service in 1861 as commander of the Union post at Rolla, Missouri, he transferred to a brigade command in Maj. Gen. Samuel R. Curtis's Army of the Southwest. At the battle of Pea Ridge in March 1862, Dodge's men performed admirably, repulsing several Confederate attacks and contributing much to the Union victory. Though slightly wounded, he handled his troops commendably and received accolades for his calm demeanor under fire. He was promoted to brigadier general for his actions at Pea Ridge, but his Civil War career soon veered away from the battlefield.[3]

While recuperating from his wound, Dodge learned that Congress was poised to pass the Pacific Railroad Act, which would lay the groundwork for construction of a transcontinental railroad. When the war had broken out in 1861, several of Dodge's business partners had urged him not to seek military command and instead to wait for opportunities to profit from the inevitable railroad expansion. "There must be money in this war some place," declared his friend Herbert M. Hoxie, "& we ought to have our share." Though refusing Hoxie's advice to "keep clear" of the army, Dodge agreed to resign his post if Congress passed the railroad bill.[4] He reneged on that promise, and instead of quitting the army to build the western railroad for profit, he remained in the service to rebuild Southern railroads for the Union.

In June 1862, Dodge received orders to reconstruct the Mobile and Ohio Railroad between Columbus, Kentucky, and Corinth, Mississippi.[5] This 150-mile span constituted a major supply line for Grant's army in northern Mississippi and West Tennessee and, because of its logistical importance, Confederate cavalry and guerrillas led by Nathan Bedford Forrest and William H. Jackson routinely tore up stretches of track, destroyed bridges, and preyed upon Union pickets and patrols. Repairing the damage left in their wake and protecting trestles, switches, and depots fell to Dodge. To accomplish both tasks he created a "pioneer corps," consisting of Wisconsin lumberjacks culled from the ranks, to rebuild the road while the remainder guarded vulnerable points along the line and served in construction battalions when needed.[6]

Perhaps the most inviting targets for Confederate raiders were the numerous railroad bridges spanning the rivers, creeks, marshes, and ravines found in the western sections of Kentucky and Tennessee and in northern Mississippi. Hindered by the persistent lack of cavalry, however, Dodge was forced to rely upon his slow-moving infantrymen to provide security. He first posted detachments at each bridge, but this method required more manpower than he had available. To compensate, Dodge, on his own initiative, began constructing enclosed block-houses near the trestles. Two stories high, made of heavy logs, and with a roof to shield soldiers from plunging fire from nearby heights, these fortifications permitted defenders to fire from protected positions at enemy soldiers approaching from any direction. According to Dodge, a company of men in a blockhouse could hold their own against a regiment, thereby reducing the number of troops required to protect the many railroad bridges. "It would have taken," he calculated, "a thousand men without block-houses protection for every hundred with it."[7] Only artillery, which few guerrillas and raiders had in tow, could overcome these stout defenses. Dodge did not invent the blockhouse concept, which had been in use since the colonial era and was recognized as a useful defensive technique by Dennis Hart Mahan in his 1836 treatise on fortifications, but he was one of the first to use them for defending railroad communication lines. Though the construction of blockhouses afforded better protection and saved some bridges from destruction, it did not solve the problem completely. Nevertheless, Dodge's enclosed blockhouses proved a significant development in protecting the army's logistical lifelines. Although an improviser himself, Grant failed to grasp the significance of this development until too late, perhaps because, as he admitted years later, fortification was "a branch of service that I have forgotten all about."[8] The Confederates soon reminded him of its importance.

After his meeting with Grant in Jackson in late October, Dodge left the Mobile and Ohio project for combat command at Corinth.[9] Meanwhile, Grant prepared for his next campaign. Already he had captured Forts Henry and Donelson, won a hard-fought victory at Shiloh, and fended off Confederate threats in northern Mississippi at Iuka and Corinth. By November he was poised to strike Vicksburg, Mississippi, the key Confederate bastion along the Mississippi River, using the Mississippi Central Railroad, his main line of supply, as the axis of advance. In his planning, however, he did not give the protection of his logistical lifelines high priority because, he reasoned, securing them would absorb precious manpower at a time when his whole army "was no more than was necessary to hold these lines, and hardly that if kept on the defensive." In order to avoid siphoning troops away from his offensive operations, he would rely heavily on a minimal number of garrison troops and mobile reserves to defend vulnerable sections. To Grant, penetrating deeper into Mississippi promised not only to bring Vicksburg within his grasp but also to reduce the threat to his supply lines. "By moving against the enemy and . . . driving their army before us," he reasoned, "these lines would nearly hold themselves."[10] In other words, a relentless advance on Vicksburg—not blockhouses and fortifications—offered the best means of securing his lines of communication. In September, Dodge was astonished to learn that blockhouses were not in general use along other rail lines in the region. By the commencement of Grant's offensive two months later, little had changed. Thus far, Dodge's use of blockhouses, which by then had proven effective, had failed to alter Grant's views.[11]

Confederate cavalry under Nathan Bedford Forrest and Earl Van Dorn soon revealed the flaws in Grant's thinking. In two simultaneous raids in December, Forrest and Van Dorn attacked Union supply lines in West Tennessee and Mississippi. Forrest burned railroad trestles, tore up miles of track along the Mobile and Ohio, and captured several depots and their garrisons between Jackson and Union City. Van Dorn descended on Grant's main supply base at Holly Springs, Mississippi, destroying or carrying away tons of supplies and seizing fifteen hundred prisoners. The damage inflicted on his communication lines, which took months to repair, and the loss of much-needed supplies forced him to abandon his drive on Vicksburg.[12] Besides scuttling the offensive, the Confederate attacks revealed much more. Before the raids, no earthworks or stockades protected Holly Springs, nor were orders issued to construct defenses at other posts. Moreover, no instructions were given to build protective fortifications anywhere along the Mississippi Central. In West Tennessee, the only sections of the railroads that survived the raids were those protected by Dodge's fortifications or those hastily constructed at the last minute.[13] As a testament to the value Grant placed—albeit belatedly—on Dodge's fortifications, six days after the raids he advised a commander in West Tennessee, "At all bridges the men should build blockhouses."[14] Although Grant soon abandoned many of the railroads in West Tennessee and northern Mississippi, opting instead to use the Mississippi River as the logistical lifeline for his next campaign against Vicksburg, he recognized and appreciated Dodge's ability to get the railroads running and to keep them that way. This appreciation manifested itself during the Chattanooga campaign a year later.

Dodge proved adept at protecting supply lines, but in spring 1863 he demonstrated a remarkable aptitude for destroying them as well. As Grant prepared for another attempt to capture Vicksburg, Dodge, in conjunction with Col. Abel D. Streight's ill-fated excursion through Alabama and Georgia, led an expedition up the Tuscumbia Valley in northern Alabama to disrupt the supply lines of Confederate general Braxton Bragg's army in Middle Tennessee. Federal troops destroyed huge quantities of corn, bacon, oats, and rye, torched several tanneries and cotton mills, smashed sixty flatboats and ferries on the Tennessee River, and demolished the railroad between Tuscumbia and Decatur. The raid, Dodge reported, "has rendered desolate one of the best granaries of the South."[15] This expedition against the enemy's source of supply was a harbinger of things to come, especially after Grant and William Tecumseh Sherman realized that starving enemy armies and showing Southern civilians the futility of continued resistance offered the best means of ending the war.

After Grant captured Vicksburg in July 1863, his attention soon focused on events in southeastern Tennessee, particularly the predicament facing Maj. Gen. William S. Rosecrans's Army of the Cumberland in Chattanooga. Stung by defeat at Chickamauga in September and besieged by Braxton Bragg's Confederates, Rosecrans faced a severe shortage of supplies and nerve. On October 23, Grant arrived in Chattanooga and realized that feeding the army demanded top priority. After replacing Rosecrans with Maj. Gen. George H. Thomas, Grant focused on logistics. First, he opened the famous "Cracker Line," which helped alleviate some of the suffering.[16] He then turned toward securing better rail connections with the large Federal base at Nashville. The Nashville and Chattanooga Railroad constituted the only operable rail link and, realizing that his massive supply needs would overburden the single track, Grant had to find another option. Remembering Holly Springs, he also hoped to secure his communications against Confederate raiders. Learning that Dodge, now leading a division in the Army of the Tennessee, accompanied Maj. Gen. William T. Sherman's forces rushing toward Chattanooga, Grant saw a solution to his supply problem. Recalling that the Iowan was "a most capable officer" as well as "an experienced railroad builder," on November 5, 1863, he ordered Dodge to halt his advance at Pulaski, Tennessee, and to rebuild the railroad between Nashville and Decatur, Alabama, a major connecting line to the Memphis and Charleston road that ran to Stevenson, Alabama. At Stevenson, the Memphis and Charleston joined the Nashville and Chattanooga, which then wound its way northeastward into Chattanooga. If successful, Dodge would provide Union forces in the town with two major lines of supply instead of one.[17]

Apparently, Grant appreciated Dodge's qualifications but not enough to let him proceed unsupervised at the outset. After ordering him to undertake the repairs of the Nashville and Decatur Railroad, Grant sent a staff officer, Col. George G. Pride, to act as "superintendent" of the project and "to take direction of the work." However, Pride never assumed this position due to a falling out with Grant, who remarked that he no longer had "any intention of ever having [Pride] at Head Quarters again." Dodge was again on his own.[18]

As in West Tennessee, he faced a daunting task. The rugged terrain and the many rivers, creeks, and deep valleys traversed by the railroads made repairs difficult. Raiders had burned nearly all the railroad bridges and had left many rails twisted like metal ribbons around trees. Many engines and much of the rolling stock had also been consigned to the flames. Confederate guerrillas and cavalry, estimated to number around one thousand men, still roamed the area. "The moment they see we intend to repair this railroad," Dodge predicted, "they will begin to burn." He also lacked appropriate tools for the job and, operating without a supply line of his own, had little hope of attaining them or meeting his other logistical needs. To make matters worse, he possessed neither an accurate map of the area nor a topographical engineer to produce one.[19]

Faced with seemingly insurmountable obstacles, Dodge improvised. Augmenting his eight thousand troops with black laborers impressed into service, he spread his men out to rebuild and, using blockhouses, to protect important sections of the line, including thirty major bridges. Mounted infantry provided more active protection, and these units fought several small engagements, including actions at Athens, Florence, and Gaines's Ferry. Dodge's men foraged for their subsistence, obviating the need for supply lines. Army blacksmiths, using confiscated forges, produced the necessary tools, and scores of soldiers wielding axes cut timber for bridges, railroad ties, and fuel for the engines. "No emergency could arise," Dodge wrote in his report, "but what some officer or man could be found to meet and master it." His self-sustaining operation proved successful. Within four months his men had rebuilt the 110 miles of the Nashville and Decatur Railroad and constructed 182 bridges of varying size.[20] Although the rail connection was not fully operational until after the Union victory at Chattanooga in late November, Dodge's improvisational feat proved important for future Federal operations, especially Sherman's Atlanta campaign. As Federal armies advanced toward this key Southern city in 1864, they depended on the railroads from Nashville for their logistical needs and, because of Dodge's defensive preparations, these lines survived numerous attacks. Moreover, as Sherman's engineers advanced with the troops, they followed Dodge's lead and constructed blockhouses at all bridges and stations.[21]

Historians have lauded Dodge's accomplishments during the Chattanooga campaign. George Edgar Turner has proclaimed that his success demonstrated that Grant "had found a Haupt of his own," a reference to Herman Haupt, the highly skilled and resourceful engineer on the U.S. military railroads in Virginia. Highlighting the important yet unheralded role of those individuals involved in logistics, Steven E. Woodworth has argued that Dodge contributed "significantly to the

Federal effort around Chattanooga without ever appearing on the battlefield."[22] More important, Dodge won the admiration of Grant. In
1864 he not only pushed Dodge's promotion for major general but also
referred to him in correspondence as "a gallant and superior officer."
Years later Grant wrote as if still awed by Dodge's improvisational
skills and his ability to keep the armies' haversacks and cartridge boxes
full, although he credited him with completing the task in forty days
when, in fact, the Nashville and Decatur was not declared open until
nearly four months after the work had begun.[23]

By late 1863 Grant recognized and valued Dodge's railroad construction expertise. But that was not all. When he spoke of his subordinate as being "a gallant and superior officer" and that "I know no officer whos [sic] judgement I would more readily endorse than that of
Gen. Dodge," he was referring not just to Dodge's combat record and
his engineering skill. He also had in mind Dodge's tenure as an intelligence officer. When the terms "intelligence," "secret service," or
"spies" are used with reference to the Civil War, the names Belle
Boyd, Rose O'Neal Greenhow, and Allan Pinkerton—not that of Grenville M. Dodge—spring to mind. But from November 1862 until July
1863 Dodge oversaw the largest intelligence operation the war had yet
seen, earning him even more renown among those who profited from
it. Chief among those beneficiaries was Ulysses S. Grant.

When Dodge moved from building railroads to commanding a division in October 1862, his career was soon to take an interesting turn.
By this time he had proven himself to be an able combat officer and a
competent engineer. The months spent rebuilding the railroad in West
Tennessee, however, had only stoked his desire to return to the battlefield. "I prefer to go to Grant," he informed his wife, "take a fighting
division, and take my chances." Once he commanded troops in Corinth,
a crucial rail junction, supply center, and staging area for future campaigns, Dodge's wish had apparently come true. And since Grant was,
at that moment, preparing his first campaign against Vicksburg, the
next battles promised to be important. "I ache to get in this fight,"
Dodge wrote. In the end, he played an important role in the coming
campaigns against Vicksburg, but one far different from what he had
imagined.[24]

Shortly after arriving in Corinth, Dodge received word that Grant
indeed wanted him to take the field in the upcoming campaign and that
Maj. Gen. Lew Wallace would relieve him there. However, a change in

Wallace's orders scuttled those plans, and Dodge remained in Corinth.[25] As Dodge waited in vain for relief, the arrival of several unexpected visitors at his headquarters altered the course of his career under Grant's command. On November 12, 1862, three spies, employed by Maj. Gen. William S. Rosecrans, who had recently departed Corinth to take command of the Army of the Cumberland, arrived with startling news that Confederate troops detached from Braxton Bragg's Army of the Tennessee, at that time operating outside Nashville, were en route to northern Mississippi. Realizing the importance of this intelligence, Dodge forwarded a summary to Grant's headquarters.[26] The report seemed to confirm one of Grant's major concerns: that Bragg would dispatch reinforcements from Middle Tennessee to defend Vicksburg or to attack his outposts in northern Mississippi. To ensure that any attempt to transfer Southern troops to Mississippi would be detected, Grant wired Dodge on November 18 and asked for help: "Can you get information from the East, say as far as Florence [Alabama]? I want to hear from along the Tennessee [River] from Tuscumbia eastward to know if any rebel troops are crossing there." A few days later, John A. Rawlins, Grant's chief of staff, elaborated on these orders, instructing Dodge to "send out spies and scouts [to the] east and obtain all information possible."[27] Interpreting these instructions to mean that he had "carte blanche to take care of that front," Dodge created a secret service organization more elaborate and extensive than Grant expected or intended.[28] Although he sent spies and scouts as far as Mobile and Atlanta, his primary responsibility was to watch the eastern flank of Grant's department, especially the Tennessee River, for Confederate reinforcements coming from Middle Tennessee.[29]

Although no evidence suggests that Grant knew of it, Dodge had had prior experience with intelligence operations. While stationed at Rolla, Missouri, in late 1861, he became involved, somewhat by accident, in "secret service" activities, a euphemism of the time for anything related to information collection and counterintelligence. Maj. Gen. John C. Frémont, then in command of the Western Department, had repeatedly sent Dodge reports about enemy movements near Rolla and ordered him to verify them. For several weeks, Dodge's cavalry wore itself out chasing these rumors, which were often proved false. Finally, a cavalry officer approached him with an idea: "I have plenty of men in my company," stated the officer, "[that] I can send out to everyone [sic] of these places and keep them there, or they can go from here and ascertain the truth." Intrigued, Dodge began recruiting spies, usually Unionists who lived in strategic locations outside his lines, to monitor Confederate movements, and he sent scouts, mostly Union soldiers recruited from the ranks, into enemy lines to gather information. "Their reports soon came in," Dodge later wrote, "and were forwarded to head-quarters, where it became known that the reports received from me were accurate."[30] At the battle of Pea Ridge, Dodge's intelligence system paid off. The day before the battle, one of his scouts informed Maj. Gen. Samuel L. Curtis, who did not expect a Confederate attack and whose forces were not yet concentrated, that the enemy approached and intended to fight. This news, corroborated by other sources, gave Curtis time to prepare for the onslaught and avert a surprise. Pea Ridge ended in a Union victory and, according to Dodge, "this information saved us."[31] Though he claims too much for his scout, who brought in only one of several reports indicating the Confederates' rapid advance, Dodge had proven that he knew how to get information on the enemy.[32]

As Grant embarked on his first attempt to capture Vicksburg in late November 1862, Dodge remained behind but was elevated to command the entire District of Corinth. Though disappointed about missing the upcoming campaign, he knew that Grant needed him where he was. Brig. Gen. Marcellus Crocker told him that, during a conversation with Grant, the general remarked that Dodge was "a good man for any place but he could not be spared from Corinth." Grant later confessed that he was "peculiarly fitted" for his new command due to his prewar experience on the frontier. He knew how to improvise in emergencies and always "acted promptly without waiting for orders," both of which were essential qualities for Dodge's unique mission.[33]

Confident that he could make important contributions to the campaign even from a distance, over the next few months Dodge created an intelligence organization that stretched from Corinth to Atlanta and into the interiors of Mississippi, Alabama, and Tennessee. From an original nucleus of eleven operatives, mostly remnants of Rosecrans's old secret service, Dodge's corps of scouts and spies burgeoned to over one hundred thirty operatives by late 1863, although only two dozen or so were on his payroll during any one month. Scouts regularly ventured from Corinth into enemy lines to monitor troop movements while spies stayed in Confederate territory and sent periodic reports to Corinth by messenger. Dodge employed at least fourteen key spies, or what he called "principal outside scouts," on a regular basis. They lived in or traveled to Vicksburg, Meridian, Selma, Mobile, Chattanooga, and Atlanta. Until October 1863, when a change of command in Corinth forced the issue, Dodge refused to reveal their names for fear their identities would become known in the South and compromise his operations, not to mention costing his agents their lives.[34] The First Alabama Cavalry (Union), formed by Dodge in fall 1862 from Unionists in northern Alabama and commanded by his chief of staff, Col. George E. Spencer, became a source for scouts and spies, producing at least twenty-two secret service recruits. "These mountain men were fearless and would take all chances," claimed Dodge, making them perfect candidates for espionage duty. Moreover, their families, many of whom remained behind Confederate lines, were also valuable sources of information. From November 1862 though July 1863, Dodge's scouts and spies completed over two hundred missions and traveled thousands of miles.[35]

Grant placed great value on Dodge's operations and defended his subordinate against attempts by other senior Union officers to control or compromise them. In early January 1863, Dodge learned that his post quartermaster could no longer provide adequate funds to pay his scouts and spies. Moreover, the quartermaster, citing army regulations, also refused to remunerate any personnel who failed to sign a voucher, which contained the name, the nature of the service, and the amount each spy or scout received in compensation. Dodge refused to allow this, arguing, "There are citizens living in the South who give me the most valuable information [who] will not sign a voucher for fear of consequences in the future." If a person living in the South spied for the Federal army and then signed a voucher—a far from confidential document—he or she risked having the nature of the service revealed, which could lead to all manner of threats and violent retribution from fellow Southerners, both during and after the war.[36] Alabama Unionist William Hugh Smith, who escaped to Union lines in 1862 and then spied for Dodge, provides an example of the past coming back to haunt a former secret service employee. Before becoming a "scalawag" governor of Alabama during Reconstruction, Smith served as a circuit court judge. However, his judicial career took a nasty turn when lawyers arguing cases before him uttered "insulting phrases concerning his war record." The abuse became unbearable, and Smith resigned.[37] Knowing that secret service recruitment, not to mention the effectiveness of his current operatives, would suffer if word spread that the army would not protect their anonymity, Dodge seized control over the money and disbursements from his quartermaster and kept the records himself. He also began selling confiscated cotton and using the proceeds for secret service. When the matter reached Grant's desk, he made no effort to reverse his subordinate's action.[38]

Paying secret service personnel also represented a vexing problem, especially since scouts and spies took enormous risks and expected to be compensated well in return. "I have collected a corps of rather efficient men," Dodge wrote in January, "[but] unless I can have funds to use I cannot hold them together." In response, Grant ordered that the revenue generated from the sale of trade permits, which allowed the buyer to traffic in cotton within the department for a fee of one hundred dollars, be collected by the department provost marshal, Col. William S. Hillyer, and deposited in a "secret service" account in Memphis. Following Dodge's lead, he later expanded the sources of revenue to include money procured from the sale of cotton and other property confiscated from secessionists.[39] Grant even allowed one district commander to supplement his secret service budget with an eight thousand dollar "assessment" levied on Southern civilians who had the misfortune of living near a Union depot raided by the enemy. As Dodge's network grew to meet Grant's intelligence needs, he needed every penny he could find. In March alone, he required nearly five thousand dollars to cover his secret service expenses.[40]

Not everyone, however, approved of this unconventional arrangement. The first objection came from Dodge's immediate superior in Memphis, Maj. Gen. Stephen Hurlbut. In early March 1863, Dodge had exhausted his secret service funds and asked Hillyer for five thousand dollars from the account in Memphis. As Grant was busy preparing for his next campaign against Vicksburg, Hillyer forwarded the request to Hurlbut. Seeing that Dodge had recently received a large amount from the Memphis secret service fund, Hurlbut grew suspicious. He instructed Hillyer to suspend payment until Dodge could justify to whom and for what purposes he had disbursed his previous allotment. Dodge refused, claiming that not even the commanding general possessed that sort of information and had never asked for it. When the matter reached Grant, he immediately sided with Dodge, thereby protecting the anonymity of operatives and maintaining the effectiveness of his intelligence network.[41]

The second objection came from Washington. In the midst of the Vicksburg campaign, Hillyer, testifying before a military commission investigating cotton sales on the Mississippi, stated that Dodge possessed large amounts of money for secret service. When asked to whom he reported his disbursements, Hillyer replied that he did not know. "The court seemed to put some stress on this point," he warned Grant, and advised him to issue an order requiring that all officers receiving secret service funds "report to you what they have done with it." Grant managed to avoid further inquiries from the commission without issuing this order, thereby allowing Dodge to continue as before, trusting in him to be faithful in his use of government money.[42] And this trust was no small matter. Between November 1862 and July 1863, Dodge expended over twenty-one thousand dollars on secret service, and Grant never knew where one penny of it went.[43] Although he never knew the true extent of Dodge's operations, both episodes demonstrate that he understood not only the essential role of intelligence but also that in Dodge he had found the right man to oversee its collection.

Perhaps the best evidence of the value of Dodge's intelligence network is the impact it had on Grant's operations. Three significant examples, all from Grant's successful campaign against Vicksburg in 1863, demonstrate that his confidence in Dodge was not misplaced. The first incident occurred a few weeks before Grant crossed the Mississippi River and landed below Vicksburg, the first step in a remarkable campaign that ended in Union victory. Before the Federals embarked, however, reliable information about Vicksburg remained scarce. To rectify this, Grant ordered Dodge to send one of his agents into the city for information. He selected W. I. Morris, who returned to Corinth on April 13 after spending several days in Vicksburg. Morris reported that the enemy faced serious supply shortages and that the garrison, numbering around twenty-five thousand men, was stretched from Grand Gulf on the Mississippi north to Greenwood on the Yazoo River. Moreover, he indicated that the Confederates had formidable defenses east of town, consisting of miles of fortifications several lines deep. "Every Hill and ridge has a work upon it," he claimed. However, Morris noted that the Confederates apparently had little fear of an attack by land from the east. Most of their big guns were posted in the defenses along the Mississippi and Yazoo Rivers north of town, where their front was "very firm."[44] This news demonstrated that the Steele's

Bayou and Yazoo Pass expeditions, which had earlier failed to find an avenue of approach north of Vicksburg, had at least "tended to confuse and mislead" the enemy as to Grant's true plan.[45] The failure of the earlier expeditions had convinced Grant finally to abandon an advance from the north and instead land south of Vicksburg and attack the defenses in the rear of the city; Morris's intelligence indicated that he was poised to strike where the enemy expected it least.[46]

The second episode occurred in April when Dodge sent his chief of staff (and later commander of the First Alabama Cavalry) Col. George E. Spencer into enemy lines toward Tuscumbia, Alabama. Spencer was not officially on the secret service payroll but had developed an innovative method for penetrating Confederate security and gaining information. Approaching enemy lines under a flag of truce, Spencer would tell pickets he carried important dispatches concerning, for example, prisoner exchanges, and they would forward him under escort to their commanders. As Spencer rode through enemy camps he counted regiments, wagons, and artillery pieces and constructed an order of battle. Though claiming he made these trips "more for amusement than anything else," the future Reconstruction senator from Alabama provided a valuable service. On this occasion, Spencer went under flag of truce to Tuscumbia, traveling through Confederate forces in the area. He learned the composition of the enemy forces in the Tuscumbia Valley, brought back several Southern newspapers, and provided evidence that the Confederates had been reinforced. This information proved valuable for Dodge's upcoming raid in the Tuscumbia Valley, during which he scattered Confederate forces, disrupted Bragg's supply lines, and "rendered useless the garden spot of Alabama for at least one year."[47]

The final case in point occurred after Union forces had crossed the Mississippi, won several victories below Vicksburg, and captured Jackson, Mississippi. At that moment, Grant remained unsure whether the Vicksburg garrison, commanded by Gen. John C. Pemberton, would venture out of its fortifications to attack his scattered army. He knew that Gen. Joseph E. Johnston's "Army of Relief," which the Federals had just expelled from Jackson, posed a significant threat, especially if it acted in concert with the Vicksburg forces to trap the Union army. Early on May 16, Grant finally gained a better grasp on the situation. As luck would have it, a spy known only as Sanborn, whom Dodge had sent to watch Johnston's army, arrived with important news.[48] According to Dodge, Sanborn reported Johnston's position and strength, indicating that Grant could defeat Pemberton long before the Army of Relief could come to his aid. Armed with this information, supplemented by intelligence on Pemberton's situation that arrived the same morning, Grant moved aggressively to engage the Vicksburg commander.[49] Sanborn's intelligence proved correct. At the battle of Champion Hill later that day Pemberton fought alone and Grant won a stunning victory. Pemberton's army retreated, met defeat again on the Big Black River, and finally filed back into the Vicksburg defenses. Though Pemberton's men waited anxiously, Johnston never came. In fact, Dodge's scouts and spies continued to monitor Johnston's movements during the remainder of the campaign, allowing Grant to sustain siege operations while protecting his rear from the Army of Relief.[50] On July 4, 1863, after nearly two months under siege, Vicksburg surrendered. This important Union victory had many authors, not the least of whom was Grenville Dodge.

Aside from these more prominent contributions, Dodge also provided less visible yet extremely valuable services to Grant during the campaign. Through spies and scouts posted on the Tennessee River and along other likely avenues of approach, he monitored Confederate troop movements in Tennessee and northern Mississippi and alerted Grant to dangers lurking in his rear. Dodge spent much of his time sorting through daily intelligence reports, interviewing deserters, refugees, and local civilians, examining captured mail, searching enemy newspapers for bits of news, sending cavalry after guerrillas, and dispatching operatives to places like Bear Creek and Okalona.[51] But Grant knew the value of these rather mundane activities and understood that his own operations against Vicksburg succeeded, in no small measure, because of them. "Gen. Dodge," he wrote in June 1863, "is one of the most valuable officers we have."[52]

By spring 1864, Dodge had risen in prominence within the Army of the Tennessee as a result of his unique service. With his name at the top of Grant's recommendation list, on June 7, 1864, Dodge received his second star and was assigned to command the left wing of Maj. Gen. James B. McPherson's Sixteenth Corps for the upcoming Atlanta campaign.[53] Severely wounded outside Atlanta, he returned to Iowa to convalesce. When he returned to duty, Grant selected him to head the Department of the Missouri, which later included the Department of Kansas, where he once again used his intelligence collection skills tracking guerrillas and Indians. He also became forever associated with the Old West when one of the most notorious cowboy towns in Kansas chose Dodge City as its name.[54] Even after the war, Grant thought well of his former subordinate from Iowa. In 1869, Secretary of War John A. Rawlins, who was terminally ill, recommended Dodge, by then a former congressman, as his successor. However, Dodge's affiliation with the Union Pacific Railroad, a potential conflict of interest given the railroad's numerous dealings with the War Department, compelled Grant to appoint William H. Belknap instead.[55] Despite this disappointment, Dodge remained a loyal admirer of his former commander and deeply mourned his death in 1885.

Whether fighting the war of spies or supplies, Dodge contributed much to Union success in the West. Though gaining few laurels in combat, he achieved prominence within the Army of the Tennessee because Grant understood the importance of maintaining logistical lines and gathering intelligence and held in high esteem officers who performed these tasks well. Moreover, success in this war demanded improvisation, and Grant, being one of the foremost practitioners of the art, saw in Dodge a kindred spirit. From blockhouses and bridges to supply lines and spies, Grenville Dodge left an indelible imprint on the war, though he set foot on few battlefields. Perhaps Grant's comment in late 1862 best captures the essence of the Iowan's unique and vital service to the Union during the Civil War: "You have a much more important command," he told Dodge, "than that of a division in the field."[56]

Grant's Ethnic General

Peter J. Osterhaus

ᘿ *Earl J. Hess*

Peter Joseph Osterhaus was the only immigrant to serve as a division commander in Ulysses S. Grant's army by the midpoint of the war. Indeed, there were only three ethnic officers who served as brigade commanders in any field armies Grant commanded during the period 1861 through 1863. Unlike other generals, Grant had relatively few immigrant officers or regiments to work with during the first half of the war. Most of the thoroughly ethnic units in his army during the Vicksburg campaign came from the Army of the Southwest, which had conducted the campaign and battle of Pea Ridge in the early months of 1862. These units were recruited mainly from the ethnic population of St. Louis and represented one-third of the infantry and cavalry regiments, and half of the artillery batteries, of that field army. In contrast, Grant's Army of the Tennessee at Vicksburg could count only about 3 percent of its infantry and cavalry regiments and about 10 percent of its artillery batteries as distinctively ethnic units.[1]

Osterhaus was part of Grant's ethnic inheritance from the Army of the Southwest when the units of that disbanded field force were incorporated into his growing army in December 1862. Grant displayed a remarkable tolerance for the ethnic soldiers of his command. In other armies, these immigrants often caused a great deal of political trouble that flowed over into military matters. They often used their ties to the ethnic community to further their own careers or to garner more publicity for their regiments than was justified. Grant was relatively free of such troubles, and therefore he treated his ethnic officers as he treated his native-born subordinates. Osterhaus epitomized the ethnic officer who refused to use his heritage as leverage to promote his career. He was an able commander on the regimental, brigade, and division levels, and he came into his own during the Vicksburg campaign, reaching new heights of leadership. Grant relied heavily on him to command troops to his rear at the Big Black River while most of his army was laying siege to the Confederates inside Vicksburg. Osterhaus offered a stark contrast to officers like Franz Sigel, his former mentor, who created ethnic dissension in their self-centered efforts to use ethnicity as a political weapon for promotion.

Osterhaus was born on January 4, 1823, in Coblenz, Westphalia. He received a good civil education and entered the coal business as a merchant. He was subject to Prussian law because that east German state controlled the Rhineland, following the defeat of Napoleon. He served one year in a Jaeger battalion, a specially organized unit armed with rifles, to satisfy his compulsory military service to the king of Prussia. Osterhaus learned a great deal about military life and decided to serve in the Landwehr, the Prussian reserve, after his Jaeger tour of duty ended. He was commissioned an officer and attended the compulsory two-week training period every year.[2]

Osterhaus was not a Prussian and he did not receive a Prussian military education, as some historians have erroneously asserted. Instead, he was a progressive west German who sympathized with the revolutionary movement that swept across the German states in 1848 and 1849. He offered his services to the Baden revolutionaries and was put in command of the post of Mannheim. He apparently missed the fighting when Prussian troops crushed the Baden uprising, escaping to France and sailing to the United States to settle in the small German community in Belleville, Illinois. His wife and baby soon joined him there, just across the Mississippi River from the much larger city of St. Louis.

Osterhaus spent the years preceding the outbreak of the Civil War making an obscure living for his family in the retail business. He moved to St. Louis in 1860 and immediately joined the army when the firing on Fort Sumter spurred Lincoln to issue a call for troops. The German Americans filled several three-month regiments under the command of Brig. Gen. Nathaniel Lyon. Captain Osterhaus intensely drilled his command, Company B, Second Missouri Infantry, in both English and German. Soon he was elected major of the regiment.

Osterhaus took part in the capture of the pro-Confederate Missouri State Militia at Camp Jackson on May 10, 1861. He next participated in Lyon's Missouri campaign, which resulted in the occupation of the state capital of Jefferson City and Federal control of the Missouri River Valley. Osterhaus saw his first combat when Lyon fought a skirmish with the Missouri State Guard, another prosecessionist force commanded by Maj. Gen. Sterling Price, near Boonville on June 17. He led the two rifle companies of the Second Missouri to skirmish with the State-Guardsmen and performed admirably under fire. He later performed magnificently in the battle of Wilson's Creek on August 10, securing Lyon's right flank on Bloody Hill and repelling repeated Confederate attempts to outflank the Union line. Then he took his battalion of the Second Missouri to support artillery in the center. His men also helped to cover the Federal retreat from Bloody Hill after Lyon's death.

After Wilson's Creek, where Osterhaus gained his first major notice in the press and among the high command in Missouri, he recruited the Twelfth Missouri Infantry for three years' service. His short tenure as colonel instilled a high level of drill and discipline in this mostly German regiment. He then commanded a brigade in Maj. Gen. John C. Frémont's Missouri campaign. Moreover, he displayed admirable political sense when he refused to join his fellow immigrant officers in denouncing the Lincoln administration for relieving Frémont of his command in November because of his dilatory movements and corrupt administration. Osterhaus preferred to take no sides in the controversy.

He was given command of a division when the army retired to Rolla, Missouri. Once again he refused to speak out when another ethnic controversy developed in late December 1861. Brig. Gen. Franz Sigel resigned his command to protest the appointment of Brig. Gen. Samuel Ryan Curtis to lead the newly fashioned Army of the Southwest. Though German partisans all across the North supported Sigel, who nevertheless withdrew his resignation to become Curtis's second in command, Osterhaus remained silent so as not to antagonize anyone in this ethnically divided field army. He later accurately said that in political and public life he was "an utterly unknown person—homo novus." Yet he had the common sense not to make enemies, and he also was of a naturally modest character.

The major themes of Osterhaus's early life and war career were taking shape as the Pea Ridge campaign began. He avoided playing the political game but relied instead on solid achievements in the field to bring him fame and promotion. Commanding one of the four divisions in Curtis's army while also exercising command of one of its two brigades, Osterhaus played a major role in the Union victory. Curtis bloodlessly recaptured Springfield and pursued Price's state guard into northwestern Arkansas. When Price and Gen. Ben McCulloch, under

Maj. Gen. Earl Van Dorn's overall command, counterattacked near
Elkhorn Tavern on March 7, 1862, Curtis relied on Osterhaus to lead a
mixed force of infantry, cavalry, and artillery to the area of Leetown,
a small village to the right rear of the army, to determine the location
of the enemy, who had completely outflanked Curtis. Osterhaus performed extremely well in deploying his outnumbered force to halt
McCulloch's advance, force him to deploy his division, and engage in
battle long before the Confederates struck Curtis's rear. Federal reinforcements and the death of McCulloch and his successor led to a
smashing Union victory at Leetown. The next day Osterhaus was instrumental in selecting the most advantageous ground on which to deploy Sigel's wing of the army as it concentrated with the other wing
south of Elkhorn Tavern to conduct the final attack on Van Dorn's
army.

Pea Ridge brought Osterhaus the promotion he deserved. He had
been mentioned for a general's commission by Frémont following the
battle of Wilson's Creek, but no serious move was made on his behalf
until Curtis formally recommended it after Pea Ridge. Still, Osterhaus
had no political pull, and the recommendation languished in the Senate
for several months before he was made a brigadier general of volunteers on June 9, 1862.

Following Pea Ridge, Osterhaus took a leading role in Curtis's
march across Arkansas through the Ozark Mountains, the army resting
at Batesville. Curtis advanced Osterhaus's division about halfway from
Batesville to Little Rock, halting him near Searcy on the Little Red
River by May 10. For nearly a month Osterhaus commanded the forward outpost of the army, unable to move on to the state capital because of Curtis's overextended supply line from Rolla. He performed
his duties admirably, building a bridge over the stream with lumber he
had milled at a local sawmill, sending patrols up and down the Little
Red to cover his flanks, and dispatching foraging expeditions into the
countryside south of the river as food grew more scarce in the region.
His men engaged in several sharp skirmishes with the Confederates.[3]

Osterhaus evacuated his forward position on June 3 and returned
to Batesville when Curtis decided to move eastward to the Mississippi
River. The march "was a tough piece of work," Osterhaus later remembered; "it led through the dismal Cane brakes and swamps thickly set
with cypress trees of the River Cache and other sluggish watercourses;
there were no buildings or Roads, and torrentlike rainstorms impeded

our progress." He complained of malarial symptoms and of diarrhea for the first time in his life. The army reached Helena on the Mississippi on July 12.[4]

The German was forced to go to his St. Louis home on sick leave twice, on July 16 and August 30, with only a two-week stay on duty in Helena in between. He grew thinner and a bit debilitated. At one point he needed assistance to walk, and he began to take quinine frequently. Yet the stubborn general returned to Helena to resume command of his division on October 2. Five days later, the troops there embarked on steamboats and headed upriver on the erroneous report that southeastern Missouri was to be invaded by Confederate troops. His health already fragile, the strain of this move drove Osterhaus to bed. He suffered from diarrhea and pleurisy on the river and was ordered by his surgeon to go home when the division reached St. Genevieve. For the first time in his career, he was absent from his command while it was on an active campaign. The troops made a futile move to Ironton before they returned to the river and sailed back to Helena.[5]

Osterhaus recuperated in bed from mid-October to December 21 and finally felt able to return to the field by the Christmas season. Curtis, now commander of all troops in the Missouri Department, assumed he would "desire his German troops" and tried to arrange it, but the old division had already embarked for Maj. Gen. William T. Sherman's strike for Vicksburg. His Germans also wanted Osterhaus to return and lead them, but the division set off on the Chickasaw Bayou campaign before he was well enough to join it. Osterhaus left St. Louis on December 31 and was given a new command, that of the Second Division of Brig. Gen. George W. Morgan's Thirteenth Corps.[6]

Osterhaus approached his new assignment with nervous trepidation; it posed a new set of challenges for him. For the first time he would come under the scrutiny of Grant and participate in a larger and more important campaign. His new division was bigger than any previous command he had held; the small divisions of the now-defunct Army of the Southwest could not compare with it. The Second Division was divided into three infantry brigades, with a total of ten regiments from Illinois, Indiana, Kentucky, and Ohio. It also had three battalions of Missouri and Illinois cavalry and two batteries of Michigan and Wisconsin artillery. In contrast, his division at Pea Ridge had had only five infantry regiments and two batteries. None of the units in this new command was predominantly German. Osterhaus was now an ethnic commander of American troops and the only immigrant general among Grant's division leaders.[7]

For the rest of his life Osterhaus would remember his first meeting with Grant. When he reached Grant's headquarters in Memphis sometime shortly after January 1, the commanding general "greeted me gruffly with a word. He was smoking the eternal cigar. I told him I was glad to be distinguished by the change [of command], but that I feared the result might not be very happy. I was a German and my [division] was no [division] of German soldiers. I thought, I told him, that they had had so much hard luck that they might think their getting a German general was the last straw." Grant listened patiently to this unsolicited confession, but he was unmoved. With a load of work to do and no reason to doubt Osterhaus's competence, he simply told the German, "Now you will go and take charge of your [division]."[8]

Osterhaus continued down the Mississippi and met his new command on its way up from the battlefield at Chickasaw Bayou, some time between January 2 and 6. Immediately, orders were issued by Maj. Gen. John A. McClernand, who also had just arrived to take charge of the expedition, to attack Arkansas Post up the Arkansas River. Osterhaus turned in the same kind of solid, intelligent leadership in this campaign that he had previously displayed at Pea Ridge. His division held the extreme left of the Union line as it deployed opposite the Confederate fort; his own left rested on the bank of the river. Osterhaus's greatest contribution to the quick reduction of this stronghold was his direction of the artillery. He thoroughly scouted the terrain and personally sited the location for Capt. Jacob T. Foster's First Wisconsin Battery, which was armed with twenty-pounder Parrotts. He also ordered the men to cut brush and pile it up in front of the guns to shield them from enemy view. At noon on January 11, the army opened fire. Osterhaus was greatly impressed by the performance of the twenty-pounders, for this was the first time he had seen them in action. They pounded the northeastern bastion of the fort at the short range of eight hundred yards, silenced one Confederate sixty-four pounder in the casemate of the fort, and silenced another sixty-four pounder mounted en barbette that was harassing the gunboats bombarding the post. After two hours of firing, the German advanced a battery of six-pounders to within two hundred yards of the outlying rebel trenches. There, supported by two infantry regiments, the light guns softened up the Confederate infantry position, but Osterhaus could not push his foot soldiers through because of a deep gully that lay in the way. The Confederates gave up at 4:00 P.M. Other division commanders had been just as aggressive as Osterhaus, but none of them had so effectively used his artillery as the German. McClernand praised him, along with several others, as displaying "the fitting qualities of brave and successful officers."[9]

The success of the Arkansas Post expedition raised the division's opinion of their new German commander. The gunners especially thought well of him because he paid so much attention to their work and praised them after the firing ended. "You have done more good than all the gunboats," he told the artillerymen. Osterhaus assured them that he "had seen artillery practice in the old country and in this, but that was the most accurate he ever saw." The infantry also "cheered themselves hoarse for this was our first victory and we had allmost become discouraged."[10]

Osterhaus further contributed to their morale after the army reembarked on transports on January 13. He was appalled by the living conditions on the boats, finding them in a "lamentably filthy condition." The transports had been the army's home for a month, with only a few brief stays on land during the two campaigns. They were filled with trash, human waste, bedbugs, and lice, and the men were ill with diarrhea and other complaints. Some of the boats were so crowded that the men had no room to lie down for proper sleep, and the lower decks were packed with horses and mules, which at times seemed to be cleaner than the men themselves. The surgeon of the Twenty-second Kentucky lamented that the "fetid and poisonous" air on board the steamers was "enough to make robust men sick." Osterhaus ordered the soldiers to bathe in the river, and he remembered how loudly they shouted when given the opportunity to clean up. "I never heard a complaint after that that their commander was a foreigner," he recalled with pride.[11]

Grant arrived from Memphis soon after the Arkansas Post expedition and assumed command of the army. Reorganization followed, with the assignment of McClernand to command the Thirteenth Corps and a reshuffling of Osterhaus's division so that it had two instead of three brigades. His command also was redesignated the Ninth Division of the Thirteenth Corps.[12]

After what seemed to be a long and tedious voyage, the division landed at Milliken's Bend on January 21 but immediately received orders to steam on to Young's Point, reaching there later that night. Osterhaus's men remained there until the rising waters of the Mississippi forced them to return to Milliken's Bend on March 2. They did not participate in Grant's efforts to dig a canal to bypass Vicksburg or to open an alternative approach to the bluffs on the east side of the river. But Osterhaus and his men did have to battle disease throughout the months of February and March. The campsite at Young's Point was on sandy soil that clung to the men's feet every time they left their tents, and even though the Milliken's Bend campsite was higher and drier, it was situated on a narrow levee. The winter weather was mostly "wet, gloomy, cold, and disagreeable," according to surgeon Benjamin Franklin Stevenson. Sickness became rampant, and the hospitals filled to overflowing. Dysentery and scurvy were common complaints as demoralization set in. These were, according to a soldier in the Sixty-ninth Indiana, "the dark days of the war."[13]

Osterhaus's health continued to suffer in this environment. He took a great deal of medicine that winter and wrote plaintively about the conditions on the Mississippi. The flat bottomland was covered with "extensive sheets of water," forcing the troops to confine themselves to the levees, where there was hardly enough room for tents, hospitals, corrals, and everything else the army needed. The dead were also buried on these levees, and often lost again. "It was most melancholy to see from the Camps on the Levee Coffins with departed Comrades, floating by; the swollen stream had torn from the levees a part of the ground reserved for a cemetery, and carried the remains to a watery grave. But such is War."[14]

Despite this, Osterhaus's reputation among his superiors was secured. When McClernand was asked to assign Brig. Gen. Charles Hamilton to his command, he protested that his two division commanders had proven their worth in the field and had "gained the confidence of their men." He did not want to replace Osterhaus or Brig. Gen. Andrew J. Smith. Grant replied that he had no intention of losing either commander and found another way to place Hamilton in a useful position.[15]

Osterhaus played a leading role in exploring a route for Grant's army around Vicksburg through the watery bottomlands of Louisiana. In late March he was ordered to push southward from Milliken's Bend toward Richmond, which his vanguard captured after a brief skirmish with Confederate cavalry. His men built a bridge over Roundaway Bayou with logs taken from local buildings and pushed on to Smith's Plantation on Bayou Vidal.

This place was two miles north of New Carthage, the first spot south of Vicksburg where Grant could contact his supporting transports and gunboats; but further reconnaissance proved that the town was isolated by the floodwaters of the Mississippi. On April 4, Osterhaus, McClernand, and members of their staffs personally scouted along the levee bordering Bayou Vidal, crossing two breaks on a skiff. Osterhaus lost his nerve at one of these crevasses and tried to climb out of the unsteady boat but instead fell into the cold, rushing water. Back on dry ground, though thoroughly wet himself, he pressed on with the group until they reached the third crevasse, within sight of New Carthage. While the group peered into the waterlogged town, Confederate skirmishers opened fire on them, and Osterhaus grabbed McClernand, both to save him from the bullets and to prevent him from falling into the water. "Damn you, stand fire," McClernand yelled at everyone, mistakenly thinking they were about to beat an undignified retreat; "don't you run, stand fire, damn you." This caused everyone to laugh. After a short skirmish, the group returned to Smith's Plantation.[16]

It was not possible to use New Carthage as an embarkation point, yet Osterhaus was instructed to occupy the town to prevent the Confederates from using it to interfere with river traffic. He sent a detachment to seize it, stationing them on the nearby James's Plantation, whose slightly higher ground commanded the town. Joshua James was a staunch rebel with four sons in the Southern army, and Osterhaus could not resist teasing him while he was there. The Confederates attacked Osterhaus's outpost on April 8 and 15 but were repulsed.[17]

Grant opened an alternate route to bypass Bayou Vidal that connected Smith's Plantation with Judge John Perkins's Plantation, a short distance downriver from New Carthage. He also ran gunboats and empty transports past the Vicksburg batteries on the night of April 16 and boarded Osterhaus's division, along with other Thirteenth Corps troops, to support Rear Adm. David D. Porter's attack on Grand Gulf, a Confederate stronghold on the east bank of the river. However, on April 29 Porter's gunboats failed to reduce the rebel batteries there, forcing Grant to use a route already explored by Osterhaus. Grant had asked that Osterhaus personally undertake this important job five days before the attack on Grand Gulf. Accompanied by a small part of his division, the German moved out from Perkins's Plantation to Hard Times Landing and then continued south, passing Grand Gulf on the Louisiana side of the river, to opposite the mouth of Bayou Pierre.

There he learned from local residents that Bruinsburg, a few miles farther south, was a feasible place for Grant to cross his army. From there, the Federals could quickly march to the high ground at Port Gibson, bypassing Grand Gulf and heading for Vicksburg or Jackson.[18]

As soon as the Grand Gulf attack failed, McClernand's three divisions were unloaded from the transports at Hard Times Landing. The fleet ran past the batteries at the Gulf and reloaded the Thirteenth Corps farther south. On April 30, Osterhaus led his men over the river. He had been in his element on this expedition, having plenty of experience scouting enemy territory, commanding outposts, and leading the way for Curtis's army in Arkansas the previous summer. Grant clearly recognized and trusted the German general's skills. Osterhaus also had an excellent working relationship with his corps commander. Moreover, he clearly understood the necessities of campaigning in rough terrain far from a base of supplies. He was careful to have his division feed itself by foraging on the rich plantations in the Louisiana delta during the march to Bruinsburg, and he collected one thousand bales of cotton for shipment to Milliken's Bend as well.[19]

Osterhaus demonstrated his tactical ability in the battle of Port Gibson on May 1. McClernand's corps took the lead, marching northeast from the river, and encountered a rebel force four miles short of that town. McClernand took two divisions to the right at a fork in the road and dispatched Osterhaus's division along the left fork, thus separating his corps. Osterhaus encountered fewer Confederates than did the other two divisions, but they were excellently positioned where the road crossed a commanding ridge. He could approach this stronghold only along narrow ridges bordered with deep gullies that were filled with thick growths of cane and brush. Osterhaus handled his division of 3,197 men and two batteries with skill, refusing to be rushed into an unwise assault. He tried to soften up the rebel position with well-directed artillery fire that smashed the Confederate guns but failed to move the infantry off the ridge. He sent for reinforcements and spent the next three hours carefully scouting the rugged terrain for a way to approach the enemy. By the time Brig. Gen. John E. Smith's brigade arrived, he was ready. While Smith worked his way toward the Confederate right, Osterhaus personally led an assault by the Forty-ninth Indiana and the 114th Ohio against the rebel center. It succeeded beautifully, the enemy position collapsed, and the battle came to an end by dusk.[20]

The Union victory opened the way for Grant to operate in the interior of Mississippi. His army set out toward the northeast, with the Thirteenth Corps keeping to the left. Osterhaus's division reached Raymond on the night of May 14 to garrison the town, but word soon arrived that the Confederates under Lt. Gen. John C. Pemberton were coming out of Vicksburg to meet Grant. The Thirteenth Corps was ordered north to delay them until the rest of the army could be concentrated. Osterhaus's men left Raymond at dawn on May 15 and reached the railroad connecting Vicksburg and Jackson at Bolton's Station a few hours later. The result was the climactic battle of Champion's Hill, fought on May 16 to the west of Bolton's Station. Osterhaus's division of 2,704 men advanced toward Pemberton's position in the center, with Brig. Gen. Alvin P. Hovey's division one mile to his right and Andrew Jackson Smith's division four miles to his left. He operated in a "chaos of ravines and narrow hills, sloping very abruptly into sink-hole valleys," and covered with dense vegetation. The landscape prevented him from deploying his whole force, and he could see no more than one hundred yards ahead along the narrow road. Yet his vanguard steadily pushed on until reaching a cleared area, where this road joined Hovey's route. Osterhaus met stiffer resistance here and engaged in a static firefight with the Confederates. Hovey's division bore the brunt of the fighting for several hours while Osterhaus and Smith advanced, but Confederate resistance collapsed in the evening.[21]

The next day the victorious Federals came across a fortified bridgehead where the railroad crossed the Big Black River. Brig. Gen. Eugene A. Carr's division deployed to the right of the tracks while Osterhaus positioned his command to the left. Ever ready for artillery work, the German personally scouted the best position for Foster's twenty-pounder Parrotts, telling the gunners, "I shows you a place where you gets a good chance at 'em." He and Foster were supervising the placement of two guns on high ground near the railroad when the Confederate artillery opened fire. A shell exploded among them, igniting a limber chest while a gunner held the lid open to retrieve a few rounds. That man was killed, the drivers were blown off their horses, one shell fragment hit Foster on the shoulder, and another struck Osterhaus on the inner side of his left thigh. The German remained on the field for a time to see the guns in action, then turned the command of his division over to Brig. Gen. Albert L. Lee. Carr's division later attacked and broke the bridgehead, leading to a frenzied Confederate re-treat.[22]

The wound was slight, but it bothered Osterhaus for the rest of his life. Indeed, his old complaint of malaria and dysentery continued to afflict him throughout the Vicksburg campaign. His personal servant noted that he was attended by the division surgeon, who also had treated his wound, on a regular basis while commanding his men during the march to Vicksburg. At times he was forced to ride in an ambulance. But none of this kept him out of action for long. Osterhaus resumed command of his division on May 18 after it had crossed the Big Black River and was heading for Vicksburg. He could barely ride short distances on horseback but "considered the circumstances imperative" for his resumption of command. He scouted the landscape despite his injury and led the division in a slow advance toward the Confederate defenses on May 19. The men reached a point within three hundred yards of the works after crawling over felled timber and through a rugged series of ravines. Osterhaus personally laid out an artillery emplacement, which his men dug under the cover of darkness that night. Another emplacement constructed on the night of May 20 gave the division two good places from which to soften up the Confederate works.[23]

A general assault was planned for May 22. Osterhaus received his orders at six o'clock the previous evening and immediately called his brigade leaders into conference, wanting them "to come to a thorough understanding as to the anticipated attack." The exact mode and point of this assault was left up to Osterhaus and the other division leaders; thus he conducted "a very minute survey" of the ground and concluded that the only place to do it was in the center of his division. Here there was a steep slope up to the rebel works, with fewer piles of felled timber impeding the way. Rugged spurs on the ridge slope would help to hide his men as they advanced, and a semiprotected area near the base of the ridge would give cover for the three assault columns as they assembled. Each column consisted of two regiments. Osterhaus could not have prepared more thoroughly. His guns opened at dawn and continued to pound the rebel lines until 10:00 A.M. His three columns made it to the top of the ridge, as he anticipated, but none could penetrate the substantial fortifications. The men took shelter where they could find it, some close enough to hear the Confederate officers talking to their men. They kept up a desultory skirmish fire on the rebels until darkness offered them an opportunity to withdraw in safety.[24]

Osterhaus lost 269 men in this attack, the failure of which forced Grant to lay siege to the city. The German did not participate in this operation, for on May 23 he received orders to take part of the division back to the Big Black River railroad bridge. A Confederate force was gathering at Jackson, looking toward the relief of Vicksburg, and Grant needed troops to guard his rear. Whether Grant or McClernand decided that Osterhaus should command them is unclear. Both men thought highly of him; McClernand even recommended him for promotion to major general for his work in the campaign.[25]

Osterhaus reached the burned bridge on the morning of May 24 with a small force consisting of his First Brigade and two sections of artillery. He found two companies of the Sixth Missouri Cavalry already there. The German quickly obeyed Grant's instructions to push men east of the river and destroy the railroad tracks at least as far as Edward's Station. He systematically tore up rails and destroyed bridges; burned any property of potential use for the rebels; confiscated cotton, sheep, and cattle; and rounded up able-bodied African Americans to provide labor for the army. He found that no Confederate forces were operating west of a line that included Raymond and Clinton, but his small force was still inadequate to meet the needs of his important mission. He worked assiduously over the next several weeks to cajole his superiors into sending more men. His greatest need was for more cavalry, and McClernand's staff gradually shifted the needed troops his way. Steadily increasing rebel activity west of the Raymond-Clinton line soon rendered these small reinforcements inadequate. Osterhaus pressed for more troopers and added requests for more infantry as well; his five regiments amounted to only 1,250 men. He asked for another brigade from the Ninth Division to be pulled out of the siege lines and sent to him, and most of his requests for help were answered. Osterhaus also mounted the 118th Illinois Infantry so it could more easily patrol the area between the bridge and Edward's Station.[26]

The steady increase in Confederate troop strength at Jackson and the greater activity of rebel patrols forced Grant to dispatch twelve hundred cavalry and a brigade of infantry to watch the river crossings north of Osterhaus's position. The commanding general also instructed the German to have his men thoroughly obstruct all roads that led to fords in his area, except those used by Union patrols. Osterhaus also began to fortify his position on the high bluffs west of the river, but with only a few black laborers, the work went slowly. He asked Grant's headquarters for one hundred more former slaves, with entrenching tools, to push the work along. He eventually accumulated nearly three hundred black laborers by the end of the siege. The fortifications extended south and north of the bridge along the edge of the bluff for about three-fourths of a mile, with retrenchments on both flanks to cover the Federal camp adequately from a surprise attack.[27]

The most valuable contributions Osterhaus made while commanding on the Big Black River were in his reconnaissance efforts and in keeping his superiors well informed of enemy activity. He communicated mostly with McClernand's and Grant's chiefs of staff, Lieut. Col. Walter B. Scates and Lieut. Col. John A. Rawlins, but often wrote directly to both commanders when they communicated with him on a particular issue. "I shall not fail to inform you of anything I learn," he wrote to McClernand early in June. The German reported fully and critically, refusing to disturb his commander's peace of mind with unsubstantiated rumors or undigested reports, basing his information on the increasingly heavy mounted patrols that he sent into the countryside east of the river. To keep in closer touch, Osterhaus established a telegraph line to connect his post with army headquarters and the new Thirteenth Corps commander, Maj. Gen. Edward O. C. Ord. He also closely interrogated passing civilians, especially former slaves, and evaluated the validity of their reports with a close eye. One man named George McCloud, "a very intelligent contraband" who could read and write, had worked in the Confederate arsenal at Demopolis, Alabama. McCloud provided a wealth of detailed information, and Osterhaus thought enough of his word to pass him on to Grant's headquarters. But the German's wariness, and his delight in the game of intelligence gathering, came through when he described McCloud as "an interesting, perhaps a useful, man—perhaps a rogue."[28]

The most difficult part of his assignment on the Big Black River was dealing with issues not directly related to the military mission. The region east of the river was essentially a no-man's-land controlled by neither army, and his post became an entry port for any communications that passed between the belligerents. Osterhaus had to create a policy for handling rebel officers who brought messages for Grant under flags of truce. He also worked to collect sick and wounded Federal soldiers who had been left behind after Grant fought his way from

Jackson to Vicksburg. Many were taken in from the immediate vicinity of the May 17 battlefield at the Big Black River, but about six hundred were still suffering in makeshift field hospitals at Champion's Hill. These men were constantly harassed by roving Confederate patrols, which frequently entered the hospitals to "capture" the wounded and make them sign paroles. Osterhaus did not have the facilities to handle such a number. When ambulances were made available, he carefully proceeded with a message to the Confederate authorities at Jackson, sent under a flag of truce, to make certain there would be no interference with his mission of mercy.[29]

Osterhaus needed advice when it came to dealing with the civilians in this no-man's-land, especially women. When a Mrs. Elmira J. Kelley asked him for permission to take her fifteen-year-old son through the lines to Cincinnati to put him in school, the German admitted to Rawlins, "I am at a loss, what to do." Mrs. Kelley was a Southern patriot, but "rather of a mild species." What to do with another woman, a Mrs. Faulkes, was another matter. She was widely known to be visiting many Federal headquarters, seemed to know much more about military matters than she ought, and was sighted by Osterhaus's patrols as she repeatedly crossed the Big Black. He put scouts on her trail to watch any further movements.[30]

Overall, Osterhaus performed his important duties on the Big Black with consummate skill; Grant was perfectly satisfied with his performance. In the latter stages of the siege, Maj. Gen. William T. Sherman took charge of the growing number of troops along the Big Black. He informed Osterhaus on July 4, the day Vicksburg surrendered, that he had orders to take the Fifteenth and Thirteenth Corps to Jackson and to deal with the rebels there. Sherman relied on Osterhaus's judgment as to whether the area around the Big Black River bridge could be used as a depot for supplying this move, and he requested copies of any maps Osterhaus had created covering the area east of the river. Sherman also helped to inform Ord of the German's capabilities, as Osterhaus and his new corps leader were "comparative strangers."[31]

Osterhaus's Ninth Division was in the vanguard of one column of Sherman's expedition to Jackson. He led two infantry brigades, one cavalry brigade, and two batteries, a total of 3,012 men, toward Jackson on July 6. He encountered stiff resistance near Clinton on the morning of July 9, forcing him to deploy his infantry and attack. The rebels gave way, and Osterhaus continued toward Jackson, arriving there on July 10. He pushed his skirmishers within 250 yards of the strong Confederate earthworks that day, then shifted his division farther to the right the next day, building fortifications to secure the point against a light Confederate attack. Only artillery firing took place on July 12, when Foster's Parrott guns dismounted a large rebel cannon. Osterhaus was ordered to advance under cover of a heavy curtain of artillery fire on July 13. He pushed his line to a point within 150 yards of the rebel works and spent the next day fortifying this advanced position. His hardworking men were relieved on July 16 and camped in the rear for rest. The next day, the Confederates evacuated Jackson for the second time. The Ninth Division helped to destroy the public buildings and left the capital on July 21 as the rear guard of the Thirteenth Corps, reaching Vicksburg on July 24.[32]

Osterhaus received Ord's praise for his effective use of artillery. He minimized losses while his infantry advanced to within close range of the enemy, suffering no more than six killed and seventy-three wounded in the Jackson campaign. This was to be his last action with the Thirteenth Corps, which was reorganized on August 1. His Ninth Division, which "had become dear to me," was disbanded, and the corps was shipped off to Natchez. Osterhaus went to St. Louis on a sick leave, still bothered by malarial symptoms, diarrhea, and a sensitive digestion. He had taken medicine a great deal during the time on the Big Black River. When he returned from Missouri, the German was given command of the First Division, Fifteenth Corps, replacing Maj. Gen. Frederick Steele, who was given command of an expedition to capture Little Rock, Arkansas. Osterhaus was delighted as the division contained most of the troops he had commanded during the Pea Ridge campaign. He took charge of his new unit on September 1 in its encampment at the Big Black River railroad bridge, the same spot where he had spent so many weeks during the Vicksburg campaign. Three weeks later, he received orders to move out for Chattanooga, the next campaign of his career.[33]

Any appraisal of Osterhaus as a division leader under Grant has to start with his relations with his subordinates and his superiors. The men who found themselves under his command uniformly respected, even liked, their leader. The ethnic soldiers whose company he left in December to enter the Thirteenth Corps missed him throughout the Vicksburg campaign, often commenting in their correspondence that

they wished he could succeed in returning to their division. That wish
came true in September. The American-born recruits in the Ninth Division also enjoyed his leadership. Kentucky surgeon Benjamin Franklin
Stevenson called Osterhaus "the most approachable of men." They
often related stories about how he refused to honor the wishes of local
civilians for the return of property stolen by soldiers, preferring to side
with his "boys." Surgeon Stevenson characterized him as a "thorough
German and a magnificent fellow, who is much liked by the soldiers.
He never says 'go, boys,' but 'follow me.' Brave to a fault." Col. Marcus M. Spiegel of the 120th Ohio, although a Rhinelander himself, was
wary of German officers because he usually found them to be venal and
petty, yet Osterhaus's warm personality won him over. He was "one of
natures Noblemen and the best and most active Generals I yet met in
America." The two developed a close personal friendship. Osterhaus
offered him "a fine German Dinner," kindness and respect, and good
conversation; Spiegel thought him "a good man, intelligent and a
splendid Scholar."[34]

Osterhaus found it easy to deal with his superiors. Lacking ambition and respectful of authority, he uncomplainingly offered his talents
to his commanders. McClernand relied heavily on him for difficult assignments during the Vicksburg campaign. Although Ord never came
to know him well, he praised his work in the Jackson campaign. Sherman thought well of him and supported his transfer to the First Division of the Fifteenth Corps.

Osterhaus's relationship with Grant was positive as well. In his
later years, the German regarded Grant as "one of the strongest military figures of the nineteenth century, a man who would have been
great in any of the European wars of the last hundred years." Like Mc-
Clernand, Grant relied on Osterhaus for difficult and responsible assignments. The personal relations between the two men are obscure.
Osterhaus in later life claimed that he often was given the task of taking
care of Grant's son, Frederick Dent Grant, as the twelve-year-old boy
accompanied his father during the campaign. The German enjoyed letting Fred ride his black horse and accompanied him on short excursions around camp. Yet there is no indication that Grant and Osterhaus
were friends.[35]

Assistant Secretary of War Charles A. Dana offered an insightful
evaluation of Osterhaus after accompanying Grant's army during the
campaign, calling him "a pleasant, genial fellow, brave and quick,

[who] makes a first-rate report of a reconnaissance. There is not another general in this army who keeps the commander in chief so well informed concerning whatever happens at his outposts." Yet Dana thought Osterhaus was weaker in instilling discipline than some officers: "On the battlefield he lacks energy and concentrativeness." Dana based this last judgment on the German's habit of advancing cautiously, using artillery fire to pry the enemy out of his positions so as to reduce infantry casualties. Despite this limitation, Osterhaus was recommended for promotion by Ord on July 27. Even though Grant endorsed the recommendation, the German had to wait a full year before receiving his much deserved elevation to major general.[36]

Osterhaus's performance in the Vicksburg campaign and his eventual promotion demonstrated his basic attributes as a commander. His rise through the ranks was based on what one modern historian has called "unquestioned competence in the field." He was a superb division leader. His skill at exploring unknown territory was unsurpassed; he had an excellent eye for terrain and a keen ability to fit his tactical plan to it. A superb artillerist, he was sharply interested in that arm of the service and paid a lot of attention to the guns during an engagement. He could develop excellent plans to coordinate the artillery and the infantry, not a common ability among Civil War field commanders. And Osterhaus's easygoing personality allowed him to get along with subordinates and superiors alike, the key to easing the stigma attached to foreigners in the army. It was readily apparent that he was not a typically stiff European but had acclimated himself to the informal atmosphere of the American volunteer army. His Rhineland upbringing and his middle-class background were essential preparations for his career in the U.S. Army.[37]

Osterhaus's relationship with Grant was mutually beneficial. The two men respected each other's ability but apparently never drew close on a personal level. The German had unusual opportunities to communicate and work directly with the army leader because his talents at reconnaissance and commanding outposts were noticed by Grant and used to the full. The normal layer of separation, that of the corps level, often was punctured by Grant's need to have Osterhaus at his fingertips. The German came into his own as a field leader in the Vicksburg campaign, and it was largely due to Grant's trust in him.

Notes

Introduction

1. Douglas Southall Freeman, *Lee's Lieutenants: A Study in Command,* 3 vols. (New York: Charles Scribner's Sons, 1942–1944).

Sherman and Grant

1. The standard works on Grant and Sherman are William S. McFeely, *Grant: A Biography* (New York: Norton, 1981), and John F. Marszalek, *Sherman: A Soldier's Passion for Order* (New York: Free Press, 1993). The newest Grant biography is Geoffrey Perret, *Ulysses S. Grant, Soldier and President* (New York: Random House, 1997). A harsh assessment of Sherman is Michael Fellman, *Citizen Sherman: A Life of William Tecumseh Sherman* (New York: Random House, 1995). Joseph T. Glatthaar, *Partners in Command: The Relationships Between Leaders in the Civil War* (New York: Free Press, 1994), includes a fine chapter on Grant and Sherman: " 'If I got in a tough place, you would come—if alive,' Grant, Sherman, and Union Success in the West."

2. McFeely, *Grant,* 20; Marszalek, *Sherman,* 23.

3. *New York Times,* September 10, 1885.

4. *Cincinnati Commercial,* December 11, 1861.

5. Nathaniel Cheairs Hughes, Jr., *The Battle of Belmont: Grant Strikes South* (Chapel Hill: University of North Carolina Press, 1991); U. S. Grant, *Personal Memoirs of U. S. Grant,* 2 vols. (New York: Library of America, 1990), 1:190.

6. Grant to Halleck, January 28, 1862, Andrew Foote to Halleck, January 28, 1862, Halleck to Grant, January 30, 1862, U.S. War Department, *War of the Rebellion: Official Records of the Union and Confederate Armies,* 128 vols. (Washington, DC: GPO, 1881–1901), series 1, vol. 7:120–21 (hereinafter cited as *OR;* except as otherwise noted, all references are to series 1); B. Franklin Cooling, *Forts Henry and Donelson: The Key to the Confederate Heartland* (Knoxville: University of Tennessee Press, 1987); Grant to S. B. Buckner, February 16, 1862, in Grant, *Memoirs,* 1:208.

7. Special Orders no. 87, December 23, 1861, in William T. Sherman, *Memoirs of General W. T. Sherman,* 2 vols. (New York: Library of America, 1990), 1:236; Henry W. Halleck to Sherman, February 13, 1862, Sherman, *Memoirs,* 1:239.

8. William T. Sherman to John Sherman, February 23, 1862, William T. Sherman Papers, Library of Congress (LC); Grant, *Memoirs,* 1:213; Grant thanks Sherman for "the kind tone of your letter" and hopes Sherman "will win for yourself the promotion, which you are kind enough to say belongs to me" (Grant to Sherman, February 19, 1862, in John Y. Simon, ed., *The Papers of Ulysses S. Grant,* 22 vols. to date [Carbondale: University of Southern Illinois Press, 1967–], 4:249).

9. Halleck to George B. McClellan, March 3, 4, 1862, McClellan to Halleck, March 3, 1862, Halleck to Grant, March, 4, 1862, *OR,* 7:679–80, and 10, pt. 2:3.

10. L. Thomas to Halleck, March 10, 1862, in Adam Badeau, *Military History of Ulysses S. Grant,* 3 vols. (New York: D. Appleton, 1868), 1:63; President's War Order no. 3, March 11, 1862, Grant to Halleck, March 13, 1862, Halleck to Grant, March 13, 1862, *OR,* 10, pt. 2:28–30, 32.

11. Sherman, *Memoirs,* 1:246–48.

12. The most complete account of Shiloh is Larry J. Daniel, *Shiloh: The Battle That Changed the Civil War* (New York: Simon and Schuster, 1997).

13. Grant, *Memoirs,* 1:223.

14. Grant to Sherman, April 4, 1862, Sherman to Grant, April 5, 1862, *OR,* 10, pt. 2:91, 93–94.

15. Grant, *Memoirs,* 1:231; Sherman to Ellen Sherman, April 11, 1862, Sherman Family Papers, University of Notre Dame Archives (hereinafter cited as SFP, UNDA).

16. Grant, *Memoirs,* 1:234; Sherman, *Memoirs,* 1:266; Sherman to Henry Coppee, June 13, 1864, *OR,* 52, pt. 1:559.

17. Grant to H. N. McLean, April 9, 1862, *OR,* 10, pt. 1:108; John Russell Young, *Around the World with General Grant,* 2 vols. (New York: American News Company, 1879), 2:469.

18. A study of Sherman's relationship with Civil War reporters is John F. Marszalek, *Sherman's Other War: The General and the Civil War Press* (1981; paperback rev. ed., Kent, OH: Kent State University Press, 1998).

19. Sherman, *Memoirs,* 1:271; Grant, *Memoirs,* 1:247, 252.

20. Sherman, *Memoirs,* 1:275–76; Perret, *U. S. Grant,* 2–13, says that Grant meant only to leave for a monthlong visit to his wife and children.

21. Grant, *Memoirs,* 1:258; Sherman to Ellen Sherman, June 6, 1862, Sherman to Grant, June 6, 1862, copy, SFP, UNDA.

22. Sherman to Ellen Sherman, May 1, August 5, 1862, SFP, UNDA.

23. The most detailed account of the Vicksburg campaign is Edwin C. Bearss, *The Vicksburg Campaign,* 3 vols. (Dayton, OH: Morningside Press, 1985–1986). Michael B. Ballard is presently preparing a volume that promises to provide a definitive account of this battle.

24. Grant, *Memoirs,* 1:286.

25. Halleck to Grant, November 10, 1862, in Simon, ed., *Grant, Papers,* 6:288n; Grant to Sherman, December 8, 1862, *OR,* 17, pt. 1:601.

26. John Y. Simon, ed., *The Personal Memoirs of Julia Dent Grant* (Carbondale: Southern Illinois University Press, 1988), 109.

27. Marszalek, *Sherman's Other War,* 117–53; Ellen Sherman to Sherman, April 4, 1863, SFP, UNDA; Grant to Thomas W. Knox, April 6, 1863, Sherman to Knox, April 7, 1863, Sherman to Grant, April 8, 1863, *OR,* 17, pt. 2:894–95.

28. Grant, *Memoirs,* 1:364n–65n.

29. Sherman to John A. Rawlins, April 8, 1863, Sherman, *Memoirs,* 1:338–39.

30. Grant to Sherman, April 27, 1863, *OR (Navy),* 24:591; Sherman to Grant, April 28, 1863, two letters, *OR,* 24, pt. 3:242–44; Sherman to John Sherman, April 23, 1863, Sherman Papers; Sherman to Ellen Sherman, April 29, 1863, SFP, UNDA.

31. Grant, *Memoirs,* 1:338.

32. Sherman to Grant, July 4, 1863, *OR,* 24, pt. 3:472; Sherman to Ellen Sherman, June 2, 1863, SFP, UNDA; Grant, *Memoirs,* 1:364; Sherman, *Memoirs,* 1:359; Grant to Abraham Lincoln, July 22, 1863, *OR,* 24, pt. 3:540–42.

33. Grant, *Memoirs,* 1:390.

34. Ibid., 1:354; Sherman to Ellen Sherman, July 5, 1863, SFP, UNDA.

35. Grant to Ellen Sherman, July 7, 1862, Sherman Papers. Here and elsewhere, Grant frequently included James B. McPherson with Sherman as the men to whom he owed his success. McPherson died in battle near Atlanta on July 22, 1864. Clearly, even when McPherson was alive, Sherman was the Union officer whom Grant most respected.

William H. L. Wallace

1. *OR,* pt. 1:185.

2. Isabel Wallace, *Life and Letters of General W. H. L. Wallace* (Chicago: R. R. Donnelley and Sons Company, 1909), 1–16 (quotes, 14, 16).

3. Ibid., 18.

4. Ibid., 40–49.

5. Ibid., 49–52.

6. Ibid., 53.

7. Ibid., 64.

8. W. H. L. Wallace to Ann Dickey Wallace, April 24, 1861, Wallace-Dickey Family Papers, Illinois State Historical Library, Springfield (hereinafter WDFP).

9. Ibid.

10. Ibid., W. H. L. Wallace to Ann Wallace, April 26, 1861.

11. Douglas Hapeman diary, Illinois State Historical Library, Springfield.

12. Regimental Order no. 2, WDFP.

13. Ibid., Wallace to Maj. John B. Wyman, May 8, 1861 (two letters), and W. H. L. Wallace to Ann Wallace, May 12, 1861.

14. Ibid., S. H. Freeland to W. H. L. Wallace, May 7, 1861; N. R. Casey to W. H. L. Wallace, May 9, 1861; Regimental Order no. 7, May 10, 1861; Regimental Order no. 8, May 11, 1861.

15. Ibid., W. H. L. Wallace to Ann Wallace, May 14, 1861; Hapeman diary.

16. *OR,* 3:243, 491, 501, 503, 533–34; ser. 2, vol. 1:504; W. H. L. Wallace to Ann Wallace, October 6, 9, 10, 14, 15, 1861, WDFP.

17. T. E. G. Ransom to W. H. L. Wallace, October 27, 1861, WDFP.

18. Ibid., Cyrus E. Dickey to Ann Wallace, November 4, 1861.

19. Nathaniel Cheairs Hughes Jr., *The Battle of Belmont: Grant Strikes South* (Chapel Hill: University of North Carolina Press, 1991), 46–47; William B. Feis, "Grant and the Belmont Campaign," in *The Art of Command in the Civil War,* ed. Steven E. Woodworth (Lincoln: University of Nebraska Press, 1998), 37–40.

20. Feis, "Grant and the Belmont Campaign," 39–40; *OR,* 3:269.

21. That, in fact, is exactly what he did claim. Ulysses S. Grant, *Personal Memoirs of U. S. Grant,* 2 vols. (New York: Charles L. Webster and Company, 1885–1886), 1:270.

22. *OR,* 3:269–70.

23. Feis, "Grant and the Belmont Campaign," 37–38; W. H. L. Wallace to Ann Wallace, November 14, 1861, WDFP; Hughes, *The Battle of Belmont,* 52.

24. W. H. L. Wallace to Ann Wallace, November 14, 1861, WDFP.

25. Grant, *Memoirs,* 1:339.

26. W. H. L. Wallace to Ann Wallace, November 15, 1861, and January 5, 1862, WDFP; Hapeman diary.

27. W. H. L. Wallace to Ann Wallace, November 19, 26, 1861, and January 12, 13, 16, 19, 20, 22, 24, 25, 28, and 29, 1862, WDFP.

28. Ibid., W. H. L. Wallace to Ann Wallace, February 1 and 4, 1862; *OR,* 3:578.

29. W. H. L. Wallace to Ann Wallace, February 7, 1862, WDFP; *OR,* 3:578, and 7:129–30.

30. W. H. L. Wallace to Ann Wallace, February 7, 1862, WDFP.

31. Ibid., W. H. L. Wallace to Ann Wallace, February 11, 1862.

32. *OR,* 7:192–95.

33. W. H. L. Wallace to Ann Wallace, February 20 and 28, 1862, WDFP.

34. Ibid.

35. *OR,* 10, pt. 2:35.

36. W. H. L. Wallace to Ann Wallace, March 22, 1862, WDFP.

37. *OR,* 10, pt. 2:88.

38. Hapeman diary.

39. *OR,* 10, pt. 2:91.

40. W. H. L. Wallace to Ann Wallace, April 5, 1862, WDFP; Grant, *Memoirs,* 1:334–35.

41. W. H. L. Wallace to Ann Wallace, April 5, 1862, WDFP.
42. *OR,* 10, pt. 1:178, 181, 185.
43. Ibid., 279.
44. Ibid., 149, 279.
45. Hapeman diary.

CHARLES FERGUSON SMITH

1. Bruce Catton, *Grant Moves South* (Boston: Little, Brown, 1960), 169, 504–5n.
2. Ulysses S. Grant, *Personal Memoirs,* 2 vols. (New York: Charles L. Webster and Company, 1885–1886), 1:311.
3. Smith's life can be followed in "Major General Smith," *Portrait Monthly of the New York Illustrated News,* 1, 1 (July 1863):51; George W. Cullum, *Biographical Register of the Officers and Graduates of the U.S. Military Academy,* 8 vols. (Boston: Houghton & Mifflin, 1891), 1:353–57; John Y. Simon, "Charles Ferguson Smith," in *Biographical Dictionary of the Union: Northern Leaders of the Civil War,* ed. John T. Hubbell and James W. Geary (Westport, CT: Greenwood Press, 1995), 484–85; Brooks D. Simpson, "Charles Ferguson Smith," in *American National Biography,* ed. John A. Garraty and Mark C. Carnes, 24 vols. (New York: Oxford University Press, 1999), 20:149–50.
4. John Y. Simon, ed., *The Papers of Ulysses S. Grant,* vol. 1, *1837–1861,* 22 vols. to date (Carbondale: University of Southern Illinois Press, 1967–), 388–89.
5. Catton, *Grant Moves South,* 50–51.
6. Simon, ed., *Grant, Papers,* vol. 2, *April–September 1861,* 198n; see also Kenneth P. Williams, *Lincoln Finds a General: A Military Study of the Civil War,* 5 vols. (New York: Macmillan, 1949–1958), 3:57.
7. Williams, *Lincoln Finds a General,* 3:241 and 301n; Geoffrey Perret, *Ulysses S. Grant: Soldier and President* (New York: Random House, 1997), 139; Nathaniel Cheairs Hughes Jr., *The Battle of Belmont: Grant Strikes South* (Chapel Hill: University of North Carolina Press, 1991), 9.
8. Simon, ed., *Grant, Papers,* vol. 3, *October 1, 1861–January 7, 1862,* 3, 25n, 31n, 42, 43, 71–72, 78, 84–85n, 114, and n; Catton, *Grant Moves South,* 64.
9. Williams, *Lincoln Finds a General,* 3:80; Catton, *Grant Moves South,* 87–88; *OR,* 3:267–74, 300–301; Hughes, *Battle of Belmont,* 46, 50, 56.
10. *OR,* 3:299–304.
11. Ibid., 4:308–9, 345–46; 7:444–46, 448–49.
12. Ibid., 7:462–64, 471–72; 8:369; Grant, *Memoirs,* 1:285.
13. *OR,* 7:468–70, 473–74, 477, 480, 482–83, 484–85, 488–89; 8:369, 395, 401, 402–3, 419.
14. Ibid., 8:532–33, 66–75, 521–22, 524, 526–29, 530–31, and 7:515; Grant, *Memoirs,* 1:285.

15. *OR,* 7:531–33, 547–49.

16. Ibid., 8:503; 7:533–34, 535, 537–38, 539–47.

17. Ibid., 7:73, 551–53, 557–58, 560; Grant, *Memoirs,* 1:286.

18. *OR,* 7:561, 573.

19. Ibid., 7:120–21, 571; *OR (Navy),* 22:457, 485–86, 511–15, 520, 525, 526.

20. For coverage of the Fort Henry operation, see Benjamin Franklin Cooling, *Forts Henry and Donelson: Key to the Confederate Heartland* (Knoxville: University of Tennessee Press, 1987), chap. 6.

21. Ibid., chap. 7.

22. Ibid., chap. 8; Simon, ed., *Grant, Papers,* 4:211–16 and n.

23. Simon, ed., *Grant, Papers,* 4:112, 123–40, 162–65; for a succinct coverage of Confederate actions during the Twin Rivers campaign, see Steven E. Woodworth, " 'When Merit Was Not Enough': Albert Sidney Johnston and Confederate Defeat in the West, 1862," in his anthology, *Civil War Generals in Defeat* (Lawrence: University Press of Kansas, 1999), chap. 1.

24. Simon, ed., *Grant, Papers,* 4:166–83.

25. Catton, *Grant Moves South,* 169–70.

26. Ibid., 174; Smith quoted in Darryl Lyman, *Civil War Quotations* (Conshohocken, PA: Combined Books, 1995), 220, 221; Simon, ed., *Grant, Papers,* 4:224.

27. Catton, *Grant Moves South,* 174–75.

28. Simon, ed., *Grant, Papers,* 7:82n; Lyman, *Civil War Quotations,* 220–21.

29. *OR,* 7:633, 637–38.

30. Ibid., 7:637, 638–39.

31. See Catton, *Grant Moves South,* chap. 9.

32. Catton closely discusses the Grant-Halleck imbroglio in *Grant Moves South* (chap. 10) as does Williams, *Lincoln Finds a General,* 3:301–7; Perret, *U. S. Grant,* 177–82, seems to see Halleck in a more sinister role.

33. Simon, ed., *Grant, Papers,* 4:344n, 360n, 367n; Catton, *Grant Moves South,* 212–14; Williams, *Lincoln Finds a General,* 3:310.

34. *OR,* 10:45–46, 49, 51, 52, 55, 62; Simon, ed., *Grant, Papers,* 4:421, 429.

35. Simon, ed., *Grant, Papers,* 4:429–30n; Williams, *Lincoln Finds a General,* 3:334; Brooks D. Simpson and Jean V. Berlin, eds., *Sherman's Civil War: Selected Correspondence of William T. Sherman* (Chapel Hill: University of North Carolina Press, 1999), 648–49; *OR,* 10, pt. 1:26.

36. *OR,* 10, pt. 1:181, 185, 331.

37. Ibid., 10, pt. 2:623, also 132, 621; Cullum, *Register,* 1:357; Simon, ed., *Grant, Papers,* 7:303n.

38. *OR,* 10, pt. 2:130; Irving McKee, *"Ben Hur" Wallace: The Life of General Lew Wallace* (Berkeley: University of California Press, 1947), 53.

39. Simon, ed., *Grant, Papers,* 10:33–34; 15:354–55; 16:59, 242, 255; 17:287n.

40. Lyman, *Civil War Quotations,* 220–21.

41. Grant's quote, in this case, followed his conclusion that "it is probable that the general opinion was that Smith's long services in the army and distinguished deeds rendered him the more proper person for such command as Halleck had bestowed, in the aftermath of their imbroglio concerning Grant's visiting Nashville and not properly communicating on a regular basis after Fort Donelson. Sherman's comment (quoted by Catton, *Grant Moves South,* 271) was made privately in 1885 and reflected his conclusion, at least, that only Smith's injury caused Halleck to return Grant to expeditionary command, leading to Shiloh. See also Grant, *Memoirs,* 1:328, and Simpson and Berlin, eds., *Sherman's Civil War,* 647–49.

Lewis Wallace

1. Lewis Wallace, *Lew Wallace: An Autobiography,* 2 vols. (New York: Harper and Brothers, 1906), vol. 2:589.

2. William B. Skelton, *An American Profession of Arms: The Army Officer Corps, 1784–1861* (Lawrence: University Press of Kansas, 1992), 295; Irving McKee, *"Ben-Hur" Wallace: The Life of General Lew Wallace* (Berkeley: University of California Press, 1947), 46; Benjamin Franklin Cooling, *Forts Henry and Donelson: The Key to the Confederate Heartland* (Knoxville: University of Tennessee Press, 1987), xiii.

3. Robert E. Morsberger and Katherine M. Morsberger, *Lew Wallace: Militant Romantic* (New York: McGraw Hill, 1980), 3–53; McKee, *"Ben-Hur" Wallace,* 1–32.

4. Wallace, *Autobiography,* 1:261–69, quote at 262; Morsberger and Morsberger, *Militant Romantic,* 54–66; McKee, *"Ben-Hur" Wallace,* 31–40; Glenn H. Worthington, *Fighting for Time: The Battle That Saved Washington* (1932; repr., Shippensburg, PA: White Mane Publishing/Beidel Printing House, 1985), 47.

5. Cooling, *Forts Henry and Donelson,* 117; James M. McPherson, *Battle Cry of Freedom: The Civil War Era* (Oxford: Oxford University Press, 1988), 332; Ezra J. Warner, *Generals in Blue: Lives of the Union Commanders* (Baton Rouge: Louisiana State University Press, 1964), xviii–xix. Despite the pressing requirement to make a high proportion of political appointments, Lincoln, in 1861, by percentage of those selected, actually made fewer political appointments than did Jefferson Davis for the Confederate army. Sixty-five percent of Lincoln's appointments to general-officer rank were professional soldiers, compared to 50 percent of those appointed by Davis that same year (see Herman Hattaway and Archer Jones, *How the North Won: A Military History of the Civil War* [Urbana: University of Illinois Press, 1983], 29–31).

6. Harold Lew Wallace, "Lew Wallace's March to Shiloh Revisited," *Indiana Magazine of History* 59 (March 1963):25; Morsberger and Morsberger, *Militant Romantic,* 23, 63–64, 429. Wallace molded a career of remarkable diversity— immersed in the literary, military, and social-political history of the United

States—now legendary for the celebrated novel he authored in 1880: *Ben-Hur: A Tale of the Christ;* McKee, *"Ben-Hur" Wallace,* 53; Stephen E. Ambrose, *Duty, Honor, Country: A History of West Point* (Baltimore: Johns Hopkins University Press, 1966), 187 n. 46; Skelton, *An American Profession of Arms,* 210–11. Since Wallace was a veteran of such battles as Fort Donelson and Shiloh, recent biographers believe that he developed a realistic knowledge of battlefield horrors but that he never escaped his eagerness to play a role in the "pomp and circumstance of glorious war." Thus, even at the age of seventy-one, at the outbreak of the Spanish-American War, he was carried away by the same "spread-eagle and evangelical oratory" that had led him into two earlier wars. Once again, he offered his services to Pres. William McKinley and the nation. To Secretary of War Russell A. Alger, Wallace proposed to raise a brigade of black troops and lead them in the impending conflict. With the support of former president Benjamin Harrison and Indiana governor James Mount, the old veteran nearly earned a major general's commission and an appointment to a field command (see Morsberger and Morsberger, *Militant Romantic,* 428–29).

7. H. L. Wallace, "Lew Wallace's March to Shiloh Revisited," 25; Morsberger and Morsberger, *Militant Romantic,* 62, 107, 109–10; Cooling, *Forts Henry and Doneslon,* 117.

8. Wallace, *Autobiography,* 1:337–38, 342, 345, 351. Wallace's commission to brigadier is dated September 3, 1861; Morsberger and Morsberger, *Militant Romantic,* 64; Bruce Catton, *Grant Moves South* (Boston: Little, Brown and Company, 1960), 87–88. Gen. Don Carlos Buell held a different opinion of Smith and expressed no enthusiasm for the old warrior when he informed George B. McClellan, "I have not seen Smith for seven years, and am afraid to judge him. I have never rated him as highly as some men"; see Kenneth P. Williams, *Lincoln Finds a General: A Military Study of the Civil War,* 5 vols. (New York: McMillan Company, 1949–1958), 3:168, and *OR,* 7:487–88.

9. Wallace, *Autobiography,* 1:337; *OR,* 3:141, 144–45, and 52, pt. 1:190. Maj. Gen. John C. Frémont ordered Smith to assume the Paducah command on September 7, 1861. The post was administered separately from Grant's district, and Smith answered directly to Frémont; see Wallace, *Autobiography,* 351–53, and 353 n. 1; Morsberger and Morsberger, *Militant Romantic,* 64–65. Grant and Smith discussed Grant's plan to attack Belmont, Missouri. The raid occurred on November 7, 1861. Smith agreed to make a simultaneous diversion/feint against Columbus.

10. Morsberger and Morsberger, *Militant Romantic,* 64; Williams, *Lincoln Finds a General,* 3:168.

11. McKee, *"Ben-Hur" Wallace,* 53; Morsberger and Morsberger, *Militant Romantic,* 62, 64–66.

12. Skelton, *An American Profession of Arms,* 212, 354, 359; Bernarr Cresap, *Appomattox Commander: The Story of General E. O. C. Ord* (San Diego: A. S. Barnes, 1981), 92, 365n; Robert R. McCormick, in *Ulysses S. Grant: The Great*

Soldier of America (New York: D. Appleton-Century Company, 1934), 70–72, coined the phrase "Grant Men." A number of officers, notably William T. Sherman, James B. McPherson, Edward O. C. Ord, Philip H. Sheridan, James H. Wilson, and John A. Rawlins, became members of a nebulous organization known as "Grant Men," a professional military clique that proved their competence in the Western Theater. All rose to high position behind Grant as he won further successes and ultimate promotion to general in chief, commanding all armies in the United States.

13. Cooling, *Forts Henry and Donelson,* 63–121; Morsberger and Morsberger, *Militant Romantic,* 67–69. Halleck authorized Grant to proceed with the attack on January 30, 1962; Halleck to Grant, January 30, 1862, in *OR,* 7:121–22.

14. Cooling, *Forts Henry and Donelson,* 176–80, 182–84, 188–89, 191, 194–98; William S. McFeely, *Grant: A Biography* (New York: W. W. Norton and Company, 1981), 98–104; Captain William S. Hillyer to Lew Wallace, February 16, 1862, Wallace Collection, William Henry Smith Memorial Library of the Indiana State Historical Society. In the battle on February 15, Wallace's Third Division suffered 293 casualties.

15. McFeely, *Grant,* 102–3; *OR,* 7:159–60. In 1885, Grant finally acknowledged Wallace's performance at Fort Donelson and proclaimed that "he had, at an opportune time, sent [John] Thayer's brigade to the support of McClernand and thereby contributed to hold the enemy within his lines" (Ulysses S. Grant, *Personal Memoirs of U. S. Grant,* 2 vols. [New York: Charles L. Webster and Company, 1885–1886], 1:306).

16. McFeely, *Grant,* 99–100; Wallace, *Autobiography,* 1:365–433; *OR,* 7:236–40, and 159–60; Grant, *Memoirs,* 1:287–315; Benjamin Franklin Cooling, *Jubal Early's Raid on Washington* (Baltimore: Nautical and Aviation Publishing Company of America, 1989), 55. In his writings on the campaign, Wallace provided twice the narrative as did Grant.

17. David Wilson Reed, *The Battle of Shiloh and the Organizations Engaged* (Washington, DC: GPO, 1902), 7–8, 10; Bruce Catton, *U. S. Grant and the American Military Tradition* (New York: Grossett and Dunlap, 1954), 82–83; Grant, *Memoirs,* 325–26, 330–34; *OR,* 10, pt. 2:41, 50–51. On March 16, 1862, Halleck instructed Grant: "As the enemy is evidently in strong force, my instructions not to advance so as to bring on an engagement must be strictly obeyed." Four days later Halleck again cautioned Grant, stating, "Don't let the enemy draw you into an engagement now. Wait till you are properly fortified and receive orders."

18. J. F. C. Fuller, *The Generalship of Ulysses S. Grant* (Bloomington: Indiana University Press, 1929), 105; *OR,* 10, pt. 1:330–31; Reed, *The Battle of Shiloh,* 11–14.

19. Stanley F. Horn, *The Army of Tennessee: A Military History,* 2d ed. (Norman: University of Oklahoma Press, 1955), 131; Wallace, *Autogiography,* 1:459–62; Robert C. Johnson and Clarence C. Buel, eds., in *Battles and Leaders*

of the Civil War, 4 vols. (New York: 1956), 1:607–8; Wiley Sword, *Shiloh: Bloody April* (New York: William Morrow and Company, 1974), 216; Grant, *Memoirs,* 336–37; Ulysses S. Grant, "The Battle of Shiloh," in Johnson and Buel, eds., *Battles and Leaders,* 1:467–68. Grant stated he reached Pittsburg Landing at 8:00 A.M.

20. Grant, "Battle of Shiloh," 468; Sword, *Shiloh: Bloody April,* 218; Reed, *The Battle of Shiloh,* 15, 51; Wallace, *Autobiography,* 1:459–62; *OR,* 10, pt. 1:175; Johnson and Buel, eds., *Battles and Leaders,* 1:608.

21. Johnson and Buel, eds., *Battles and Leaders,* 1:468, 607; Grant, *Memoirs,* 336–37; Reed, *The Battle of Shiloh,* 15, 51; Wallace, *Autobiography,* 1:463–64; *OR,* 10, pt. 1:170, 175.

22. Reed, *The Battle of Shiloh,* 51, 93; Johnson and Buel, eds., *Battles and Leaders,* 607, 609; Grant, *Memoirs,* 334; Wallace, *Autobiography,* 1:451–53; *OR,* 10, pt. 1:91. Grant advised Sherman on April 4, 1861: "I have directed General W. H. L. Wallace . . . to reinforce General L. Wallace in case of an attack with his entire division, although I look for nothing of the kind, but it is best to be prepared." Grant then added, "and should such a thing be attempted, give all the support of your division and General [Stephen] Hurlburt's, if necessary."

23. Wallace, *Autobiography,* 1:451–53; Wallace, "Lew Wallace's March," 23; Stacy D. Allen, "Shiloh! The Second Day's Battle and Aftermath," *Blue and Gray Magazine* 14, 4 (1997):9–10; Grant, *Memoirs,* 351.

24. Fuller, *Generalship of Ulysses S. Grant,* 108–10; Reed, *The Battle of Shiloh,* 16, 45; Allen, "Shiloh!" 9.

25. Wallace, *Autobiography,* 1:463–64; *OR,* 10, pt. 1:170, 175.

26. *OR,* 10, 1:179; Wallace, *Autobiography,* 1:466–67.

27. *OR,* 10, 1:170, 179–80; Reed, *The Battle of Shiloh,* 51; Johnson and Buel, eds., *Battles and Leaders,* 1:608.

28. Johnson and Buel, eds., *Battles and Leaders,* 1:608; Williams, *Lincoln Finds a General,* 3:372; *OR,* 10, pt. 1:181–82, 186–87.

29. *OR,* 10, pt. 1:187–88; Williams, *Lincoln Finds a General,* 3:379–81; Wallace, *Autobiography,* 1:469–71.

30. Wallace, *Autobiography,* 1:471–73.

31. Johnson and Buel, eds., *Battles and Leaders,* 1:476; Grant, *Memoirs,* 1:346–48; Morsberger and Morsberger, *Militant Romantic,* 109–14; McKee, *"Ben-Hur" Wallace,* 53–54; Johnson and Buel, eds., *Battles and Leaders,* 1:610; Joseph W. Rich, "Gen. Lew. Wallace at Shiloh: How He Was Convinced of an Error After Forty Years," *Iowa Journal of History and Politics* 18, 2:301–8. While on a visit to Shiloh National Military Park in 1901, General Wallace told Maj. D. W. Reed, Battlefield Commission secretary and historian, "that if he had known the exact conditions of the Confederate forces it might have been a good plan to have continued his march and attacked the enemy in the rear" (D. W. Reed to Joseph W. Rich, February 13, 1909, at 308).

32. *OR*, 10, pt. 1:174–76, 178, 188–89; McKee, *"Ben-Hur" Wallace*, 54.

33. Morsberger and Morsberger, *Militant Romantic*, 69; Wallace, *Autobiography*, 1:399; Cooling, *Forts Henry and Donelson*, 170–71, 176–77.

34. Johnson and Buel, eds., *Battles and Leaders*, 1:468; *OR*, 10, pt. 1:175, 170.

35. *OR*, 10, pt. 1:179–85; Johnson and Buel, eds., *Battles and Leaders*, 1:607; Grant, *Memoirs*, 336 n. 351–52. Knefler wrote to Wallace in February 1868 and stated that the note was "a written order to march and form a junction with the right of the army." He added, "The order was placed in my hands as Assistant Adjutant-General; but where it is now, or what became of it, I am unable to say. Very likely, having been written on a scrap of paper, it was lost."

36. *OR*, 10, pt. 1:179, 185; John Fiske, *War in the West: The Mississippi Valley in the Civil War*, 2 vols. (Boston: Houghton Mifflin Company, 1900), 1:80–81. Fiske challenges the idea that "Napoleon in his best days left but little room open for contingencies and misunderstandings."

37. McFeely, *Grant*, 102, 442. Most Grant scholars believe that he possessed the capacity to select able subordinate commanders; however, McFeely is a notable exception. He believes that Grant was "disillusioned about almost all of his generals," including Sherman and Sheridan, and held reservations about all his lieutenants, whether professional or volunteer soldiers.

38. Horace Porter, *Campaigning with Grant* (New York: Century Company, 1897), 6–7; *OR*, 52, pt. 1:313; McFeely, *Grant*, 102, 146–47. Horace Porter served on Grant's staff from April 1864 through the conclusion of the war. He was amazed that Grant did his own paperwork. "At this time [October 1863], as throughout his later career, he wrote nearly all his documents with his own hand," he observed, and added that Grant "seldom dictated to any one even the most unimportant despatch."

39. Wallace, *Autobiography*, 1:466–70; *OR*, 10, pt. 1:178–88; Johnson and Buel, eds., *Battles and Leaders*, 1:610.

40. *OR*, 10, pt. 1:179–80, 187. Rowley wrote in 1863: "I can only say that to *me* [the march] appeared intolerably slow, resembling more a reconnaissance in the face of an enemy than a forced march to relieve a hard-pressed army" (emphasis in original).

41. Ibid., 187–88; Morsberger and Morsberger, *Militant Romantic*, 69.

42. Johnson and Buel, eds., *Battles and Leaders*, 1:609; Reed, *The Battle of Shiloh*, 15, 51–52.

43. *OR*, 19, pt. 1:981; Stephen W. Sears, *Landscape Turned Red* (New Haven, CT: Ticknor and Fields, 1983), 197, 257, 286.

44. Grant, *Memoirs*, 1:352n; Catton, *Grant Moves South*, 310. According to Mark Mayo Boatner, *The Civil War Dictionary* (New York: David McKay Company, 1959), 2, the definition of an acoustic shadow ("silent battle") "is a phenomenon that results in sound being inaudible to persons a short distance from the source while the same sound may be heard over a great distance away in another

direction." Dense forest, extreme variations in terrain, atmospherics (fluctuations in barometric pressure), weather (wind), or the combination of variables can cause the effect.

45. Reed, *The Battle of Shiloh,* 21–23, 98, 102, 110; Grant, *Memoirs,* 1:348–51, 366–67, 371; *OR,* 10, pt. 1:98–99; Stephen E. Ambrose, *Halleck: Lincoln's Chief of Staff* (Baton Rouge: Louisiana State University Press, 1962), 45–46, 168; *OR,* 34, pt. 3:332.

46. Ambrose, *Halleck,* 45; *OR,* 10, pt. 1:98–99.

47. Morsberger and Morsberger, *Militant Romantic,* 112.

48. Merle E. Sumner, ed., *The Diary of Cyrus B. Comstock* (Dayton, OH: Morningside Press, 1987), 255–56.

49. Morsberger and Morsberger, *Militant Romantic,* 106–7; Francis B. Heitman, *Historical Register and Dictionary of the United States Army, from Its Organization, September 29, 1789, to March 2, 1903,* 2 vols. (Washington, DC: GPO, 1903), 1:20–22, 28–30; *OR,* 10, pt. 2:144, and 52, pt. 1:245; Ambrose, *Halleck,* 41–54, 56–57.

50. McKee, *"Ben-Hur" Wallace,* 52; *OR,* 17, pt. 2:14–15, 29–30; Wallace, *Autobiography,* 2:585–88; Morsberger and Morsberger, *Militant Romantic,* 109.

51. Morsberger and Morsberger, *Militant Romantic,* 109; McKee, *"Ben-Hur" Wallace,"* 52–53; Wallace, *Autobiography,* 2:589–91.

52. Wallace, *Autobiography,* 2:579–80; Morsberger and Morsberger, *Militant Romantic,* 107; *OR,* 7:261.

53. Wallace, *Autobiography,* 2:591; James Lee McDonough, *War in Kentucky: From Shiloh to Perryville* (Knoxville: University of Tennessee Press, 1994), 150–51; Morsberger and Morsberger, *Militant Romantic,* 115–20; McKee, *"Ben-Hur" Wallace,* 58–62.

54. *OR,* 27, pt. 2:308, 327; Wallace, *Autobiography,* 2:641–53; McKee, *"Ben-Hur" Wallace,* 63–64.

55. *OR,* 52, pt. 1:313–14.

56. Heitman, *Historical Register and Dictionary of the United States Army,* 1:20–22, 28–30; Wallace, *Autobiography,* 2:603.

57. Morsberger and Morsberger, *Militant Romantic,* 129.

58. Wallace, *Autobiography,* 2:662–66; *OR,* 30, pt. 3:182–84.

59. *OR,* 30, pt. 3:183–84; Wallace, *Autobiography,* 2:663, 665. Sherman sent the confidential inquiry to Rawlins the very same day (August 27, 1863) that he wrote the long letter to Wallace and advised him not to call for a court of inquiry. In the letter Sherman also informed Wallace "that Grant was now up river, and when he returns I will endeavor to convey to him your proper expressions of confidence without in the least compromising your delicate sense of honor." On October 9, 1863, Sherman informed Wallace that he and Grant had "had a full and frank conversation" about Wallace's chances for a command in the department. Sherman stated that Grant did not wish to change the existing structure of departmental personnel.

60. Wallace, *Autobiography,* 2:577–80, 590, 653; Morsberger and Morsberger, *Militant Romantic,* 109; Carl Sandburg, *Abraham Lincoln: The War Years,* 4 vols. (New York: Harcourt Brace, 1939), 2:40. Sandburg provides a conversation between Lincoln and a visitor to the White House, whereupon Lincoln states, "Halleck wants to kick Wallace out, and [Sen. Henry S.] Lane wants me to kick Halleck out." See also Morsberger and Morsberger, *Militant Romantic,* 130–31.

61. For additional comments from Grant on McClernand, see *OR,* 24, pt. 1:37, 43, and Grant, *Memoirs,* 1:426, 440–41. Based on his remarks it is clear that Grant believed McClernand "unmanageable" and that he did not have "either the experience or the qualifications" to fit him for command. Like any professional, Grant would desire to work among colleagues. The volunteer generals like McClernand and Wallace were of a different cast from the regulars. In this most political of wars, Grant sought the positional authority to pick and place officers who in his opinion were the most capable. Based on merit secured by military success and recognized ability, Sam Grant earned the opportunity to wield such high authority and ably established an effective unified command. Knowledgeable in his administrative and operational responsibilities throughout the war, Grant capably selected and managed subordinates.

ANDREW HULL FOOTE

1. *Boston Journal,* n.d., in Frank Moore, comp., 12 vols. *The Rebellion Record* (New York, 1862–1867), 4:374; Henry Walke, *Naval Scenes and Reminiscences of the Civil War* (New Haven, 1877), 55.

2. H. J. Maihaffer, "The Partnership," U.S. Naval Institute *Proceedings* 93 (May 1967):55.

3. John D. Milligan, "Andrew Hull Foote: Zealous Reformer, Administrator, Warrior," in *Captains of the Old Steam Navy: Makers of the American Naval Tradition, 1840–1880,* ed. James C. Bradford (Annapolis; Naval Institute Press, 1986); "Andrew Hull Foote," in *American National Biography,* ed. John A. Garraty and Mark C. Carnes (New York: Oxford University Press, 1999), 117; see also Kenneth J. Blume, "Admiral Foote," *Portrait Monthly of the New York Illustrated News,* October 1873, 21; Association of Graduates, USMA, *Register of Graduates and Former Cadets of the United States Military Academy* (West Point: 1990), 253.

4. Milligan, "Andrew Hull Foote," 127–28. The best and most recent full-length biography of Foote is Spencer C. Tucker, *Andrew Foote: Civil War Admiral on Western Waters* (Annapolis: Naval Institute Press, 2000), although no more enlightening on the Foote–Grant relationship than other cited sources in this essay.

5. U.S. Navy Department, 30 vols. *Official Records of Union and Confederate Navies in the War of the Rebellion* (Washington, DC: GPO, 1894–1927), series 1, vol. 22:314, and 307–8 (hereinafter *ORN*); Richard S. West, Jr., *Mr. Lincoln's*

Navy (New York; Longmans, 1957), 161, and West, *Gideon Welles: Lincoln's Navy Department* (Indianapolis; Bobbs-Merrill, 1943), 20–21; Gideon Welles, *Diary of Gideon Welles, Secretary of the Navy Under Lincoln and Johnson,* ed. Howard K. Beale and Alan W. Brownsword, 3 vols. (Boston: Houghton Mifflin, 1909–1911), 1:74–75, 2:135.

6. Milligan, "Foote," 123–25; West, *Mr. Lincoln's Navy,* 161–63; also *ORN,* vol. 22:314–22.

7. Kenneth P. Williams, *Lincoln Finds a General: A Military Study of the Civil War,* 5 vols. (New York; Macmillan, 1949–1958), 3:56–57; *ORN,* vol. 1, 22:323.

8. *ORN,* vol. 1, 22:323.

9. West, *Welles,* 163; Milligan, "Foote," 124–25; James Russell Soley, "The Union and Confederate Navies," in *Battles and Leaders of the Civil War,* ed. Robert Underwood Johnson and Clarence Clough Buel, 4 vols. (New York, 1887), 1:619.

10. Geoffrey Perret, *Ulysses S. Grant: Soldier and President* (New York; Random House, 1997), 139–40; joint activities in this period may be judged from appropriate correspondence in *ORN,* vol. 1, 22:318–98, and in John Y. Simon, ed., *The Papers of Ulysses S. Grant,* 22 vols. to date (Carbondale: University of Southern Illinois Press, 1967–), 3:5, 36, 48n, 56n, 59, 61, 62n, 68, 73n, 95–97, 99–100.

11. *ORN,* ser. 1, vol. 22:366; Rowena Reed, *Combined Operations in the Civil War* (Annapolis: Naval Institute Press, 1978), 72.

12. *ORN,* ser. 1, vol. 22:398–99; on the Belmont operation, see Nathaniel Cheairs Hughes Jr., *The Battle of Belmont: Grant Strikes South* (Chapel Hill: University of North Carolina Press, 1991), and William B. Feis, "Grant and the Belmont Campaign: A Study in Intelligence and Command," in *The Art of Command in the Civil War,* ed. Steven E. Woodworth (Lincoln: University of Nebraska Press, 1998).

13. *ORN,* ser. 1, vol. 22:391, 394, 399–400, 405, 434–35, 438–39.

14. Perret, *U. S. Grant,* 149; Henry Walke, "The Gun-Boats at Belmont and Fort Henry," in Johnson and Buel, eds., *Battles and Leaders,* 1:360, 361; *ORN,* ser. 1, vol. 22:428–80.

15. Feis, "Grant and the Belmont Campaign," 22, 42–43.

16. Simon, ed., *Grant, Papers,* 3:213, 240–41, 244n, 246, 263, 274, 281–89, 319, 339, 358, 364, 392–93, 425–26, 433–34.

17. Perret, *U. S. Grant,* 157–58; Simon, ed., *Grant, Papers,* 4:3–75; see also B. Franklin Cooling, *Forts Henry and Donelson: The Key to the Confederate Heartland* (Knoxville: University of Tennessee Press, 1987), chap. 5.

18. Simon, ed., *Grant, Papers,* 4:74; Ulysses S. Grant, *Personal Memoirs* (New York, 1885), 1:286–87.

19. Grant, Memoirs, 1:287; Perret, *U.S. Grant,* citing John W. Emerson, "Grant's Life in the West," *Midland Monthly* (May 1898), 158.

20. *OR,* 7:121; *ORN,* ser. 1, vol. 22:524.

21. *ORN,* ser. 1, vol. 22:525–26; *OR,* 7:571, 572.

22. *OR,* 7:121–22.

23. Milligan, "Foote," 128–29; *OR,* 7:125–26, 586.

24. The action at Fort Henry has been covered by Cooling in *Forts Henry and Donelson,* 101–11.

25. *OR,* 7:124–25, 134, 143.

26. Ibid., 7:153–59, 591–92, 596–97, 598, 600.

27. Ibid., 7:600; see also 595, 601–4.

28. Cooling, *Forts Henry and Donelson,* 148–49.

29. Ibid., 153; Grant, *Memoirs,* 301–2; *OR,* 7:166, and for a sense of basis for Foote's trepidations, see *ORN,* 1, vol. 22:577–84.

30. Milligan, "Foote," 131–32; Cooling, *Forts Henry and Donelson,* chap. 9.

31. *ORN,* ser. 1, vol. 22:586; Grant, *Memoirs,* 304–5.

32. Williams, *Lincoln Finds a General,* 3:247; Simon, ed., *Grant, Papers,* 4:214.

33. *ORN,* ser. 1, vol. 22:616; Williams, *Lincoln Finds a General,* 3:chap. 11 especially.

34. *ORN,* ser. 1, vol. 22:622–23, 624, 639.

35. See Cooling, *Forts Henry and Donelson,* 231–38.

36. Ibid., 238–44.

37. Simon, ed., *Grant, Papers,* 7:314 and n.

38. *ORN,* ser. 1, vol. 22:626; Milligan, "Foote," 132.

39. *ORN,* ser. 1, vol. 22:714–15.

40. Simon, ed., *Grant, Papers,* 5:161; William B. Cogar, *Dictionary of Admirals of the U.S. Navy,* vol. 1, *1862–1900* (Annapolis, 1890), 64; West, *Welles,* 237; Blume, "Foote," 8:190.

41. Francis B. Heitman, *Historical Register and Dictionary of the United States Army,* 2 vols. (Washington, DC: GPO, 1903), 1:427; Simon, ed., *Grant, Papers,* 15:602.

42. See John Keegan, *The Mask of Command* (New York; Viking, 1987), chap. 3.

43. Maihaffer, "The Partnership," 57.

WILLIAM S. ROSECRANS

1. Quoted in William M. Lamers, *The Edge of Glory: A Biography of General William S. Rosecrans. U.S.A.* (New York: Harcourt Brace and World, 1961), 445–46. Lamers's book stands to date as the only complete biography on Rosecrans, and I have relied on it for much of the biographical material in this chapter and as a guide to primary materials. Despite its age it remains a fairly balanced account, although certainly a fresh look at Rosecrans seems well overdue.

2. Ulysses S. Grant to Henry Halleck, August 9, 1862, in *OR,* 27, pt. 2:160.

3. Ulysses S. Grant to Edwin M. Stanton, December 2, 1864, *OR*, 41, pt. 4:743.

4. Lamers, *The Edge of Glory*, 8–12.

5. Ibid., 12–13.

6. Ibid., 15–17.

7. William S. Rosecrans to Annie E. Rosecrans, May 25, 1861, quoted in ibid., 26; William S. Rosecrans's testimony in "Rosecrans's Campaigns," *Report of the Joint Committee on the Conduct of War*, 3 vols. (Washington, DC: GO, 1865): 3:1 (hereinafter cited as *Conduct of War Report*).

8. George B. McClellan to E. D. Townsend, July 14, 1861, *OR*, 2:297.

9. Quoted in Whitelaw Reid, *Ohio in the War: Her Statesmen, Her Generals and Her Soldiers*, 2 vols. (Cincinnati and New York: Moore, Wiltstach and Baldwin, 1868), 1:316; see also Lamers, *The Edge of Glory*, 31.

10. Jacob D. Cox, *Military Reminiscences of the Civil War*, 2 vols. (New York: Scribner's and Sons, 1900), 1:127.

11. John Beatty, *Memoirs of a Volunteer, 1861–1863*, ed. Harvey S. Ford, intro. Lloyd Lewis (New York: W. W. Norton, 1946), 191–92, 194–96; see also Peter Cozzens, *No Better Place to Die: The Battle of Stones River* (Urbana and Chicago: University of Illinois Press, 1990), 18.

12. Quoted in Reid, *Ohio in the War*, 1:315.

13. Quoted in Peter Cozzens, *The Darkest Days of the War: The Battles of Iuka and Corinth* (Chapel Hill: University of North Carolina Press, 1997), 201.

14. *Charleston Courier*, Sept. 21, 1861.

15. Henry Adams to Charles Francis Adams Jr., September 28, 1861, in Worthington Chauncey Ford, ed., *A Cycle of Adams Letters, 1861–1865*, 2 vols. (Boston: Houghton Mifflin Company, 1920), 1:49.

16. Rosecrans's testimony in *Conduct of War Report*, 15.

17. Quoted in Lamers, *The Edge of Glory*, 79.

18. Cozzens, *The Darkest Days of the War*, 28.

19. Ibid., 13–14.

20. Ibid., 35.

21. Ulysses S. Grant to Henry Halleck, August 9, 1862, *OR*, 27, pt. 2:160.

22. Ulysses S. Grant to Jesse Root Grant, August 3, 1862, in *The Papers of Ulysses S. Grant*, ed. John Y. Simon, 22 vols. to date (Carbondale: University of Southern Illinois Press, 1970–), 5:264.

23. Lamers, *The Edge of Glory*, 85, 94–95; Reid, *Ohio in the War*, 1:321; Cozzens, *The Darkest Days of the War*, 26.

24. Lamers, *The Edge of Glory*, 103–4; Reid, *Ohio in the War*, 1:322; Cozzens, *The Darkest Days of the War*, 64–65.

25. Lamers, *The Edge of Glory*, 114–15; Cozzens, *The Darkest Days of the War*, 71, 125–26.

26. Ulysses S. Grant, *Personal Memoirs of U. S. Grant*, 2 vols. (New York:

Charles L. Webster and Company, 1885–1886), 1:413; see also Cozzens, *The Darkest Days of the War,* 70, 129–30.

27. William S. Rosecrans to Ulysses S. Grant, 10:30 P.M., September 19, 1862, *OR,* 17, pt. 1:67.

28. Lamers, *The Edge of Glory,* 133.

29. Lamers, *The Edge of Glory,* 171; Cozzens, *The Darkest Days of the War,* 143–44.

30. Ulysses S. Grant to Henry Halleck, September 20, 1862, *OR,* 17, pt. 1:64.

31. Grant instead paid general tribute "to all the officers and soldiers composing this command." See Ulysses S. Grant to Henry Halleck, October 20, 1862, *OR,* 17, pt. 1:64–69.

32. William S. Rosecrans to Annie Rosecrans, September 24, 1862, quoted in Lamers, *The Edge of Glory,* 116.

33. Reid, *Ohio in the War,* 1:323; William S. Rosecrans to John Rawlins, September 29, 1862, *OR,* 17, pt. 1:74.

34. Cozzens, *The Darkest Days of the War,* 152–53; Rosecrans's testimony, *Conduct of War Report,* 20–21.

35. Ulysses S. Grant to William S. Rosecrans, October 5, 1862, in Simon, ed., *Grant, Papers,* 6:123; see also editor's note, 123; William S. Rosecrans, "The Battle of Corinth," in *Battles and Leaders of the Civil War,* ed. R. U. Johnson and C. C. Buel, 4 vols. (New York; Century Co., 1884–1888), 2:753.

36. Grant, *Memoirs,* 1:417; see also Ulysses S. Grant to William S. Rosecrans, October 7, 1862, in Simon, ed., *Grant, Papers,* 6:131.

37. William S. Rosecrans to Ulysses S. Grant, October 7, 1862, *OR,* 17, pt. 1:163–64.

38. Henry Halleck to Ulysses S. Grant, October 8, 1862, in Simon, ed., *Grant, Papers,* 6:130, 133; see also *OR,* 17; pt. 1:156.

39. Ulysses S. Grant to Henry Halleck, October 8, 1862, 7:30 P.M., in Simon, ed., *Grant, Papers,* 6:134; see also *OR,* 17, pt. 1:156; Ulysses S. Grant to Stephen A. Hurlbut, October 8, 1862, in Simon, ed., *Grant, Papers,* 6:136.

40. Stephen A. Hurlbut to Ulysses S. Grant, October 8, 1862, *OR,* 27, pt. 2:269.

41. Lamers, *The Edge of Glory,* 170; Cozzens, *The Darkest Days of the War,* 162, 194, 197–98, 242, 251, 274, 293–302. Peter Cozzens, who has written the only campaign study of Iuka and Corinth, supports Rosecrans's contention that he could have gone all the way to Vicksburg if he had been supported by Grant. He judges his delay "immaterial" in successfully destroying Van Dorn's battered and exhausted army (see *The Darkest Days of the War,* 316).

42. Ulysses S. Grant to William S. Rosecrans, October 7, 1862, and William S. Rosecrans to Ulysses S. Grant, October 8, 1862, both in Simon, ed., *Grant, Papers,* 6:131, and 6:138–39; see also *OR,* 17, pt. 1:164–65.

43. *Cincinnati Commercial,* October 9, 1862.

44. William S. Rosecrans to Ulysses S. Grant, October 11, 1862, *OR,* 17, pt.

205

erts, *The Darkest Days of the War,* 311.

45. William S. Rosecrans to Ulysses S. Grant, October 18, 1862, in Simon, ed., *Grant, Papers,* editor's notes, 6:157.

46. Lamers, *The Edge of Glory,* 172.

47. Correspondence between U. S. Grant and William S. Rosecrans, October 21, 1862, in Simon, ed., *Grant, Papers,* 6:163–65, and editor's notes, 6:163–64; see also Cozzens, *The Darkest Days of the War,* 311–13; *OR,* 17, pt. 2:238, and *OR,* ser. 2, 4:639.

48. Mortimer D. Leggett to John Rawlins, in Simon, ed., *Grant, Papers,* editor's notes, 6:166–67.

49. John Y. Simon, ed., *The Personal Memoirs of Julia Dent Grant* (New York: G. P. Putnam's Sons, 1975), 104.

50. William S. Hillyer to William T. Sherman, October 29, 1862, *OR,* 17, pt. 2:307.

51. Ibid., William S. Rosecrans to Henry Halleck, September 26, 1862, 239.

52. Quoted in Lamers, *The Edge of Glory,* 177.

53. William S. Rosecrans to Annie Rosecrans, October 22, 1862, quoted in Lamers, *The Edge of Glory,* 176.

54. Quoted in Cozzens, *No Better Place To Die,* 15.

55. Beatty, *Memoirs,* 143–44.

56. Ulysses S. Grant to Elihu B. Washburne, November 7, 1862, in *General Grant's Letters to a Friend, 1861–1880,* ed. James G. Wilson (New York: T. Y. Crowell, 1897), 22.

57. Abraham Lincoln to William S. Rosecrans, January 8, 1863, *OR,* 20, pt. 1:186.

58. Ibid., Henry Halleck to William S. Rosecrans, January 9, 1863, 187.

59. Ibid., E. M. Stanton to William S. Rosecrans, January 7, 1863, pt. 2:306.

60. Murat Halstead, an outspoken critic of Grant, wrote Salmon Chase on April 1, 1863. Quoted in Lamers, *The Edge of Glory,* 262, also 247; for more on Stones River, see Cozzens, *No Better Place to Die.*

61. Rosecrans's testimony, *Conduct of War Report,* 33; Grant, *Memoirs,* 2:18.

62. *New York Times,* November 2, 1863.

63. *Richmond Examiner,* October 26, 1863.

64. Lamers, *The Edge of Glory,* 406.

65. Charles Dana to Abraham Lincoln, June 1, 1864, *OR,* 40, pt. 1:28.

66. Ibid., Henry Halleck to Ulysses S. Grant, September 29, 1864, 41, pt. 3:468.

67. Ibid., Ulysses S. Grant to Henry Halleck, September 29, 1864, 469.

68. Ibid., Ulysses S. Grant to Henry Halleck, October 20, 1864, pt. 4:126.

69. Ibid., John Rawlins to Ulysses S. Grant, November 4, 1864, 429–30.

70. Ibid., Edwin M. Stanton to Ulysses S. Grant, December 2, 1864, 742, and Ulysses S. Grant to Edwin M. Stanton, December 2, 1864, 743.

71. William S. Rosecrans to James Garfield, December 30, 1864, James Garfield Papers, Library of Congress.

72. Gideon Welles, *Diary of Gideon Welles,* ed. Howard K. Beale and Alan W. Brownsword, 3 vols. (Boston: Houghton Mifflin, 1909–1911), 2:282–83.

73. Lamers, *The Edge of Glory,* 440–41.

74. Rosecrans, "The Battle of Corinth," 2:755–56.

75. Arthur Ducat to William S. Rosecrans, April 24, 1885, quoted in Lamers, *The Edge of Glory,* 179; see also 445.

76. Grant, *Memoirs,* 1:420.

John A. McClernand

1. Richard Kiper, *Major General John Alexander McClernand: Politician in Uniform* (Kent, OH: Kent State University Press, 1999), xii.

2. On June 23, 1863, McClernand notified Pres. Abraham Lincoln that "I have been relieved for an omission of my adjutant. Hear me" *OR,* 24, pt. 1:158.

3. John Fiske, *The Mississippi Valley in the Civil War* (New York; Houghton Mifflin 1900), 225.

4. Historian Edwin C. Bearss writes emphatically of Grant's decision: "The third alternative was full of dangers and risks. Failure in this venture would entail little less than total destruction [of his army]. If it succeeded, however, the gains would be complete and decisive" (*The Vicksburg Campaign,* 3 vols. [Dayton, OH: Morningside Press, 1985–1986], 2:21).

5. Letter from McClernand Butler Crawford (great-great-great grandson of General McClernand) to author, May 26, 1998. Quoted by Mr. Crawford from *Past and Present of Sangamon County* (n.p., n.d.).

6. Ezra J. Warner, *Generals in Blue* (Baton Rouge: Louisiana State University Press, 1964), 293–94; Mark M. Boatner, *The Civil War Dictionary* (New York: McKay Books: 1988), 525.

7. Kiper, *McClernand,* 45.

8. *OR,* 3:271, 277; John Y. Simon, ed., *The Papers of Ulysses S. Grant,* 22 vols. to date (Carbondale: University of Southern Illinois Press, 1967–   ), 3:138, 148.

9. Ulysses S. Grant, *The Personal Memoirs of U. S. Grant,* 2 vols. (New York: Charles Webster and Company, 1885–1886), 1:246; *OR,* 7:178.

10. Kiper, *McClernand,* 84; *OR,* 7:159–60.

11. *OR,* 7:160, 170–82; Charles A. Dana and James H. Wilson, *The Life of Ulysses S. Grant* (Springfield, IL, 1868), 65.

12. Grant, *Memoirs,* 1:282; *OR,* 10, pt. 1:110.

13. The reader may recall the famous photographs of Lincoln and McClellan taken at the Grove farm during the president's visit to the battlefield near Sharpsburg. A lesser known photograph of the same group shows McClernand standing

next to the president, and another photograph taken on the same occasion shows McClernand with President Lincoln and Alan Pinkerton. McClernand was no doubt telling Lincoln, "Give me command, Mr. President, and I'll whip those rebs." This may be personal conjecture, but McClernand could have done as well as Ambrose Burnside, whom Lincoln selected to replace McClellan.

14. The Battle of Chickasaw Bayou occurred on December 27–29, 1862. The principal attack was launched on December 29, during which Sherman's troops were repulsed with ease, suffering the loss of 1,776 men compared to only 187 casualties for the Confederates (*OR*, 17, pt. 1:671).

15. Ibid., pt. 2:553.

16. Ibid., 24, pt. 1:11, 13.

17. Grant, *Memoirs*, 1:358–59.

18. *OR*, 24, pt. 1:141, 159.

19. Bearss, *The Vicksburg Campaign*, 2:402–4; *OR*, 24, pt. 1:160.

20. Bearss, *The Vicksburg Campaign*, 2:646–51.

21. Ibid., 2: 680, 686–89; *OR*, 24, pt. 1:617. In his memoirs, Grant glosses over McClernand's success at Big Black River, writing simply of the engagement: "The assault was successful. But little resistance was made. The enemy fled from the west bank of the river, burning the bridge behind him and leaving the men and guns on the east side to fall into our hands" (Grant, *Memoirs*, 1:440).

22. Bearss, *The Vicksburg Campaign*, 3:773–78.

23. *OR*, 24, pt. 1:172.

24. Bearss, *The Vicksburg Campaign*, 3:862–64.

25. James H. Wilson, *Under the Old Flag* (New York: D. Appleton, 1912), 182–83.

26. *OR*, 24, pt. 1:159–61.

27. *OR*, 24, 1:162–63. Both Sherman's and McPherson's notes that followed are quoted at length to illustrate the vitriolic nature of the relationship between McClernand and his fellow corps commanders and the lack of harmony— detrimental to the army—that existed among Grant's subordinates.

28. Ibid., 164.

29. Ibid., 159, 162.

30. Ed Longacre, *From Union Stars to Top Hat* (Harrisburg, PA: Stackpole, 1972), 83.

31. *OR*, 24, pt. 1:16.

32. Ibid., 167.

33. Ibid., 167–68.

34. Ibid., 157.

35. Ibid., 169.

36. Bearss, *The Vicksburg Campaign*, 1:27.

37. Simon, ed., *Grant, Papers*, 7.

38. *OR*, 24, pt. 1:172.

39. Kiper, *McClernand*, 308.

40. Warner, *Generals in Blue*, 293.

JAMES B. MCPHERSON

1. Bruce Catton, *Grant Moves South* (Boston: Little, Brown, and Company, 1960), 149, 209–10; James J. Hamilton, *The Battle of Fort Donelson* (New York: Thomas Yoseloff, 1968), 29.

2. William T. Sherman, "The Late Major-General J. B. McPherson," *Hours at Home* 2, 6, (April, 1866):486.

3. John H. Brinton, *Personal Memoirs of John H. Brinton* (New York: Neale Publishing Company, 1914), 131.

4. Halleck to Lorenzo Thomas, March 5, 1862, Record Group (RG) 94, Records of the Office of the Adjutant General, Letters Received, National Archives and Records Administration (NARA); Grant to Halleck, February 16, 1862, RG 393, Department of the Missouri, Letters Received, NARA.

5. Tamara Moser Melia, "James B. McPherson and the Ideals of the Old Army" (Ph.D. diss., University of Southern Illinois, 1987), 45–46; Ulysses S. Grant, *Personal Memoirs of U. S. Grant*, 2 vols. (New York: Charles L. Webster and Company, 1885–1886), 1:353–54.

6. Sherman to Ellen Ewing Sherman, July 26, 1864, SFP, UNDA.

7. Willard Warner to the editor of the *Tribune*, April 8, 1876, Sherman Papers.

8. John B. Dennis to Sherman, June 22, 1872, in William T. Sherman, *Personal Memoirs of William T. Sherman* (New York: Charles L. Webster and Company, 1890), 469; Melia, "James B. McPherson," 2.

9. Grant to Lydia Slocum, August 10 [1864], in Ulysses S. Grant, *The Papers of Ulysses S. Grant*, ed. John Y. Simon, 22 vols. to date (Carbondale: University of Southern Illinois Press, 1967–   ), 11:397.

10. Horace Porter, *Campaigning with Grant*, ed. Wayne C. Temple (Bloomington: Indiana University Press, 1961), 244–45; Grant to Stanton, July 22, 1865, in *OR*, 46, pt, 1:32; Grant, *Memoirs*, 2:169.

11. Grant to Lydia Slocum, August 10, [1864], in Simon, ed., *Grant, Papers*, 11:397.

12. Tamara Moser Melia, "The Gallant Knight: The Life and Early Career of James Birdseye McPherson" (master's thesis, University of Southern Illinois, 1979), 4–10.

13. Melia, "Gallant Knight," 12–28; Dennis Hart Mahan, *Hours at Home*, 2, 6, (April 1866):436.

14. Custis [Lee] to McPherson, October 16, 1859, Barnard to McPherson, November 6, 1860, and June 25, 1861, and Steve [Merchant] to McPherson, January 14, 1860, all in James B. McPherson Papers, LC; McPherson to Emeline, December 28, 1855, and [October 1856], in James B. McPherson Family Papers, Toledo–

Lucas County Historical Society (TLCHS); W. Craig to McPherson, January 11, 1857, McPherson Papers, LC; McPherson to C. B. Comstock, October 1857, Elizabeth Comstock Papers, State Historical Society of Wisconsin, La Crosse; Boggs to McPherson, March 17, 1861, and G. W. Cullum to McPherson, January 31, 1855, both in McPherson Papers, LC; Melia, "James B. McPherson," 22–26.

15. Melia, "Gallant Knight," 38–48.

16. John D. Kurtz endorsement on letter of McPherson to General [John G. Barnard], October 15, 1861, McPherson Papers, LC; Melia, "James B. McPherson," 36; John Y. Simon, ed., *The Personal Memoirs of Julia Dent Grant* (New York: G. P. Putnam's Sons, 1975), 105.

17. Melia, "Gallant Knight," 77–88.

18. Grant to Halleck, October 5, 1862, in Simon, ed., *Grant, Papers,* 6:120–22.

19. Rosecrans to Grant, October 7, 1862, RG 393, Department of the Missouri, Telegrams Received, NARA.

20. Halleck and Stanton endorsements, October 8, 1862, on Grant to Halleck, October 7, 1862, RG 94, letters received by the Adjutant General's Office, NARA.

21. Wimer Bedford, "Memoirs of Some Generals of the Civil War," *Lippincott's* 77 (January 1906):124.

22. James Harrison Wilson, *Life of John A. Rawlins* (New York: Neale Publishing Company, 1916), 167; Matilda Gresham, *Life of Walter Quintin Gresham, 1832–1895,* 2 vols., reprint ed. (Freeport, NY: Books for Libraries Press, 1970), 1:195.

23. De B[enneville] Randolph Keim, "Life and Character of Major-General James B. McPherson," *U.S. Service Magazine* 2, 4 (October 1864):371; Melia, "James B. McPherson," 68–73, 82–83.

24. Keim, 372.

25. Melia, "James B. McPherson," 83–90.

26. Ibid., 93–100.

27. Ibid., 100–17.

28. Ibid., 117–32.

29. Sherman to John Sherman, July 19, 1863, Sherman Papers, LC.

30. Grant to Abraham Lincoln, July 22, 1863, in Simon, ed., *Grant, Papers,* 9:97.

31. Ibid., 98–99.

32. William F. G. Shanks, *Personal Recollections of Distinguished Generals* (New York: Harper and Brothers, 1866), 26.

33. Sherman to Grant, August 15, 1863, in Simon, ed., *Grant, Papers,* 9:99.

34. Ibid., Grant to Senator Henry Wilson, January 19, 1864, 10:35–36.

35. Ibid., Grant to McPherson, [October 10, 1863], 9:229–31; Sherman to Rawlins, March 7, 1864, *OR,* 32, pt. 1:179–82; Melia, "James B. McPherson," 142–55, 163–72.

36. Melia, "James B. McPherson," 173–74; McPherson to "Mother" [Cynthia R. McPherson], April 4, 1864, McPherson Papers, TLCHS.

37. Melia, "James B. McPherson," 179–200.

38. Sherman to Halleck, September 15, 1864, *OR*, 38, pt. 1:64.

39. Melia, "James B. McPherson," 204–7; Sherman to McPherson, May 10, 1864, 10:30 A.M., *OR*, 38, pt. 4:125; Sherman to Ellen Ewing Sherman, June 12, 1864, William T. Sherman, *Home Letters of General Sherman*, ed. M. A. DeWolfe Howe (New York: Charles Scribner's Sons, 1909), 296; Sherman, *Hours at Home* 2:488; William T. Sherman, *Memoirs of General William T. Sherman*, 2 vols. (New York: D. Appleton and Company, 1875), 2:34.

40. J. F. C. Fuller, *The Generalship of Ulysses S. Grant* (New York: Dodd, Mead and Company, 1929), 312; Wilson, *Life of John A. Rawlins*, 196.

41. John M. Schofield, *Forty-six Years in the Army* (New York: Century Company, 1897), 125–29.

42. Melia, "James B. McPherson," 210–52; Sherman, *Hours at Home*, 2:488; Grenville M. Dodge to William E. Strong, October 10, 1885, Strong Papers, Illinois State Historical Library, Springfield.

43. John A. Logan address, October 18, 1876, *National Republican*, and *Report of the Proceedings of the Society of the Army of the Tennessee, at the Tenth Annual Meeting Held at Washington, D.C., October 18th and 19th, 1876* (Cincinnati: F. W. Freeman, 1876), 56–77; John B. Dennis to Sherman, June 22, 1872, in Sherman, *Memoirs* (2d ed.), 469; Wilson, *Life of John A. Rawlins*, 117–18.

44. B. H. Liddell Hart, *Sherman: Soldier, Realist, American* (New York: Dodd, Mead and Company), 336, 368–69; John A. Logan speech to the Army of the Tennessee, July 13, 1865, typescript, Logan Papers, LC; Henry H. Wright, *A History of the Sixth Iowa Infantry* (Iowa City: State Historical Society of Iowa, 1923), 392–94, 411–15; John A. Carpenter, *Sword and Olive Branch: Oliver Otis Howard* (Pittsburgh: University of Pittsburgh Press, 1964), 75.

45. *Washington, DC, National Republican*, October 18, 1876, 1:1–3; William W. Belknap to B. J. Lossing, September 29, 1876, James B. McPherson Papers, Henry E. Huntington Library, San Marino, CA; Wilson, *Life of Rawlins*, 440; L. M. Dayton to Sherman, November 3, 1875, Sherman Papers, LC.

46. Sherman to W. B. Hazen, December 23, 1865, and Emily Hoffman to Sherman, November 16, 1868, Sherman Papers, LC; *Washington, D.C., National Republican*, October 18, 1876; L. M. Dayton to Sherman, November 3, 1875, R. M. Buckland to Sherman, October 18, 1875, Sherman Papers, LC; James M. Goode, *The Outdoor Sculpture of Washington, D.C.: A Comprehensive Historical Guide* (Washington, DC: Smithsonian Institution Press, 1974), 281; *Toledo Blade*, October 18, 1876, typescript copy, Wilfred S. Foerster Collection, Rutherford B. Hayes Presidential Center Library, Fremont, OH.

47. *Cincinnati Commercial*, July 23, 1881, 1:7.

48. Sherman to Slocum, July 24, 1864, *OR,* 38, pt. 5:246, and 39, pt. 2:203.

ADMIRAL DAVID DIXON PORTER

1. Porter to Welles, April 17, 19, 1863, Greer to Porter, April 17, 1863, log of the U.S. Gunboat *Benton, ORN,* series 1, 24:552–56, 682.

2. Richard S. West Jr., *The Second Admiral: A Life of David Dixon Porter, 1813–1891* (New York: Coward-McCann, 1937), 1–10; Chester G. Hearn, *Admiral David Dixon Porter* (Annapolis: Naval Institute Press, 1996), 1–11. Additional biographies of Porter include Paul Lewis, *Yankee Admiral* (New York: McKay, 1968), and James R. Soley, *Admiral Porter* (New York: Appleton, 1903).

3. Tamara Moser Melia, "David Dixon Porter: Fighting Sailor," in *Captains of the Old Steam Navy: Makers of the American Naval Tradition, 1840–1880,* ed. James C. Bradford (Annapolis: Naval Institute Press, 1986), 227; West, *The Second Admiral,* 13–17; Hearn, *Porter,* 5–6; David Dixon Porter never forgot the disgrace brought to his father's name and worked the remainder of his life to restore the honor he believed was his due.

4. Melia, "David Dixon Porter," 227–28; Hearn, *Porter,* 8–11; West, *The Second Admiral,* 18–27.

5. Melia, "David Dixon Porter," 228–29; Hearn, *Porter,* 12–20; West, *The Second Admiral,* 28–40.

6. K. Jack Bauer, *Surfboats and Horse Marines: U.S. Naval Operations in the Mexican War, 1846–1848* (Annapolis: Naval Institute Press, 1969), 75–122; Samuel Eliot Morison, *"Old Bruin": Commodore Matthew C. Perry, 1794–1858* (Boston: Little, Brown and Company, 1967), 206–42.

7. Lincoln to Porter, April 1, 1861, *ORN,* 1, 4:108–9; West, *The Second Admiral,* 77–84; Bern Anderson, *By Sea and by River: The Naval History of the Civil War* (New York: Da Capo Press, 1962), 18–24; Richard S. West Jr., *Mr. Lincoln's Navy* (New York: Longmans, 1957), 19–24; David D. Porter, *Naval History of the Civil War* (New York: Sherman Publishing Company, 1886), 100–102; Hearn, *Porter,* 36–44; Melia, "David Dixon Porter," 230; Gideon Welles, *The Diary of Gideon Welles: Secretary of the Navy Under Lincoln and Johnson,* ed. Howard K. Beale and Alan W. Brownsword, 3 vols. (Boston: Houghton Mifflin, 1909–1911), 1:12–31.

8. Brown to Meigs, Meigs to Porter, April 17, 1861, Porter to Brown, April 18, 1861, *ORN,* 1, 4:123–24; West, *The Second Admiral,* 87–104; Anderson, *By Sea and by River,* 23–24; West, *Mr. Lincoln's Navy,* 25–28; Porter, *Naval History of the Civil War,* 102–4; Hearn, *Porter,* 44–52; Melia, "David Dixon Porter," 230; Welles, *Diary,* 3:31–36.

9. Proposition of Porter in Farragut to Welles, September 13, 1862, Porter to Welles, April 25, 1862, Porter to Welles, April 30, 1862, *ORN,* 1, 18:145–46, 356–59, 361–74; West, *Mr. Lincoln's Navy,* 130–31; Alfred Thayer Mahan, *The Gulf*

and Inland Waters (New York: Charles Scribner's Sons, 1883), 52–90; West, *The Second Admiral,* 113–21; Hearn, *Porter,* 68–118; William N. Still Jr., "David Glasgow Farragut: The Union's Nelson," in Bradford, ed., *Captains of the Old Steam Navy,* 169–70; Dana M. Wegner, "The Union Navy, 1861–1865," in *In Peace and War: Interpretations of American Naval History, 1775–1984,* ed. Kenneth J. Hagan (Westport, CT: Greenwood Press, 1984), 115–16; William M. Fowler, *Under Two Flags: The American Navy in the Civil War* (New York: Avon Books, 1990), 111–27.

10. Welles to Porter, September 22, 1862, Welles to Porter, October 1, 1862, General Orders no. 150, October 2, 1862, *ORN,* 1, 23:373, 388, 389; Welles, *Diary,* 1:157; West, *The Second Admiral,* 146. Porter's assignment possibly resulted from his public criticism of Gen. John A. McClernand.

11. Welles to Porter, November 15, 1862, *ORN,* 1, 23:484; Hearn, *Porter,* 116–18.

12. Porter to Welles, October 29, 1862, Porter to Sherman, Sherman to Porter, November 12, 1862, Memorandum Regarding the Operations of the Mississippi Squadron under Acting Rear-Admiral Porter, U.S. Navy, from October 1862 to May 1863, Report of Acting Rear Admiral Porter to Welles, December 12, 1862, *ORN,* 1, 23:396, 458, 478–79, 542–54; Ulysses S. Grant, *Personal Memoirs of U. S. Grant,* 2 vols. (New York: Charles L. Webster and Company, 1885–1886), 2:246; Porter, *Naval History of the Civil War,* 284; West, *The Second Admiral,* 172–83.

13. Memorandum, *ORN,* 1, 23:396–97; Grant to Sherman, December 8, 1862, *OR,* 17, pt. 1:601; Grant to Sherman, December 8, 1862, in John Y. Simon, ed., *The Papers of Ulysses S. Grant,* 22 vols. to date (Carbondale: University of Southern Illinois Press, 1967–), 6:406–7; Porter, *Naval History of the Civil War,* 284; Rowena Reed, *Combined Operations in the Civil War,* Bison Book edition (Lincoln: University of Nebraska Press, 1993), 233.

14. Porter to Gwin, December 20, 1862, Sherman to Porter, December 29, 1862, Porter to Welles, Porter to Sherman, January 1, 1863, Porter to Foote, January 3, 1863, Porter to Welles, January 3, 1863, Sherman to Porter, January 3, 1863, Sherman to Rawlins, January 3, 1863, *ORN,* 1, 23:567–69, 584–85, 590–93, 597, 604–8; Sherman to Rawlins, January 3, 1863, *OR,* 17, pt. 1:605–10; Hearn, *Porter,* 158–67; John D. Milligan, *Gunboats Down the Mississippi* (Annapolis: U.S. Naval Institute Press, 1965), 107–11; Joseph T. Glatthaar, *Partners in Command: The Relationships Between Leaders in the Civil War* (New York: Free Press, 1994), 168–69.

15. Porter to Welles, January 11, 28, 1863, *ORN,* 1, 24:127, 107–9; McClernand to Rawlins, January 20, 1863, *OR,* 17, pt. 2:700–709; Glatthaar, *Partners in Command,* 169–70.

16. Grant to Halleck, January 20, 1863, *OR,* 24, pt. 1:8–9; Grant to Porter, January 10, 1863, in Simon, ed., *Grant, Papers,* 7:206; *Grant, Memoirs,* 1:445–49; Fowler, *Under Two Flags,* 208–9; Glatthaar, *Partners in Command,* 171.

17. Smith to Porter, November 2, 1863, *ORN,* 1, 24:243–49; Grant to Porter, February 6, 1863, *OR,* 24, pt. 3:36; Grant to Porter, February 6, 1863, in Simon, ed., *Grant, Papers,* 7:288–89.

18. Porter to Welles, March 26, 1863, Porter to Grant, March 16, 1863, *ORN,* 1, 24:474–80, 480–81; Grant to McPherson, March 16, 1863, Grant to Sherman, March 16, 1863, Grant to Porter, March 23, 1863, *OR,* 24, pt. 3:112–13, 132–33; Grant to McClernand, March 18, 1863, Grant to Banks, March 23, 1863, Grant to Porter, March 23, 1863, in Simon, ed., *Grant, Papers,* 7:440–41, 445–47, 459–61; Herman Hattaway and Archer Jones, *How the North Won: A Military History of the Civil War* (Urbana: University of Illinois Press, 1983), 343; Glatthaar, *Partners in Command,* 171–73.

19. Grant to Porter, Porter to Grant, March 29, 1863, Grant to Porter, April 2, 1863, Porter to Welles, April 17, 1863, Porter to Welles, April 19, 1863, General Order of Acting Rear Admiral Porter, April 10, 1863, log of U.S. Gunboat *Benton, ORN,* 1, 24:517, 518, 521, 552–55, 682; Grant to Sherman, March 22, 1863, Farragut to Grant, Grant to Farragut, Grant to Porter, March 23, 1863, in Simon, ed., *Grant, Papers,* 7:455–56, 456–57, 458–59, 459–61; Grant to Porter, Porter to Grant, March 29, 1863, Grant to Porter, April 2, 1863, *OR,* 24, pt. 3:151–52, 168.

20. See *ORN,* 1, 24 and 25; see also *OR,* 24, pt. 3; Grant to Kelton, July 6, 1863, in Simon, ed., *Grant, Papers,* 8:507.

21. Farragut to Welles, September 22, 1864, Welles to Porter, September 22, 1864, *ORN,* 1, 21:655–57; Welles to Lincoln, October 28, 1864, *ORN,* 1, 11:3; Grant to Stanton, July 22, 1865, *OR,* 36, pt. 1:43–44; *Welles, Diary,* 2:127–29, 146–47; Porter to Fox, October 15, 1864, October 19, 1864, in James Merrill, "The Fort Fisher and Wilmington Campaign: Letters from Rear Admiral David D. Porter," *North Carolina Historical Review* 35, 4 (October 1958):464–67; Reed, *Combined Operations in the Civil War,* 331–33; Glatthaar, *Partners in Command,* 184–85; Hearn, *Porter,* 270–72; see also Charles M. Robinson III, *Hurricane of Fire: The Union Assault on Fort Fisher* (Annapolis: Naval Institute Press, 1998).

22. Butler to Porter, December 25, 1864, Porter to Welles, December 26, 1864, Alden to Porter, *ORN,* 1, 11:250–51, 253–60, 317–18; Grant to Stanton, July 22, 1865, *OR,* 36, pt. 1:44–45; Grant, *Memoirs,* 2:388–95.

23. Grant to Porter, December 30, 1864, Porter to Grant, January 1, 3, 1865, Grant to Terry, January 3, 1865, Porter to Welles, January 14, 15, 16, 17, 1865, *ORN,* 1, 11:394, 401–2, 404–5, 432–42; Grant to Stanton, July 22, 1865, *OR,* 36, pt. 1:45–46; Grant, *Memoirs,* 2:395–99.

24. Porter to Welles, July 13, 1863, *ORN,* 1, 25:280; Grant to Stanton, July 22, 1865, *OR,* 36, pt. 1:45.

GRENVILLE M. DODGE

1. Grenville M. Dodge, "Personal Recollections of General Grant and His Campaigns in the West," in *Personal Recollections of the War of the Rebellion,*

ed. A. Noel Blakeman (New York: G. P. Putnam's Sons, 1907), 358–59; Stanley P. Hirshson, *Grenville M. Dodge: Soldier, Politician, Railroad Pioneer* (Bloomington: Indiana University Press, 1967), 64.

2. For the best descriptions of Dodge's prewar life, see J. R. Perkins, *Trails, Rails and War: The Life of General G. M. Dodge* (Indianapolis: Bobbs-Merrill, 1929) and Hirshson, *Dodge.*

3. Hirshson, *Dodge,* 53–58.

4. Herbert M. Hoxie to Dodge, April 20, 1861, box 2, Grenville Mellen Dodge Papers, State Historical Society of Iowa, Des Moines; Hirshson, *Dodge,* 44, 60.

5. Special Orders no. 114, May 22, 1862, *OR,* 10, pt. 2:210.

6. Grenville M. Dodge, "Reminiscences of Engineering Work on the Pacific Railways and in the Civil War," *Engineering News* 62 (October 28, 1909):457.

7. Grenville M. Dodge, "Use of Block-Houses During the Civil War," *Annals of Iowa* 6 (January 1904):301.

8. Philip Lewis Shiman, "Engineering Sherman's March: Army Engineers and the Management of Modern War, 1862–1865" (Ph.D. diss., Duke University, 1991), 190–91, 208–9, 511–12; Dodge, "Reminiscences," 456; Hirshson, *Dodge,* 60–61; Grant to Capt. Speed Butler, August 23, 1861, *OR,* 3:452–53.

9. Special Orders no. 5, October 30, 1862, *OR,* 17, pt. 2:310; J. T. Granger, *A Brief Autobiographical Sketch of the Life of Major-General Grenville M. Dodge* (New York: Ayer Company, 1893), 124.

10. Ulysses S. Grant, *Personal Memoirs of U. S. Grant,* 2 vols. (New York: Charles L. Webster, 1885–1886), 1:423; Shiman, "Engineering Sherman's March," 191–92.

11. Dodge to Capt. M. Rochester, September 5, 1862, *OR,* 17, pt. 1:55; Shiman, "Engineering Sherman's March," 191–92.

12. For a detailed account of the Holly Springs raid and Forrest's expedition in West Tennessee, see Edwin C. Bearss, *The Vicksburg Campaign,* 3 vols. (Dayton, OH: Morningside Press, 1985) 1:231–74, 287–318; Herman Hattaway and Archer Jones, *How The North Won: A Military History of the Civil War* (Urbana: University of Illinois Press, 1983), 311–12.

13. Dodge, "Block-Houses," 298–99; Shiman, "Engineering Sherman's March," 192; Kenneth P. Williams, *Lincoln Finds a General: A Military Study of the Civil War,* 5 vols. (New York: Macmillan, 1949–1958), 4:198–200.

14. Grant to Brig. Gen. J. E. Smith, December 26, 1862, in John Y. Simon, ed., *The Papers of Ulysses S. Grant,* 20 vols. to date (Carbondale: University of Southern Illinois, 1967–   ), 7:120.

15. Dodge to Capt. S. Wait, May 5, 1863, *OR,* 23, pt. 1:249; Hirshson, *Dodge,* 71–73.

16. Steven E. Woodworth, *Six Armies in Tennessee: The Chickamauga and Chattanooga Campaigns* (Lincoln: University of Nebraska Press, 1998), 129–68.

17. Grant, *Personal Memoirs,* 2:46–48; Grant to Maj. Gen. William T. Sher-

man, November 5, 1863, and Sherman to Dodge, November 9, 1863, *OR,* 31, pt. 3:54–55, and 100; Woodworth, *Six Armies in Tennessee,* 170–71.

18. Asst. Secretary of War Charles A. Dana to Secretary of War Edwin M. Stanton, November 21, 1863, and Grant to Julia Grant, November 30, 1863, in Simon, ed., *Grant, Papers,* 9:415, and 478.

19. Shiman, "Engineering Sherman's March," 208–9; Grant, *Memoirs,* 2:322; Dodge, "Reminiscences," 456; Dodge to Sherman, November 11, 1863, *OR,* 31, pt. 3:119–20.

20. Dodge to Maj. R. M. Sawyer, November 16, 1863, *OR,* 31, pt. 3:171.

21. Dodge to Sawyer, February 23, 1864, *OR,* 32, pt. 1:451–52; Dodge, "Block-Houses," 298–99; Grant, *Memoirs,* 2:47–48; Hirshson, *Dodge,* 88–89.

22. Dodge, "Block-Houses," 298–99.

23. George Edgar Turner, *Victory Rode the Rails: The Strategic Place of the Railroads in the Civil War* (Lincoln: University of Nebraska Press, 1992), 296; Woodworth, *Six Armies in Tennessee,* 171.

24. Grant to Col. H. R. Mizner, February 15, 1864, in Simon, ed., *Grant, Papers,* 10:126; Grant, *Memoirs,* 2:47–48; Dodge to Sawyer, February 23, 1864, *OR,* 32, pt. 1:451–52.

25. Dodge to Anne Dodge, November 14, 1862, and Dodge to Anne Dodge, November 4, 1862, Dodge Record Books, vol. 3, 912, and 897, Dodge Papers.

26. Special Orders no. 320, October 30, 1862, *OR,* 17, pt. 2:308; Grant to Dodge, November 8, 1862, in Simon, ed., *Grant, Papers,* 6:287; and Maj. Gen. Henry W. Halleck to Grant, November 10, 1862, 6:286.

27. Dodge to Grant, November 12, 1862, and Grant to Halleck, November 14, 1862, in Simon, ed., *Grant, Papers,* 6:313 and 310–12.

28. Ibid., Grant to Dodge, November 18, 1862, and Lt. Col. John A. Rawlins to Dodge, November 22, 1862, 6:373–74 and 374.

29. Ibid., Grant to Dodge, November 18, 1862, 6:374; Rosecrans to Grant, November 21, 1862, 6:374; Rawlins to Dodge, November 22, 1862, 6:374; and Grenville M. Dodge, "The Secret Service in the Civil War," Dodge Record Books, 5:1–47, Dodge Papers, SHSI.

30. William B. Feis, "Finding the Enemy: The Role of Military Intelligence in the Campaigns of Ulysses S. Grant, 1861–1865," (Ph.D. diss., Ohio State University, 1997), 217–18.

31. Dodge, "Secret Service," 1–2; Hirshson, *Dodge,* 67.

32. Maj. Gen. Samuel R. Curtis to Capt. N. H. McLean, April 1, 1862, *OR,* 8:197; Dodge, "Secret Service," 2.

33. See Curtis's report, April 1, 1862, *OR,* 8:197.

34. Dodge Record Books, 1:93, 101.

35. Dodge to Maj. Gen. Stephen Hurlbut, October 30, 1863, RG 110 (Records of the Provost Marshal Generals Bureau), entry 31, box 2, NARA; Dodge, "Secret Service," 14–15.

36. Inventory of Dodge's Scouts, box 148, Dodge Papers; Dodge Secret Service Vouchers, boxes 148 and 149, Dodge Papers; Dodge, "Secret Service," 5; Feis, "Finding the Enemy," 218; Hirshson, *Dodge,* 73–74. See also William Stanley Hoole, *Alabama Tories: The First Alabama Cavalry. U.S.A., 1862–1865* (Tuscaloosa, AL: Confederate Publishing Company, 1960).

37. Dodge to Rawlins, May 5, 1863, RG 393 (Records of the U. S. Army Continental Commands), pt. 1, entry 6159, pt. 2, NARA; Dodge, "Secret Service," 5.

38. John Craig Stewart, *The Governors of Alabama* (Gretna, LA: Pelican Publishing Company, 1975), 116–18; Walter L. Fleming, *Civil War and Reconstruction in Alabama* (New York: Columbia University Press, 1905), 510.

39. Perkins, *Trails, Rails and War,* 119–20.

40. Dodge to Rawlins, January 30, 1863, in Simon, ed., *Grant, Papers,* 7:523; General Order no. 5, January 16, 1863, *OR,* 17, pt. 2:569; Dodge, "Secret Service," 29–30. See also Rawlins to Dodge, February 26, 1863, in Simon, ed., *Grant, Papers,* 7:523.

41. Brig. Gen. Jeremiah Sullivan to Grant, January 16, 1863, in Simon, ed., *Grant, Papers,* 6:349; "Final Report of Receipts and Expenditures of Col. Wm. S. Hillyer, Provost Marshal General, Department of the Tennessee," box 1, William Silliman Hillyer Papers, University of Virginia Library, Charlottesville; Dodge Secret Service Vouchers, boxes 148 and 149, Dodge Papers.

42. Dodge, "Secret Service," 29–30; Hirshson, *Dodge,* 68.

43. Hillyer to Grant, June 30, 1863, in Simon, ed., *Grant, Papers,* 8:220.

44. Dodge Secret Service Vouchers, boxes 148 and 149, Dodge Papers.

45. Entry for April 13, 1863, in Dodge's "Report of Spys [*sic*], 1863–Feb. 1864," box 149, Dodge Papers; Maj. Gen. Richard Oglesby to Lt. Col. Henry Binmore, April 13, 1863, *OR,* 24, pt. 3:191.

46. Dodge, "Personal Recollections of General Grant," 361.

47. Grant to Col. J. C. Kelton, July 6, 1863, in Simon, ed., *Grant, Papers,* 8:485; Bearss, *The Vicksburg Campaign,* 2:19–21.

48. Dodge, "Secret Service," 16; Dodge to Oglesby, April 13, 1863, box 2, Richard Oglesby Papers, Illinois State Historical Library, Springfield, IL; Hirshson, *Dodge,* 71–73.

49. Dodge, "Secret Service," 14; Grant to Kelton, July 6, 1863, in Simon, ed., *Grant, Papers,* 8:497; James H. Wilson, "A Staff-Officer's Journal of the Vicksburg Campaign, April 30 to July 4, 1863," *Journal of the Military Service Institution* 43 (July 1908):105–6; Grant, *Memoirs,* 1:507–8.

50. Dodge, "Secret Service," 14; address by Gen. Frederick D. Grant, Society of the Army of the Tennessee, *Report of the Proceedings of the Society of the Army of the Tennessee, 1909–1911* (Cincinnati: Charles O. Ebel Publishing Company, 1913), 200; Frederick D. Grant, "A Boy's Experience at Vicksburg," in Blakeman, ed., *Personal Recollections,* 93. Grant claimed that Hurlbut employed the spy who brought Johnston's message; however, Hurlbut had few operatives of

his own and regularly "borrowed" Corinth scouts and spies for intelligence missions. Thus, Hurlbut may have authorized the mission, but Sanburn was most likely under Dodge's supervision.

51. For examples of Dodge's reports, see *OR*, 24, pt. 3:192, 291, 298, 303, 323, 326, 336, 364, and 370. See also Dodge's reports to Oglesby, April–June 1863, Oglesby Papers.

52. Grant to Lt. Col. Henry Binmore, June 20, 1863, in Simon, ed., *Grant, Papers*, 8:562.

53. Hirshson, *Dodge*, 93–105, 109–127.

54. Ibid., 109–127.

55. On Dodge's nomination as Grant's secretary of war, see correspondence in Simon, ed., *Grant, Papers*, 19:260–61 and Hirshson, *Dodge*, 173–74.

56. Grant to Dodge, December 11, 1862, *OR*, 17, pt. 2:399.

Peter J. Osterhaus

1. The three ethnic brigade commanders were Col. Julius Raith, who led the Third Brigade of Maj. Gen. John A. McClernand's First Division at Shiloh; Brig. Gen. Charles L. Matthies, who commanded the Third Brigade of Brig. Gen. James M. Tuttle's Third Division, Fifteenth Corps, at Vicksburg; and Col. Adolph Englemann, who led Englemann's Brigade of Brig. Gen. Nathan Kimball's Provisional Division at Vicksburg.

2. This sketch of Osterhaus's early life and Civil War career is from Earl J. Hess, "Osterhaus in Missouri: A Study in German-American Loyalty," *Missouri Historical Review* 78 (1984):144–67. See also Earl J. Hess, "The Twelfth Missouri Infantry: A Socio-Military Profile of a Union Regiment," *Missouri Historical Review* 76 (1981):53–77.

3. William L. Shea and Earl J. Hess, *Pea Ridge: Civil War Campaign in the West* (Chapel Hill: University of North Carolina Press, 1992), 284–303.

4. Peter J. Osterhaus, "What I Saw of the War," 6, Belleville Public Library; Samuel Prentis Curtis, "The Army of the South-West, and the First Campaign in Arkansas," *Annals of Iowa* series 1, 7 (1869):216–17; Frederick Tell Ledergerber affidavit, July 26, 1886, and John Schenk affidavit, September 9, 1886, Osterhaus Pension File, RG 94, NARA; Henry Kircher diary, July 11, 1862, Englemann-Kircher Collection, Illinois State Historical Library.

5. Peter J. Osterhaus, "Generals' Report of Service," 3:411–13, RG 94, NARA; medical certificate, August 28, 1862: Osterhaus to Major Glasser, September 2, 1862; Osterhaus to Curtis, October 20, 1862, Generals' Papers, Records of the Adjutant General's Office, RG 94, NARA. Osterhaus told Capt. Ferdinand Steinberg of the Twelfth Missouri "that he would rather die, than to leave his command." See Ferdinand Steinberg affidavit, November 26, 1886; Frederick Tell

Ledergerber affidavit, July 26, 1886; Adolph Wagner affidavit, October 27, 1887, Osterhaus Pension File, RG 94, NARA; Osterhaus, "What I Saw of the War," 6.

6. Osterhaus, "What I Saw of the War," 6–7; Osterhaus, "Generals' Report of Service," 3:413–14, RG 94, NARA; Samuel Ryan Curtis to Willis A. Gorman, December 19, 1862, *OR,* 22, pt. 1:852; Henry A. Kircher to mother, December 9, 1862, and Kircher to mother, December 22, 1862, in Earl J. Hess, ed., *A German in the Yankee Fatherland: The Civil War Letters of Henry A. Kircher* (Kent, OH: Kent State University Press, 1983), 32, 38.

7. Order of battle, Robert Underwood Johnson and Clarence Clough Buel, eds., *Battles and Leaders of the Civil War,* 4 vols. (New York: Thomas Yoseloff, 1956), 3:546.

8. Clinton B. Fisk to Samuel Ryan Curtis, January 2, 1863, *OR,* 22, pt. 2:8; Osterhaus, "What I Saw of the War," 7; Raymond E. Swing, interview with Osterhaus, *Chicago Daily News,* January 3, 1914, clipping in Peter J. Osterhaus Papers, Missouri Historical Society (MHS).

9. Osterhaus, "What I Saw of the War," 7; Osterhaus to E. D. Saunders, January 14, 1863, and McClernand to John A. Rawlins, January 20, 1863, *OR,* 17, pt. 1:708, 745–48.

10. Dan Webster and Don C. Cameron, *History of the First Wisconsin Battery Light Artillery* (Washington, DC: National Tribune, 1907), 115, 118; Richard M. Hunt reminiscences, Richard M. Hunt Papers, U.S. Army Military History Institute, Carlisle Barracks, PA.

11. Osterhaus, "What I Saw of the War," 7; George K. Pardee to wife, January 19, 1863, private collection; Benjamin Franklin Stevenson, *Letters from the Army* (Cincinnati: W. E. Dibble, 1884), 175–76; Swing interview with Osterhaus.

12. McClernand to Grant, January 18, 1863, *OR,* 17, pt. 2:574; McClernand to Grant, February 17, 1863, in John Y. Simon, ed., *The Papers of Ulysses S. Grant,* 22 vols. to date (Carbondale: University of Southern Illinois Press, 1967–), 7:350n.

13. Osterhaus, "Generals' Report of Service," 3:415, RG 94, NARA; Stevenson, *Letters from the Army,* 175–76, 178, 181; Webster and Cameron, *History of the First Wisconsin Battery,* 124; Oran Perry, "The Entering Wedge," *War Papers Read Before the Indiana Commandery Military Order of the Loyal Legion of the United States* (Indianapolis: Indiana Commandery, 1898), 360.

14. John Schenck affidavit, September 9, 1886, Osterhaus Pension File, RG 94, NARA; Osterhaus, "What I Saw of the War," 8.

15. McClernand to Grant, March 19, 1863; Grant to McClernand, March 22, 1863; Simon, ed., *Grant, Papers,* 7:452n–53n.

16. Osterhaus, "What I Saw of the War," 8; Grant to J. C. Kelton, July 6, 1863, Osterhaus to Walter B. Scates, April 18, 1863, and McClernand to John A. Rawlins, June 17, 1863, all in *OR,* 24, pt. 1:46–47, 490–92, and 139–40; Paul H. Hass, ed., "The Vicksburg Diary of Henry Clay Warmoth, Part 1 (April 3, 1863–April 27, 1863)," *Journal of Mississippi History* 31 (November 1969):336–37.

17. Hass, ed., "Vicksburg Diary of Henry Clay Warmoth," 340–43; Perry, "Entering Wedge," 365–69; Osterhaus to Scates, April 18, 1863, and McClernand to Rawlins, June 17, 1863, *OR,* 24, pt. 1:491–94, 139–40.

18. Osterhaus, "What I Saw of the War," 8; Grant to Kelton, July 6, 1863 *OR,* 24, pt. 1:46–48; Grant to McClernand, April 24, 1863, in Simon, ed., *Grant, Papers,* 8:113–14.

19. McClernand to Rawlins, June 17, 1863, and Osterhaus to Scates, April 18, 1863, *OR,* 24, pt. 1:142, 493.

20. Osterhaus, "What I Saw of the War," 8; Osterhaus to Scates, May[?], 1863, *Supplement to the Official Records of the Union and Confederate Armies,* pt. 1, vol. 4 (Wilmington, NC: Broadfoot, 1995), 367–77; Grant to Kelton, July 6, 1863, and McClernand to Rawlins, June 17, 1863, *OR,* 24, pt. 1:48–49, 143–44.

21. Osterhaus to Scates, May 26, 1863, *OR,* 24, pt. 2:12–16, and McClernand to Rawlins, June 17, 1863, pt. 1:147–50.

22. Ibid., McClernand to Rawlins, June 17, 1863, pt. 1:152–53; Osterhaus to Scates, May 26, 1863, pt. 2:16; Webster and Cameron, *History of the First Wisconsin Battery,* 143–44; Jacob T. Foster memoir, 53, State Historical Society of Wisconsin; Osterhaus statement, October 21, 1885, Osterhaus Pension File, RG 94, NARA.

23. McClernand to Rawlins, June 17, 1863, *OR,* 24, pt. 1:153, and Osterhaus to Scates, May 26, 1863, pt. 2:17–18; John Schenck affidavit, September 9, 1886, Osterhaus Pension File, RG 94, NARA.

24. Osterhaus to Scates, May 26, 1863 *OR,* 24, pt. 2:20–21, and McClernand to Rawlins, June 17, 1863, pt. 1:154–56.

25. Ibid., Osterhaus to Scates, May 26, 1863, 24, pt. 2:21, and McClernand to Rawlins, June 17, 1863, 24, pt. 1:154–56.

26. Ibid., Osterhaus to Scates, May 25, May 27, June 6, June 14, 1863, 24, pt. 2:209–11, 215, 223; Osterhaus to Grant, May 29, 1863, 211–12; Osterhaus to Rawlins, May 30, 1863, 212; Osterhaus to Edward O. C. Ord, June 21, 1863, 225; Osterhaus to Rawlins, May 26, 1863, in Simon, ed., *Grant, Papers,* 8:278n–79n; John G. Fonda to McClernand, September 1, 1863, *Supplement to the Official Records,* 4:383.

27. Scates to Rawlins, June 2, 1863, Grant to Osterhaus, June 2, 1863, in Simon, *Grant, Papers,* 8:292n–93n, 303; Osterhaus to Rawlins, June 12, 1863, *OR,* 24, pt. 2:222; Isaac F. Shepard to Rawlins, July 3, 1863, in Simon, ed., *Grant, Papers,* 8:565; Fonda to McClernand, September 1, 1863, *Supplement to the Official Records,* 4, 383.

28. Osterhaus to Rawlins, May 30, 1863, and Osterhaus to McClernand, June 7, 1863, *OR,* 24, pt. 2:212, 219; Osterhaus to Rawlins, June 14, 1863, and Rawlins to Osterhaus, June 14, 1863, in Simon, ed., *Grant, Papers,* 340n, 341n; Osterhaus to Rawlins, June 17, 1863, *OR,* 24, pt. 2:223.

29. Osterhaus to Scates, May 27, 1863, *OR,* 24, pt. 2:210–11; Grant to Oster-

haus, June 10, 1863, and Osterhaus to Rawlins, May 26, 1863, in Simon, ed., *Grant, Papers,* 8:339n, 278n–79n.

30. Elmira J. Kelley to Osterhaus, June 28, 1863, and Osterhaus to Rawlins, June 27, 1863, in Simon, ed., *Grant, Papers,* 8:571, 570–71.

31. Sherman to Osterhaus, July 14, 1863, *OR,* 24, pt. 3:458, 474–75.

32. Ibid., Osterhaus to Scates, July 25, 1863 pt. 2:579–83.

33. Ibid., Ord to J. H. Hammond, July 27, 1863, 575–76; Osterhaus, "Generals' Report of Service," 3:419–20, RG 94, NARA; Osterhaus, "What I Saw of the War," 10; Frederick Tell Ledergerber affidavit, July 26, 1886, and Adolph Wagner affidavit, October 27, 1887, Osterhaus Pension File, RG 94, NARA.

34. Henry Kircher to mother, January 3, 4, 7, and April 22, 1863, in Hess, ed., *A German in the Yankee Fatherland,* 40–53, 93–95; Stevenson, *Letters from the Army,* 247, 250; Spiegel to wife, January 29, February 2, March 22, April 27, 1863, in *Your True Marcus: The Civil War Letters of a Jewish Colonel,* ed. Frank L. Byrne and Jean Powers Soman (Kent, OH: Kent State University Press, 1985), 231, 234, 253, 260, 269.

35. Swing interview, with Osterhaus.

36. Charles A. Dana, *Recollections of the Civil War with the Leaders at Washington and in the Field in the Sixties* (New York: D. Appleton, 1909), 64; Ord to Rawlins, July 27, 1863, in Simon, ed., *Grant, Papers,* 9:72n; Earl J. Hess, "Alvin P. Hovey and Abraham Lincoln's 'Broken Promises': The Politics of Promotion," *Indiana Magazine of History* 80 (March 1984):46–47.

37. Murray M. Horowitz, "Ethnicity and Command: The Civil War Experience," *Military Affairs* 42 (December 1978):185.

Contributors

Stacy D. Allen is chief historian at Shiloh National Military Park.

Benjamin Franklin Cooling is a historian for the U.S. government and the award-winning author of *Forts Henry and Donelson: Keys to the Confederate Heartland* and *After Fort Donelson.*

R. Blake Dunnavent teaches history at Idaho State University.

William B. Feis teaches history at Buena Vista University and is the author of several articles on the Civil War.

Lesley J. Gordon is associate professor of history at the University of Akron and author of *General George E. Pickett in Life and Legend.*

Earl J. Hess is professor of history at Lincoln Memorial University and author of *The Union Soldier in Battle* and *Liberty, Virtue, and Progress: Northerners and Their War for the Union.*

John F. Marszalek is professor of history at Mississippi State University and author of *Sherman: A Soldier's Passion for Order* and *Sherman's Other War: The Soldier and the Civil War Press.*

Tamara A. Smith is an independent scholar in Bonita, California.

Terrence J. Winschel is chief historian at Vicksburg National Military Park and author of *Triumph and Defeat: The Vicksburg Campaign* and *Vicksburg: Fall of the Confederate Gibraltar.*

Steven E. Woodworth is associate professor of history at Texas Christian University and author of *Jefferson Davis and His Generals, Davis and Lee at War,* and *While God Is Marching On: The Religious World of Civil War Soldiers.*

Index

Adams, Henry, 113
Alcatraz Island, 154
Ammen, Jacob, 59
Anderson, Robert B.
  as commander of Fort Sumter, 172
  as commanding general of
    Cumberland region, 7
  physical and mental fatigue, 8
  Sherman as second-in-command to, 7
Anderson, William, 170
Arkansas Post. *See* Fort Hindman
Army, Confederate
  advance on Corinth, 118
  at Columbus, Ky., 29–31, 47
  Fort Donelson stronghold of, 34–35,
    46–47, 52–55, 69–70, 98–99,
    103–4
  Fort Henry stronghold of, 33, 36,
    46–47, 51–52, 98–99
  at Shiloh, 11–13, 38–39, 71–72
  at Vicksburg, 16–17
  See also Johnston, Albert Sidney;
    Johnston, Joseph E.
Army, Union
  at battle of Corinth, 118
  campaign against Vicksburg, 137–40
  camp at Young's Point, 206
  capture of Jackson, Miss., 139, 158,
    196, 213–14
  coordination efforts in the West,
    48–50

defeat at First Bull Run, 7
encampment at Crump's Landing,
  11–12, 21, 27
at Fort Fisher, 180–81
Halleck as commanding general of,
  15, 114–15
Indiana Zouaves, 64
L. Wallace's command of Eleventh
  Illinois, 25–32, 36
Pittsburg Landing as forward base, 71
pursuit of Confederates to Holly
  Springs, 119
Athens, action at, 189
Atlanta, battle of, 152, 163
Aztec Club, 44

Banks, Nathaniel, 16, 20, 179
Barnard, John G., 154
Baxter, A. S., 72–74, 77, 79
Bearss, Edwin C., 148
Beatty, John, 113, 122–23
Beauregard, P. G. T., 13, 51, 84, 99–100
Belmont, battle of, 8, 29–31, 46, 95–96,
  132–33
Bentonville, S.C., 165
Bickham, W. D., 119–20
Big Black River, battle of, 19, 139–40,
  143, 197, 200, 213
Bird's Point, Mo., 28–30
Blair, Francis Preston, Jr. (Frank), 144,
  164

Bowen, John S., 157
Bragg, Braxton, 115–16, 123
Brown, Harvey, 172
Buckner, Simon B., 9, 43, 53–55, 104
Buell, Don Carlos, 8, 47, 48, 56
    command of Department of the Ohio,
        47–48
    Grant's encounter with, 56
    military commission investigates, 86
    replaces Sherman, 8
    at Shiloh, 13, 71, 82, 135
Butler, Benjamin, 16, 174, 180

Cameron, Simon, 8
Camp Beauregard, 98
Camp Jackson, capture of, 200
Canal River Coal Company, 111
Canton, Miss., 160
Carr, Eugene A., 209–10
Champion's Hill, battle of, 19, 139, 143,
    158, 197, 209, 213
Charleston, Mo., 30
Charleston, S.C., 165
Chattanooga, battle of, 189
Cheshire Academy, 92
Chickamauga, battle of, 124
Chickasaw Bluffs, battle of, 136, 175,
    204
Chunky Station, Miss., 160
Columbia, S.C., burning of, 165
Comstock, Cyrus B., 84
Corinth, battle of, 118, 155, 186
Cox, Jacob, 112
Crocker, Marcellus M., 157, 192
Crump's Landing, 11–12, 21, 37
Curtis, Samuel, 96, 192, 201–3

Dallas, Ga., battle of, 163
Dana, Charles, 125, 134, 215–16
Davis, Charles H., 174
Davis, Jefferson, 163
Decatur, Stephen, 169

Dickey, Cyrus E., 29
Dickey, T. Lyle, 22, 24
Dodge, Grenville M.
    at Atlanta, 163–64
    in Atlanta campaign, 197
    in campaign against Vicksburg,
        190–91
    career prior to Civil War, 183–84
    in Chattanooga campaign, 189–90
    commands Department of the
        Missouri, 126
    disrupts Bragg's supply lines, 187
    forms First Alabama Cavalry, 13
    intelligence about Vicksburg, 195–96
    intelligence gathering at Rolla,
        191–92
    as intelligence officer, 190
    at Pea Ridge, 184, 192
    rebuilding of Nashville and Decatur
        Railroad, 188–89
    relationship with Grant, 183–86,
        190–95
    secret service corps of, 191–96
    strategy to repair Mobile and Ohio
        Railroad, 185–86
    during Vicksburg campaign, 197
Dodge City, 198
Douglas, Stephen A., 132
Ducat, Arthur, 127

Edwards Station, capture of, 143
Elkhorn Tavern, Mo., 202
Elston, Isaac, Jr., 68
Ewing, Thomas, 7

Farragut, David G., 15–16, 173
Feis, William B., 96–97
Florence, Ga., action at, 189
Foote, Andrew Hull
    in action at Fort Donelson, 102–3
    assumes cautious stance, 106–7
    at Brooklyn Navy Yard, 92

in charge of naval operations at St.
    Louis, 93
as chief of Bureau of Equipment and
    Recruiting, 107
collaboration with Grant, 99–103,
    107–8
command of Union navy at Fort
    Henry, 69
death of, 107
duty in second Anglo-Chinese war,
    92
early contacts with Grant, 94
friendship with Grant, 105–6
Grant's relationship with, 9, 45–46
role in capture of Fort Henry, 50–52
Foote, Augustus Russell Street, 107
Forrest, Nathan Bedford, 185, 186–87
Fort Donelson
    attack by Union army and navy on, 9,
        69
    battle of, 1, 9–10, 11, 34–35, 42,
        133–34, 186
    Foote and Grant at, 102–3
    Lew Wallace's actions at, 69–70
    McClernand at, 133–34, 137
    plan to capture, 101
Fort Fisher, 180–81
Fort Henry
    attack by Union army and navy on, 9,
        69
    attack on, 68–69
    capture of, 1, 9, 11, 33, 101, 186
    Grant, Smith, and Foote plan to
        capture, 50–51
    Phelps's information about, 46–47
    pressure on Halleck to take, 99
    Smith's reconnaissance of, 50
Fort Hindman, surrender of, 136,
    175–76, 204–5
Fort McAllister, 165
Fort Pemberton, attack on, 177
Fort Pickens, 172

Fort Sumter
    fall of, 7
    plan to relieve (1861), 171–72
Foster, Jacob T., 204
Fox, Gustavus, 107, 171, 179
Frémont, John C.
    character and personality of, 46
    command of Department of the West,
        44
    orders Smith to occupy Paducah, 45
    Osterhaus serves under, 201
    replaces Rosecrans, 114

Gaines's Ferry, action at, 189
Garfield, James, 166
Grand Gulf, attack on, 178, 207
Grant, Frederick Dent (son of USG),
    215
Grant, Julia Dent (wife of USG), 16,
    155
Grant, Ulysses S.
    at battle of Belmont, 96
    Cairo headquarters in Western
        Theater, 7, 66
    at Champion's Hill, 158
    character and personality of, 9, 14–15
    civilian career of, 6–7
    collaboration with Foote, 99–103,
        107–8
    as colonel in Twenty-First Illinois
        Regiment, 7
    command at Belmont, 46
    commander at battle of Iuka, 82
    as commander of Department of West
        Tennessee, 9
    criticism of Rosecrans, 110
    criticized for losses at Shiloh, 83–84
    at Fort Donelson, 52–55, 133–35
    headquarters at Savannah, Tenn.,
        11–12, 71
    judgment of Lew Wallace, 68
    on loss of C. F. Smith, 60

Grant, Ulysses S., *continued*
L. Wallace blamed for losses at
Shiloh, 84
observations of Forts Henry and
Donelson campaigns, 70
at Paducah, 66–67
personality of, 5, 99
physical appearance of, 5
praise for Dodge, 197–98
reaction to McPherson's death,
152–53, 164–65
relationship with C. F. Smith, 45–46,
48, 57–59
relationship with Dodge, 183–86,
190–95
relationship with Foote, 9, 93–96,
105–6
relationship with Halleck, 10–11, 14,
36
relationship with L. Wallace, 66–68,
76–79, 82–89
relationship with McClernand,
133–37, 158
relationship with McPherson,
151–53, 156–59, 164–65
relationship with Osterhaus,
199–200, 215–16
relationship with Porter, 160, 180–81
relationship with Rosecrans, 115–21,
123–27
relationship with Sherman, 10–20,
156, 159–60
relationship with W. H. L. Wallace,
21–22, 28–32, 42
reorganizes Army of the Tennessee,
156
replaces McClernand, 158
replaces Rosecrans, 124–25
reputation for drinking, 67
Rosecrans under command of,
109–10
service in Mexican War, 6

Sherman and McPherson as favorites
of, 87
at Shiloh, 38–40, 57, 72–82, 152
similarities to Sherman, 5
as subordinate to Halleck, 10–11
takes Paducah (1861), 8
treatment by Halleck, 10, 14
at Vicksburg, 158–59, 174–76, 186
Vicksburg campaign of, 17–19,
130–31, 137–40, 156–57, 176–78,
186–87, 192, 195
West Point education of, 5–7
Gregg, John, 157–58
Grierson, Benjamin, 157

Halleck, Henry W.
as army chief of staff under Grant, 83
cautious nature of, 99, 104–5
character and personality of, 36
as commanding general of Union
armies, 15, 114
at Corinth, 14–15
criticism of Union political soldiers at
Shiloh, 82–83
dislike of L. Wallace, 85
Grant joins, 8–9
investigation of C. F. Smith's
disciplinary actions, 67
on McPherson's military
performance, 155
meets McPherson, 154
orders Grant to take Fort Henry, 51,
68–69, 99–100
on qualities of C. F. Smith, 59
relationship with Grant, 9–11, 14, 36
replaces Frémont, 46
Sherman serves under, 8–10
strategy in western department, 98
as Union commander of western
department, 71, 96
vacillation about Fort Henry strategy,
99
Hamilton, Charles, 206
Hankinson's Ferry bridge, 157

Hardee, William, 47, 163
Hardin, John J., 23
Haupt, Herman, 189
Hill, Ambrose P., 81–82
Hillyer, William S., 69–70, 194–95
Hitchcock, Ethan Allan, 51, 56
Holly Springs, Miss., 16, 156, 157, 187
Hood, John Bell, 153, 162–64
Hovey, Alvin P., 142, 209
Howard, Oliver O., 153
Hoxie, Herbert M., 184
Hull, J. B., 173
Hurlbut, Stephen, 39–40, 119, 120, 194

Iuka, battle of, 82, 116–17, 186

Jackson, Miss., capture of, 139, 158,
    196, 213–14
Jackson, William H., 185
James, Joshua, 207
James's Plantation, 207
Johnston, Albert Sidney
    attack on Pittsburg Landing, 71
    death of, 12, 39
    falls back to Corinth, Tenn., 11
    orders army's retirement to Alabama
        and Mississippi, 105
    perceived vulnerability in western
        theater, 97–98
    Polk regroups with, 57
    strategy in western theater, 97
Johnston, Joseph E., 19
    Army of Relief of, 196–97
    in Georgia campaign, 161, 163
    retreat at Atlanta, 163
    at Vicksburg, 157, 158

Kenesaw Mountain, battle of, 163
Kiper, Richard, 129, 150
Knefler, Frederick, 79
Knox, Thomas W., 17

Lamers, William, 117
Lane, Henry S., 68
Lee, Albert L., 209
Lee, G. W. Custis, 153
Lee, Robert E.
    invades Maryland (1862), 115
    as superintendent of West Point, 153
Leggett, Mortimer, 121
Lincoln, Abraham
    concern for Union army in
        Appalachia, 47–48
    Grant's success impresses, 10
    impressions of Grant, 10
    military appointments of, 65
    orders Halleck to replace Frémont, 46
    on premonitions of Union victories,
        126
    pressure on commanders in western
        department, 97–98
    on Union victory at Stones River, 123
Logan, John A., 35–36, 132, 157, 164
Lyon, Nathaniel, 200–201

Mahan, Dennis Hart, 154, 185
McAllister, Edward, 33
McClellan, George B.
    at battle of Rich Mountain, 112
    as commander of Army of the
        Potomac, 113
    commander of Union army in
        Virginia, 57
    as general in chief of the army, 96
    Rosecrans serves under, 109
    Sherman's demands for men from, 8
McClernand, John A., 16–17, 19, 28,
    33–34
    accompanies Lincoln to Antietam
        battlefield, 135
    alienates Union army and navy, 156
    at battle of Belmont, 132–33
    at Big Black River, 139–40
    at Champion's Hill, 139

McClernand, John A., *continued*
  character and personality of, 16, 134,
    137, 141, 149–50
  civilian career, 131
  as commander of First Brigade, 132
  as commander of Thirteenth Corps,
    137–38, 149
  congratulations to his troops, 141–44
  at Fort Donelson, 69–70, 133–34,
    137
  at Fort Hindman, 176
  Grant's criticism of capacities of, 89
  leadership qualities of, 149
  political career, 132, 149
  at Port Gibson, 138, 208
  praise for Osterhaus, 205
  raises and commands force on
    Mississippi River, 135–36
  relationship with Grant, 132–37
  relieved of command, 146–48
  replacement of, 158
  role in capture of Fort Henry, 51
  service in Black Hawk War, 31
  at Shiloh, 134–35, 137
  at surrender of Fort Hindman, 136
  at Vicksburg, 140–41, 158, 174
McCloud, George, 212
McCulloch, Ben, 201–2
McFeely, William S., 79
McPherson, James B., 38, 75–77, 78, 81
  administration of Vicksburg, 159–60
  in advance on Oxford, Miss., 156
  at Atlanta, 163–64, 165
  at Champion's Hill, 139
  character and personality of, 151,
    153–54
  as commander of Army of the
    Tennessee, 152
  as commander of Seventeenth Corps,
    137–38, 160
  at Corinth, 155
  at Dallas, 163

  death of, 152
  duty on Alcatraz Island, 154
  at Fort Donelson, 156
  in Georgia campaign (1864), 161
  at Kenesaw Mountain, 163
  on McClernand's order to his troops,
    145–46
  at Raymond, 138, 157–58
  reconnaissance missions, 160
  relationship with Grant, 151–53, 156
  relationship with Sherman, 153, 154,
    156, 159
  at Resaca, 161–63
  role at Forts Henry and Donelson,
    151–52
  at Shiloh, 152
  as superintendent of West Tennessee
    railroads, 155
  as valuable subordinate officer,
    155–56, 166
  at Vicksburg, 140, 157–59, 165
  as West Point graduate, 153–54, 166
McPherson Square, Washington, D.C.,
    166
Meigs, Montgomery, 96, 172
Memphis, capture of, 84
Meridian, Miss., 160
Mexican War
  C. F. Smith's service in, 44
  W. Wallace's service in, 23–24, 41
  Z. Taylor's service in, 23–24
Milligan, James, 100
Milligan, John D., 92
Milliken's Bend campsite, 137, 206
Missouri campaign, 200–220
Morgan, George W., 203
Morris, W. I., 195–96
Morton, Oliver P., 64, 85, 88

Nashville, capture of, 70
Navy, Confederate
  gunboats on Tennessee and
    Cumberland rivers, 97, 101

gunboats on western Kentucky rivers, 47

Navy, Union
accompanying Grant along Tennessee River, 105
actions along Mississippi River, 105
at battle of Fort Donelson, 69, 102–4
at Fort Fisher, 180–81
gunboat action at Fort Henry, 100–101
gunboats sweep along Tennessee River, 101–2
at Memphis, 84
at Mississippi River Island No. Ten, 106
occupation of Clarksville, 105
river boat reconnaissance, 98
use of mortar boats, 98

Nelson, William, 71
New Orleans, capture of, 16, 173

Oglesby, Richard, 28–30
Ord, Edward O. C.
commander at battle of Iuka, 82, 116–18
in command of Thirteenth Corps, 212
praise for Osterhaus, 214, 215
replaces McClernand, 146

Osterhaus, Peter J.
in attack on Vickburg, 210–11
at Big Black River, 209
at capture of Camp Jackson, 200
at Champion's Hill, 209
character and personality, 216
command at Rolla, 201
command of First Division, Fifteenth Corps, 214, 215
in command of fortification at Big Black River, 211–13
command of Ninth Division, Thirteenth Corps, 205
command of Second Division, Thirteenth Corps, 203–4

at Fort Gibson, 208
at Fort Hindman, 204–5
health of, 203, 206, 210, 214
immigrates to United States, 200
at Jackson, 213–14
military service in Prussia, 200
in Missouri campaign, 200
at Pea Ridge, 201–2
praise for his division, 205
reconnaissance related to Grand Gulf attack, 207–8
relationship with Grant, 199–200, 215–16
at Searcy, Ark., 202
in Vicksburg campaign, 216
at Wilson's Creek, 201
wounded at Big Black River, 209–10

Pacific Railroad Act (1861), 184–85
Paducah, battle of, 8, 66–67
Pea Ridge, Mo., battle of, 184, 192, 201–2
Pemberton, John C., 19, 138, 158, 196–97, 209
Perret, Geoffrey, 45, 96
Perry, Matthew Calbraith, 171
Perry, Oliver Hazard, 169
Phelps, Ledyard, 45, 46–47, 51
Phelps, S. L., 97
Pillow, Gideon J., 8, 94
Pittsburg Landing, battle of. See Shiloh, battle of
Platt, Charles T., 170
Polk, Leonidas, 47, 57, 94
Pollock, James, 61
Pope, John, 106
Porter, David Dixon
in attacks on Fort Fisher, 180–81
as commander of North Atlantic Blocking Squadron, 179–80
at Drumgould's Bluff, 175
at Fort Hindman, 176

Porter, David Dixon, *continued*
  at Grand Gulf, 178, 207
  illness and death of, 107
  patrols on Mississippi River, 179
  plan to capture New Orleans, 173
  in Red River campaign, 179
  reinforcement of Fort Pickens,
    172–73
  relationship with Grant, 160, 180–81
  role in Yazoo Pass expedition, 177
  service in Mexican navy, 170–71
  service in U.S. Coastal Survey, 171
  at Vicksburg, 157, 169, 173–79
  on Yazoo River, 175
Porter, David (father of David Dixon
    Porter), 169–70
Port Gibson, battle of, 19, 138, 142,
    157, 208
Prentiss, Benjamin, 12, 28, 36, 39–40
Price, Sterling, 115–18, 201–2
Pride, George G., 188

Railroad Redoubt, 149
Ransom, T. E. G., 29
Rawlins, John A.
  as chief of staff to Grant, 59, 75,
    77–81, 88, 121, 125, 191, 212
  as Secretary of War, 198
Raymond, battle of, 19, 138, 157–58
Red River campaign, 179
Reed, Rowena, 179
Reid, Whitelaw, 118
Resaca, Ga., battle of, 161–64
Richmond, Miss., capture of, 206
Rich Mountain, battle of, 112, 116
Rodgers, John, 93, 94, 169
Rosecrans, Crandell, 110
Rosecrans, William S.
  actions in western Virginia, 109
  advances on Bragg at Murfreesboro,
    123
  as aide to McClellan, 111

  at battle of Corinth, 118–19
  at battle of Iuka, 116
  in battle of Rich Mountain, 112, 116
  character and personality of, 112–13,
    115, 116, 118–21, 127
  commands Department of the
    Cumberland, 121–22
  commands Department of the
    Missouri, 125
  commands Department of the Ohio,
    113
  at Corinth, 155
  critics of, 124
  defeat at Chickamauga, 124
  hostility toward Grant, 109
  in House of Representatives, 109
  as minister to Mexico (1868), 127
  political enemies of, 114
  postwar civilian pursuits, 126–27
  prewar business ventures, 111
  relationship with Grant, 115–21,
    126–27
  relations with Stanton, 114, 115, 122
  removal from command (1864), 110
  replaced by Dodge (1864), 126
  replaced by Thomas (1863), 124
  secret service corps of, 191, 192
  as strategist, 112
  transferred to western department,
    109–10
  at West Point, 110–11
Ross, James, 72
Rowley, William R., 74–80

Sanborn (Union spy), 196–97
Santa Anna, Antonio Lopez, 23–24
Scates, Walter B., 212
Schofield, John M., 153, 162–63
Scott, Winfield, 7, 44, 170–71
Seward, William H., 172
Shanks, William, 113
Sheridan, Philip H., 153
Sherman, William Tecumseh
  advice to L. Wallace, 87–88

appearance, 5
character and personality of, 5, 9–10,
    14–20
at Chickasaw Bluffs, 17–18, 136, 175
civilian career of, 6–7
as commander of Department of
    Cairo, 9
criticized for losses at Shiloh, 83
at First Bull Run, 7
in Georgia campaign (1864), 161–65
joins Halleck's command, 8
on McClernand's order to his troops,
    144–45
promotion to brigadier general, 7
reaction to McPherson's death, 152,
    164
relationship with Grant, 10–20, 156
relationship with McPherson, 153,
    154, 156, 159
role in Yazoo Pass expedition, 177
service in Mexican War, 6
service in Second Seminole War, 6
at Shiloh, 38–40, 74, 83–84, 134
similarities to Grant, 5
at Vicksburg, 140, 157–58
West Point education of, 5–7
Yellow Creek expedition of, 11
Shiloh, battle of, 11–13, 21, 38–41,
    55–59, 71–84, 134–37, 152, 186
Shirk, James W., 51
Sigel, Franz, 200, 201
Sill, Joshua W., 153
Smith, Allen, 60
Smith, Andrew Jackson, 206, 209
Smith, Charles F., 10, 11, 36–37
    character and personality of, 44, 66
    death and burial, 59–60
    disciplinary measures criticized,
        66–67
    expeditionary force at Pittsburg
        Landing, 57–58
    at Fort Donelson, 52–55, 69–70

Grant's assistance to family of,
    60–61
intelligence gathering of, 98
L. Wallace serves under command of,
    66
relationship with Grant, 45–46, 48,
    57–59
report on land and river threats, 97
role in capture of Fort Henry, 50–51
service in Mexican War, 44
West Point education and career, 44
as West Point instructor, 44
Smith, Henrietta, 60–61
Smith, John E., 208
Smith, William Hugh, 193
Smith's Plantation, 206–7
Snake Creek Gap, Ga., 161–62
Spencer, George E., 193, 196
Spiegel, Marcus M., 215
Stanton, Edwin, 59, 82, 84, 88, 126, 179
    approves McPherson's promotion,
        155
    relationship with Rosecrans, 114,
        122, 123
Steele, Frederick, 214
Steele's Bayou expedition, 177, 195–96
Stevenson, Benjamin Franklin, 206, 215
Stewart, Robert, 122
Stones River, battle of, 123, 126
Streight, Abel D., 187
Stuart, J. E. B., 153

Taylor, Zachary
    C. F. Smith serves under command
        of, 44
    Grant's service under, 6
    William Wallace serves under
        command of, 23–24, 30–32
Terry, Alfred H., 181
Thomas, George H., 84, 124, 188
Thompson, M. Jeff, 28, 29, 32
Tilghman, Lloyd, 100–101

Totten, Joseph G., 154
Tucker, John, 60
Turner, George Edgar, 189
Tuscumia Valley raid, 196

Van Dorn, Earl, 116, 118, 186–87, 202
Vicksburg
  in Confederate hands, 16–17
  McPherson's administration of, 160
  siege of, 130–31, 141, 178–79, 211
  surrender of, 1, 19, 197
Vicksburg campaign
  Grant's strategy, 17–19, 156–57,
    176–78, 186–87, 192, 195
  McClernand's role in, 16–17
  McPherson's canal built during,
    156–57
  Sherman's role in, 16–19

Walke, Henry, 107
Wallace, Lewis "Lew"
  character and personality of, 65–68
  command of Eleventh Indiana
    (Zouave) Regiment, 64
  conduct at Shiloh, 73–84
  criticism of C. F. Smith, 67–68
  criticized for conduct at Shiloh,
    83–84
  at Crump's Landing, 72
  under direct command of Grant, 68
  at Fort Donelson, 34–35, 53, 69
  on Forts Henry and Donelson
    campaign, 70
  with Grant at Shiloh, 82
  march from Stoney Lonesome to
    Shiloh, 73–82
  as military commander at Cincinnati,
    86
  political career, 64
  as president of military commission,
    86

problem of rank, 86–87
reconnaissance of Camp Beauregard,
  48
relationship with Grant, 66–68,
  76–79, 82–89
relationship with Smith, 60, 66–68
relieved of command, 85, 88
service in Mexican War, 64
service in Western Theater, 65–66
Sherman's advice and assistance to,
  87–88
Wallace, Susan Elston (Mrs. Lewis), 64
Wallace, William H. L.
  character and personality of, 24–28,
    41–42
  early life, education, and civilian
    career, 22, 24
  at Fort Donelson, 34–35, 42
  Grant's relationship with, 21–22
  promotion to brigadier general,
    35–36
  relationship with Grant, 21–22,
    28–32, 42
  service in Mexican War, 22–23, 41
  service in Union army, 24–26
  at Shiloh, 38–41
  wounding and death of, 40–41, 59
Warner, Ezra, 150
Washburne, Elihu, 7
Webster, Joseph D., 151, 152
Weitzel, Godfrey, 180
Welles, Gideon, 92–93, 107, 126, 172,
  173–74, 179
West, Richard S., Jr., 93
Williams, Kenneth P., 104
Wilson, James Harrison, 141
Wilson's Creek, battle of, 201, 202
Woodworth, Steven E., 189–90

Yates, Richard, 135, 147
Yazoo Pass expedition, 176–77, 196

CPSIA information can be obtained
at www.ICGtesting.com
Printed in the USA
LVHW092322250723
753490LV00031B/565

9 780700 635252